Our City

Community Activism In Bristol

Edited by Suzanne Audrey

⬥Tangent Books

Our City: Community Activism In Bristol
First published 2024 by Tangent Books

Tangent Books
31 Balmain Street, Bristol BS4 3DB

www.tangentbooks.co.uk
richard@tangentbooks.co.uk

ISBN 978-1-914345-37-1
Commissioned and edited by: Suzanne Audrey

Design: Joe Burt, Wild Spark Design

A CIP record of this book is available at the British Library.

Printed by CMP, Poole on paper from a sustainable source

CONTENTS

Introduction

THIS BOOK IS about our city, Bristol. Two key factors shaped the context of the events described here. The first is austerity. Cuts to local authority funding began in 2010 under the Conservative and Liberal Democrat coalition government, and continued under successive Conservative governments through to 2024. The second is the mayoral system of governance that began in Bristol in 2012 and ended in 2024. Throughout this period, the Council adopted a 'strong leader' model through which decision-making powers were concentrated in the role of a directly elected mayor.

This was the context within which individuals, groups and organisations contributed to the recent history of Bristol. Some identified and promoted a cause, some found themselves unexpectedly drawn into a campaign, while others raised questions and scrutinised decisions. Some people celebrated success, some had no choice but to accept defeat, and others fight on.

The book has three main sections – promoting inclusion, community campaigning, and city planning. But there are obvious overlaps. Those who promote inclusion often campaign for their communities, communities feel the impact of poor city planning which can undermine inclusion, and so on...

We begin with six examples of promoting inclusion. Overcoming barriers to cycling, creating safe places for Bristol's queer communities, providing toilets that welcome everyone, resisting cuts to special educational needs provision, reclaiming independent living for disabled people, and championing the reparations movement. Each contributes to making Bristol a more inclusive city.

Bristol was awarded the accolade of the UK's first 'cycling city' in 2008. But barriers persist, and cycling is not as inclusive as it should be. Zoe Banks Gross describes the progress and setbacks she has experienced while developing projects to get more mums on bikes, make our streets family friendly, and provide cycling lessons for women from Black, Asian and other minority ethnic groups.

Andy Leake celebrates safe spaces for Bristol's diverse queer community, including people of colour and the trans community. As well as a thriving nightlife, there are clubs and collectives for an ever-growing array of LGBT+ interests. While acknowledging there is still work to be done, Andy believes that Bristol's reputation as an LGBT+ friendly city is undeniable.

In 2018, Bristol City Council closed 18 of its public toilets and asked businesses and organisations to sign up to a community toilet scheme, giving free public access to their facilities. The determination of Watershed, to provide toilets that are safe and welcoming for everyone, met with some criticism. But they stuck to their principles, with heart-warming results.

Also in 2018, three mothers of children with special educational needs successfully challenged Bristol City Council in the High Court over proposals to cut £5m from SEND funding. Jen Smith's chapter is a shocking tale of poor decision-making by Council leaders that undermined relationships with parents and carers, and compounded problems with special educational needs provision.

Bristol Reclaiming Independent Living (BRIL) also challenged Bristol City Council. A cabinet decision, to consult on a proposed Fair and Affordable Care Policy, threatened independent living and was vigorously opposed by BRIL. Their detailed submission, including pro bono legal advice, contributed to the policy being withdrawn. But concerns remain about the extent to which disabled people's voices are heard.

The voices of people of African heritage have been championed by the reparations movement. The chapter on Atonement and Reparations describes the process through which Bristol became the first UK core city to officially back the campaign for reparations, leading to the launch of new initiatives focussing on Bristol's history, racial justice and the future of African heritage communities in our city.

The next six chapters focus on community campaigns. Ursa the Bear, boaters' rights, allotmenteering, public access to green space, street trees, and Bristol's last working farm, have all come under threat in recent years. But the citizens of Bristol have refused to give them up without a fight.

Richard Jones recalls the battle to save Ursa the Bear. While standing on the toilet block in Bristol's Bearpit roundabout, Ursa welcomed people to our city and was part of a broader movement of creative community activism. Despite her popularity, she was removed when the Council 'took back control' of the Bearpit. But her spirit lives on.

Members of Bristol's boating community also feared being removed from the city when the Mayor accused them of abusing the system. After campaigning in vain to be consulted about fees and licences, the Bristol City Docks Fees and Charges Review was imposed upon them. But George Colwey believes Bristol's boating community has been strengthened by their struggle.

Consultation did take place about allotment rule changes and rent increases, and raised considerable alarm. Holly Wyatt describes how allotment tenants across Bristol came together to form Bristol Allotmenteers Resist. Protests outside City Hall, and a petition that triggered a Full Council debate, led to some proposals being withdrawn and others deferred.

Helen Powell recounts a rollercoaster journey defending open public access to Stoke Lodge Playing Fields, which has involved the Local Government Ombudsman, the Information Commissioner's Office and the High Court. The Village Green status is still under threat, but Helen celebrates the strength derived when a community fights for a cause that is dear to its heart.

Despite Bristol City Council declaring an ecological emergency, George Cook recounts how the nature-rich land at Yew Tree Farm is under threat from encroaching development, including by the Council itself. Farmer Catherine Withers and nature-loving Bristolians continue their fight to protect the farm, and George acknowledges the importance of Bristol's wildlife champions.

Vassili Papastavrou, of Bristol Tree Forum, is one of Bristol's wildlife champions. While applauding previous policy makers who gave our city tree-lined streets and generous green space, he is concerned that largescale development is leading to a loss of green space and important trees across the city. Vassili argues that policies must be enforced to protect Bristol's urban trees.

The final group of chapters relates to planning in our city and decisions that do not stand up well to scrutiny. A focus on numbers, rather than city design, has set the context for some controversial decisions relating to Bristol's city-centre arena, St Mary le Port, Bristol Zoo Gardens,

Cumberland Basin, and Broadwalk shopping centre.

George Ferguson, the first elected mayor of Bristol, acknowledges the importance of responding to the housing crisis but argues that a short-sighted political reaction, to build fast and high in an attempt to tick off promised numbers, is not the solution. Other factors must be considered to ensure our city is sociable and sustainable for generations to come.

Marvin Rees began his term as Bristol's mayor with a controversial decision to cancel the planned arena at Temple Meads in favour of YTL's proposal for a private arena on the edge of the city. Joanna Booth documents the convoluted process through which this was accomplished, despite opposition from councillors and the public.

Joe Banks questions how plans for three out-of-scale buildings were approved for the historic site at St Mary le Port. Concerns about democratic accountability and due process have led him to question the involvement of the mayoral administration in the planning system, facilitated by a tight network of consultants, developers, and corporate architects.

The fight to save Bristol's historic Zoo Gardens from redevelopment as a housing estate is told in two parts. Tom Jones describes the campaign to save the Zoo at its Clifton site. Fellow campaigners Alistair Sawday and Iain Boyd highlight the broader battle against profiteering developers, and propose an alternative vision for the historic gardens.

Anna Haydock-Wilson focuses on the ways in which citizens relate to their neighbourhoods. Her chapter focuses on the Hotwells community, and local feelings about Council-led plans to rebrand the Cumberland Basin as Western Harbour. An initial flawed consultation caused outrage, but Anna hopes a fresh start will bring opportunities to enhance this unique environment.

Laura Chapman recalls how a controversial planning application to develop Broadwalk shopping centre escalated into a scandal. When the planning committee's unanimous decision to reject the proposal was overturned, evidence pointed to interference by the mayor's office in conjunction with the developer and the planning committee chair. A high court judge was sufficiently concerned to grant an impending judicial review.

The final chapter of the book focusses on scrutiny and local democracy. In 2012, the mayoral system had promised a strong, accountable leader. But as scrutiny was increasingly undermined, and councillors sidelined, the demise of the mayoral system appeared inevitable. In 2022, Bristol voted to abolish its elected mayor and implement a new committee system.

Read on to discover more about these events that happened in our city, Bristol.

Promoting Inclusion

Zoe and Felix. Credit: Zoe Banks Gross

Kidical Mass, Bristol. Credit: Rob Browne

Growing active lifestyles in under-represented communities

Zoe Banks Gross, whose background is in environmental science and community development, has aspirations for Bristol to be a city where more people feel confident to walk, wheel or cycle, especially those from underserved backgrounds...

———

BRISTOL HAS DEEP inequalities when it comes to health. As a new parent, I became interested in creating more opportunities for new parents and families to cycle and founded a group called East Bristol Kidical Mass in 2014. This project benefited from funding in the beginning, helping to grow the group, highlighting the need to increase equity in cycling opportunities.

Bristol City Council previously had public health and physical activity teams which nurtured volunteers and assisted in developing projects and people who were interested in improving health outcomes in the city. This included the Kidical Mass project as well as managing a city-wide running programme designed to get people off the couch and able to run five kilometres. These roles and programmes were cut prior to the Covid pandemic even though there were still persisting health inequalities across the city.

Research from Professor Sir Michael Marmot, spanning from before 2010 through the early 2020s, shows the need to address health inequalities across England. A socially just, more equitable city of the future would have high-quality walking, wheeling and cycling infrastructure facilitating access to greenspace, everyday amenities and school and work. Bristol needs strong leadership to create a fairer, healthier city in the future.

The seed

In 2010, I was excited to move to Bristol, which had recently been given the moniker of Cycling City [1]. Since leaving the US in 2001, I had lived without owning a car, and cycling was my main form of transport. Riding my bike to and from work or to do the shopping was normal for me. But it was not always enjoyable and I was one of the few people who chose to travel this way. When I actually arrived in Bristol, I was pregnant. This didn't stop me from exploring the city, often on my bike. And it was how I got to my midwife appointments, until I could no longer fit my growing belly and my bike through our narrow Victorian doors at the same time. It would take over a year to get back on my bike, and even longer to cycle confidently with my baby in a seat on the back of my bike.

As soon as I did start cycling with the kiddo, I kicked myself for having waited so long. I'd been worried my centre of gravity had changed or that I would not be able to balance with the additional weight, which considering that I had commuted on my bike for years, was a bit silly. Around this time, late 2013, I also had become involved in a few local community activities – I got involved with a community energy group and I became interested in coordinating a Playing Out play street on my road [2].

Germination

Attending a local neighbourhood forum meeting on behalf of the community energy group, I heard about some funding for communities for active travel. My brain spun pretty quickly to an idea of starting a group for other parents like me who needed a little help or support getting back to cycling with their kids. At the time, there were a few types of child seat for the back or front of the bike and trailers that could hold a couple of little ones. I had also seen cargo bikes from the Netherlands which held 2-3 kids in a bucket on the front.

Being able to try out a few different options was something I thought might help parents who were trying to decide what might work best for them. Especially before making an investment, seeing how different seats would work (or not) for parents and kids, seemed like another step which would help people on the journey back onto bikes and into family cycling.

I spoke to an active travel officer from Bristol City Council, connected with a local Healthy Living Centre and with people from the Council's public health team to see if my idea resonated and how I could get it off the ground.

Digging in, with the right conditions

Setting up this project opened up a new world of public health and physical activity to me. My career before having a child was focused on ecology and environmental science, working in public and private sector, as well as some time in academia. I had never really engaged much outside my natural science sphere, nor had I been involved in organised sport or physical activity.

When I spoke to one of the council officers in the public health team about why I wanted to set up the project, she suggested I attend a Local Health Champion Training Course. This Level 2 Royal Society for Public Health course opened my eyes to how stark the health inequalities were in Bristol. We learned about the contrast in health outcomes in different parts of the city, and recommendations from a Fair Society, Healthy Lives: Marmot Review [3], which had a profound impact on me: "The starting point for this Review is that health inequalities that are preventable by reasonable means are unfair. Putting them right is a matter of social justice."

This new knowledge affected how I approached setting up Kidical Mass as well as other physical activity initiatives. Part of what pushed me to lead Kidical Mass, and deliver other physical activity sessions, was the desire to make a difference to local people's lives, especially if they were already worse off than people in other parts of Bristol.

Lawrence Hill, Bristol, where the Kidical Mass project is based, was in the most 10% deprived areas in England in 2015 and 2019 [4] and residents are less likely to live longer, healthier lives than people in more affluent parts of the city. As someone living in this ward, my own and my family's health was also a concern. In 2017, a report was published on air quality in Bristol, showing that the highest percentage (10.5 – 11) of mortality related to NO2 and PM 2.5 was Lawrence Hill [5]. Bristol City Council was required to implement a Clean Air Zone, which was enforced from November 2022 [6, 7]. Unfortunately, the coverage of the CAZ is lacking in the Lawrence Hill ward, which was a surprise considering it had the worst outcomes due to air pollution, the lowest level of car ownership, as well as a high proportion of the population being under 16.

This – and learning that active travel, like cycling, could help people live longer, healthier lives – really inspired me to progress with my idea to start a family cycling group, focused on getting mums back on their bikes. As well as get children used to cycling as a form of transport from an early age. Not only can active travel help increase physical activity levels, but it has very little greenhouse gas emissions, especially in comparison to using petrol or diesel cars.

Working with Wellspring Healthy Living Centre (now merged with Barton Hill Settlement, Wellspring Settlement) an application for funding was submitted to cover training for Ride Leaders, a variety of bike seats, a trailer and a Dutch cargo bike. Wellspring already had a shed full of bikes, which was located nearby, just off the Bristol and Bath Railway Path, a traffic-free shared walking and cycling route in East Bristol. These bikes were mostly suited to adults. It was possible to affix seats to a few of them to allow participants to "taste" different options on a led ride. Inspired by a movement in the US, Kidical Mass [8], I named the project East Bristol Kidical Mass. Working with Wellspring, we planned regular rides, some during the week, and some on weekends, trying to accommodate for different working patterns. I was delighted when the funding was approved for our project, and proceeded quickly with training and planning.

Establishing the seedling

May of 2014, and over the following years myself and other volunteers would lead dozens of rides. It was really exciting to see so much interest in the project – and so many local people discovering that they could cycle to access greenspaces, like the Railway Path, but also to access the city centre. Most of the participating adults were confident cyclists before having kids, more women joined the initial rides, but despite being in an area with a higher proportion of people from ethnic minority backgrounds, not many came from these backgrounds.

Shoots and leaves

The public health team at the Council suggested that I undertake the Cycle Instructor Training which they would cover and I could pay them back by delivering instruction as a volunteer for a set period of time. This was a great opportunity to learn how to properly teach other people to cycle, and I was interested in figuring out how to make the Kidical Mass rides more accessible for everyone, so it fitted well.

That summer I started assisting cycle instruction sessions at Easton Community Centre for women from Black, Asian and other minority ethnic groups. The Community Centre had several bikes on the premises which people could borrow for the sessions or pay a nominal fee to use at other times. These sessions were set up so that women could learn as a group and it worked really well. They enjoyed the atmosphere of women instructors who created a welcoming, non-judgemental space for learning. We ensured that they could wear clothing they felt comfortable in, for example, many of these women were Muslim and wore hijab, they had headscarves and usually wore skirts or dresses, and we showed them how to maintain their style of dress, but still cycle (e.g. clothes pegs to keep fabric out of the bike chain!) Being a woman of colour myself and instructing these courses also demonstrated that cycling was something for them, not just the people often depicted in the media (white men in Lycra.)

After the initial sessions where I volunteered my time, I was paid to deliver further sessions. Seeing these women, who often had never learned to ride as they weren't taught as girls, gain the ability and confidence to cycle, was amazing. They often had to overcome significant barriers to get to the point where they could learn, and many said that learning how to cycle gave them the confidence to learn how to do other things like swim or drive a car. And some of these women, with some basic skills, were later able to join the Kidical Mass rides with their children.

Teaching women to cycle who had never cycled as girls also taught me a lot about why some people don't cycle – whether they had never seen anyone that looked like them do it, or if they had associated it with sport, potentially involving sweat and/or mud, or had otherwise seen cycling as an activity for men and not women. Several of the women mentioned the fact that the bikes used for their lessons didn't really suit them – that if they were going to cycle, they would not want to be on a hybrid style city bike, but rather be on a bicycle which reflected them more, something stylish and pretty. This influenced writing the next funding bid where we asked for money to buy lightweight bikes for kids as well as lightweight, Dutch style, step through bikes for women. When these bikes arrived, and we began using them for cycle training sessions as well as Kidical Mass, it was notable how interested all of the women were in riding these bikes.

Although I never would have considered myself an activist, or community-focused person, Kidical Mass seemed to have a cascade effect on me. As a volunteer, I led regular bike rides for the first year. The second year of Kidical Mass, I proposed additional elements: dedicated refresher session rides for mums to gain confidence before joining a led ride, as well as a trial of basic cycling skills for reception aged children, and some instruction for mums of school aged children. Interest was high for each of these, and it was incredibly inspirational to see little kids get on pedal bikes and learn to ride, sometimes at the same time their mums were learning too. The refresher sessions helped mums get confident enough to join a larger ride, but they also said they felt more confident to get back to cycle commuting and other activities with their kids.

Working with a school and seeing first-hand the impact on the children who participated (there were about 30) galvanised me to go on to trial the Daily Mile at the same school:

The Daily Mile is a social physical activity, with children running, wheeling or walking – at their own pace – in the fresh air with friends. Children can occasionally walk to catch their breath, if necessary, but should aim to run, jog or wheel for the full 15 minutes. [9]

After this second year of Kidical Mass – which increased participation, widening the reach and also increased the numbers of kids and parents with basic cycling skills – I was ready to continue to scale up. The children who had been in the trailer, or on the seat on a parent's bike, were now cycling on their own, and some families were interested in longer rides. I continued to lead rides as a volunteer alongside two other regular volunteers, but was interested in scaling up, getting more volunteers, more Kidical Mass in other parts of the city, and trialling more basic skills sessions for Early Years.

Considering that I was never someone who identified as sporty, that I didn't like PE or gyms, I had accidentally become an activist in getting people active. Seeing the impacts that Kidical Mass was having, as well as the women who were learning to cycle, I also continued to undertake other training offered by the Council, including a taster session in sports coaching, then the Community Sports Leadership Award training and Leadership in Running Fitness.

Alongside the cycling activity, I began leading 'Couch to 5k' (C25K) running courses [10]. Being part of the journey for people to become more active, spending more time outside, was rewarding. These courses were held in parts of the city experiencing higher health inequalities, offering local people an opportunity to participate in a free running course. Most of the participants in the C25K courses were women, and many had struggled with being physically active in the past. Some of these women had also experienced harassment whilst running, being verbally abused because of their gender, appearance and/or ethnicity. Running as a group created a safe space for them to exercise, and to connect with other people and greenspace.

Challenges

Unfortunately, the funding stream which had provided the resource for Years 1 (May 2014-2015) and 2 (2015-2016) of Kidical Mass, was not available after 2016. This was definitely a blow to the project, but myself and the other volunteers were able to continue to offer free, regular led bike rides. We had more rides over the summer months, and just kept the group/project afloat with good will and the fact that most of us had children who were keen to join these rides.

I led C25k groups from 2015 until the end of 2019, when the Council said it could no longer afford to pay the instructors to lead these running groups. That year was also the last that I taught cycling to women in inner city Bristol, also because there wasn't any funding available. Watching programmes that I had been involved in get cut back, alongside the knowledge that the health inequalities I was addressing weren't shrinking, was difficult.

Achievements, setbacks, aspirations

From the seed of an idea to get more mums back on their bikes in 2014, I ended up also teaching cycling, leading running groups and getting into coaching. This was all possible due to the infrastructure of Bristol City Council in the early time frame, as well as supportive, knowledgeable officers at the Council who were well connected with the voluntary and community sector.

As austerity measures cut deeper, and the Council was restructured, the numbers of officers dwindled as the funding did. This was part of a perfect storm which meant that, when the pandemic hit, people from underserved backgrounds were experiencing high levels of inequality and poor health outcomes. The follow up research from Professor Sir Michael Marmot, Health Equity in England, The Marmot Review 10 years on, [11] showed that health inequalities had not only *not* been addressed sufficiently, but they had widened over the last ten years: "the more deprived areas, with greatest need, had the greatest reductions in per person spending."

Bristol's health inequalities are stark, and Sport England's most recent Active Lives data shows that levels of physical activity are also not improving for people who are from lower socio-economic classes [12]. This dataset also shows that women get less physical activity than men, and the people from Black, Asian and other minority ethnic groups are less active than those who are white.

Future growth

Currently, our city is full of barriers for becoming more active. Behaviour change interventions (e.g. free classes to learn to cycle, or get support to run 5k) are no longer funded by the Council. If some funding is found, this is often for short periods of time and does not always meet the needs of the communities most in need. Our walking and cycling infrastructure needs to improve significantly to ensure that everyone feels welcome walking, running, cycling or wheeling. People need to be able to access greenspace easily, as well as use active travel for everyday trips, like the school run, grocery shopping or to work. My aspiration for Bristol is a more equitable city, where more people feel confident to walk, wheel or cycle, especially those from underserved backgrounds. ∎

ACKNOWLEDGEMENTS

I never would have started Kidical Mass or become a cycle instructor without inspiration from Ben Bowskill and support from Celia Davis, the Community Active Travel Officers at the time. Kate Cooke at Bristol City Council was instrumental in connecting the dots and spurring me on with public health training opportunities. I am grateful for the other volunteers who led rides – Rae Pears, Abiir Shirdoon, Will Pomeroy and Jo Elms – it wouldn't have been possible without you. Also, thanks to my partner Bernhard Gross and kiddo, Felix Gross, who joined so many of the rides, adding to the fun, but also aiding in logistics.

REFERENCES

1. Bristol named UK's first 'cycling city'. Allegra Stratton and agencies. *The Guardian*, 19 June 2008. Available at: https://www.theguardian.com/politics/2008/jun/19/transport.transport1 (Accessed 5 June 2024)

2. https://playingout.net (Accessed 5 June 2024)

3. Fair Society, Healthy Lives. The Marmot Review, February 2010. Available at: https://www.instituteofhealthequity.org/resources-reports/fair-society-healthy-lives-the-marmot-review/fair-society-healthy-lives-full-report-pdf.pdf (Accessed 5 June 2024)

4. Bristol City Council. Deprivation in Bristol 2019 Summary findings of the 2019 English Indices of Deprivation within Bristol Local Authority Area, October 2019. Available at: https://www.bristol.gov.uk/files/documents/1905-deprivation-in-bristol-2019/file (Accessed 5 June 2024)

5. Air Quality Consultants Ltd. Health Impacts of Air Pollution in Bristol, February 2017. Available at: https://www.bristol.gov.uk/files/documents/599-health-impacts-of-air-pollution-in-bristol-february-2017/file (Accessed 5 June 2024)

6. Bristol City Council. Bristol's Clean Air Zone. Available at: https://www.bristol.gov.uk/residents/streets-travel/bristols-caz (Accessed 5 June 2024)

7. Bristol Clean Air Zone launches for some of the most polluting cars. *BBC News*, 28 November 2022. Available at: https://www.bbc.co.uk/news/uk-england-bristol-63778390 (Accessed 5 June 2024)

8. https://kidsonbike.org (Accessed 5 June 2024)

9. https://thedailymile.co.uk (Accessed 5 June 2024)

10. https://c25k.com (Accessed 5 June 2024)

11. Marmot Review, 10 Years on. February 2020. London: Institute of Health Equity. Available at: https://www.health.org.uk/publications/reports/the-marmot-review-10-years-on (Accessed 5 June 2024)

12. Active Lives. Adult Survey November 2022-2023 report, April 2024. Available at: https://www.sportengland.org/research-and-data/data/active-lives?section=access_the_reports (Accessed 5 June 2024)

Vince Ugly and Miss Venus Wailer at The House of Savalon Birds of Paradise edition. Credit: Darren Shepherd

Gender criminal at the Conqueer fashion show. Credit: Matt Hickmott

Making space for Bristol's diverse queer community

Andy Leake, freelance journalist specialising in queer culture, celebrates Bristol's rich and varied LGBT+ scene...

———

BRISTOL'S LGBT+ SCENE has undergone an explosive transformation in recent years. An old guard of collectives and event organisers has inspired layer upon layer of a new generation of queer groups. Spaces are being created for all subsections of the LGBT+ community. My work as *Bristol24/7*'s LGBT+ Editor has been to write articles representing Bristol's diverse queer community – from vogue performance spaces centring queer people of colour, to drag collectives celebrating non-binary and trans performers.

Bristol's queer nightlife has reached a point where on some weekends, you have to make a choice of which LGBT+ night you want to attend. There's art-rave, industrial music enthusiasts Conqueer, a friendly techno crowd at Queerky and cutting-edge music at pioneer night People Like Us. You can explore LGBT+ Italo-Disco nights or bouncy, fun house music at Don't Tell Your Mother. Sex positivity reigns at nights like Club Love.

What do all of these nights have in common? Bristol's immensely friendly LGBT+ community. There's also a movement in the community towards events outside of nightlife spaces. As people search for opportunities for sober socialising, more groups are emerging. From queer choirs, hiking and running groups to supper clubs that donate their profits to the city's trans community. Niches are being carved out, creating a rich and varied LGBT+ community.

A network of queer collectives

I've lived across the world, and something I highly value when I'm moving to a new city is a vibrant queer scene. The difference between the terms queer, gay and LGBT depends on who you ask. For me, queer is an umbrella term, it unites the community under one label. The terms gay and LGBT+ separate people into boxes, so I prefer to say queer. When I first moved to Bristol, the city was recovering from years of Covid restrictions, I was told there wasn't much of a queer scene left. I thought, surely for a city this size, there must be more going on than two gay clubs. Through going on dates and chatting with people in bars, I discovered a network of queer collectives.

I want to explain the difference between a commercial gay club, and a queer event run by the community. Gay clubs like Bristol's OMG and Queenshilling tend to attract crowds of non-queer people. They can be fun. However, they're not necessarily safer spaces for all subsections of the LGBT+ community. There was historically little visibility for queer people of colour and the trans community.

The first queer club night I learned about was run by a performance collective called The House of Savalon. It was created by drag artist Astro-Zenica and heavyweight performer Elektra Duboir. Always resolutely themed, the House of Savalon parties introduced me to some of Bristol's most prominent community leaders and performers. Their first event I went to was birthday party themed. One of the highlights of that event was a segment where Astro brought audience members onto the stage and asked for their birthday wishes. One person wanted to be famous, so Lady Gaga's Paparazzi was cued, as the audience shone phone lights on them. The second person's wish was for a 40 inch HD TV Screen. Audience members were invited onto stage, where they recreated a scene from a nature documentary framed inside an HD TV. Swiftly followed by a best dressed competition and fashion show, it was a silly, carefree atmosphere.

The House of Savalon also ran a performance residency, called Get Qweird. This was a programme of weekly events at Lost Horizon. Newer drag performers were invited to perform once a week, every week, for two months. It was an experimental testing ground for new material. The performers were then showcased at The House of Savalon's club nights. The club nights were usually held in the lofty tunnels of Loco Klub, underneath Temple Meads station. Performances ranged from perfectly choreographed live performances any pop princess would envy, to eclectic rappers and gravity-defying pole dancing. As I'd learn with a lot of Bristol's queer scene, tied in between all of these performances was an undertone of protest. Whether it was denouncing homophobes, or challenging the status quo on trans identity, queer issues were aired and debated.

After the performers finished, the dance floor would open up. Attendees embraced the themes fully. Speaking to Astro-Zenica for a Bristol24/7 article, the themes were introduced as a great way to break the ice, bonding the audience through a common look. The House of Savalon Birds of Paradise edition encouraged attendees to channel the extravagant, flamboyant birds-of-paradise. There were bold displays of creativity; bright colours, feathered eyelashes and costumes based on birds caught in an oil slick. The Birds of Paradise edition opened with a gorgeous all-trans performance created in defiance of the Section 35 appeal. The appeal was the UK government's controversial decision to block Scotland's Gender Recognition Reform. This was an unfortunate step away from Scotland's trans community being able to have their gender legally recognised.

The House of Savalon events slowed down once host Astro-Zenica moved away from Bristol. However, the Get Qweird residencies saw some go from performing for the first time, to creating their own collectives. One influential performer to emerge from The House of Savalon's Get Qweird residencies is the artist known as Gender Criminal. Starting as a performer, Gender Criminal now fathers the trans and nonbinary drag collective House of Boussé. Their events usually run at queer-owned venue, Cloak, on Gloucester Road. The atmosphere at House of Boussé is always fun, showcasing a range of talent across the gender identity spectrum. Their events feature poetry readings, lip sync performances and lots of comedy. The nights are held together by Gender Criminal's passionately political hosting. It served as a place for fun as well as a place to distribute resources. Art and activism mingle to spread awareness of an issue and achieve political action.

When I spoke with Gender Criminal, for an article about a solidarity event and fundraiser called Queers for Palestine, he told me that art is inherently political [1]. It is a response to the world around us. The event raised money and energy, but also created a place to unite the community around a common aim. Gender Criminal has been central to many topical conversations that happened across Bristol. To me he represents a younger generation of politically intelligent and engaged queers.

Creating safer spaces

A night run in part by Gender Criminal, Quaverz, ran into some difficulties regarding a venue, the Crown, and its security policy. When running a queer event, there are precautions and measures that are needed to create safer spaces. There were issues with the Crown's security, clashes over how to deal with the welfare of attendees, and no officially designated gender-neutral toilets [2]. After the incident, The Crown outlined a series of new policies which tackled anti-racism, LGBTQ+ inclusivity, anti-sexual assault and other issues. The incident with Gender Criminal's night helped shape their new welfare policy. Incidents like this show how queer events can help shape Bristol's venues, making them safer and more welcoming spaces.

Speaking of creating intentional safer spaces, a group that's grown hugely in influence is Bristol's Ballroom Community. Ballroom is an international community started in 1980s New York by the Black and Latin American communities. It is a space to celebrate and champion queer and trans people of colour. Ballroom events consist of different performance categories, where performers compete to win that category and a grand prize. Categories include Vogue (a dance style made famous by TV Shows like Pose and Madonna's 'Vogue' music video), Face (where competitors show off their best facial features), and Runway walks and Realness (where walkers attempt to pass as straight). When ballroom communities gather and compete against one another, it's known as a ball. It's captivating to see mind-blowing performances, but also an environment where everyone is celebrated. Across the spectrums of race, body type, sexuality, gender expression, all are welcome and uplifted. Watching ballroom events definitely helped me in my own journey of expressing my queerness more visibly.

Performers belong to houses, with their leaders known as fathers and mothers. They are called houses as young queer people of colour were often forced to leave their families, due to homophobia. The ballroom community becomes their chosen family. Houses are well-established and run out of major cities like London and Paris. A sign of having an authentic ballroom scene is having some of its members belong to houses. There is a long and highly esteemed history of ballroom. The art form has been increasingly appropriated in mainstream culture due to the popularity of shows like Rupaul's Drag Race and vogue dancing. People may say they love ballroom, duckwalks and dips, without knowing their cultural significance. As a result of this, there is a huge amount of importance in creating authenticity in a city's ballroom scene.

When I first met Aysha, the 'Mother' of Bristol's Ballroom Community, the community was still establishing itself. I interviewed her in Spring 2023 for one of my *Bristol24/7* articles [3]. I'd seen the ballroom community performing at a few queer club nights. The scene was in its beginning phases. A lot of the community's practices centred on education. They ran workshops, where attendees were taught the history of each category. You don't have to be queer or a person of colour to participate. However, an awareness of the history and culture of ballroom is important. For example, Realness, where walkers attempt to pass as straight has a strong history behind it. Queer people of colour had to practise how they could hide their sexuality. It was an important survival tactic to remain safe in less open-minded environments. Aysha told me in those earlier stages, to build an authentic scene you have to share knowledge of ballroom culture.

The next time we met, the community had expanded rapidly. Having found a few determined and proactive members, the group found its feet. Watching them at Bristol Pride was overwhelming. They raised the roof by throwing a mini ball, performing to a packed out, sweaty tent. The amount of love they received from the crowd made me emotional. I was watching their hard work pay off in real time. Walkers from Bristol Ballroom began to perform in other cities, from Cardiff, to London, to Paris. At functions in other cities, they'd always be talking up their hometown. That's how Bristol has been put on the ballroom community map.

A thriving scene

The first time I really clocked that the ballroom scene was thriving was when I went to one of their social events, called Fruitea. This was described as a practice ball, where walkers could train in a fun, friendly environment. Fruitea has been running at Bristol's Trinity Centre. The high ceilings and stained glass create an appropriately dramatic backdrop to the talent displayed at these events. Some Bristol Ballroom Community members have been invited to join houses. Therefore, prominent members of these houses now attend Bristol Ballroom Community functions, elevating the levels of performance.

At the start of the events, they do a roll call. This is when legendary and iconic members of the community are introduced, and celebrated. I remember watching members of the House of Telfar during roll call. They were all so talented in every category. From doing backflips and frontflips in dance categories, to Fashion Week-level walks in the runway categories. To me, Fruitea was a huge step up in terms of what was expected from a Bristol Ballroom event. It's still an incredibly friendly scene. The smoking area outside of Trinity is always full of people hugging, cackling and chatting away in excitement. This atmosphere is carried through all of the community's events.

In April 2024 Bubblegum and Maze Louboutin hosted Bristol's first ever Kiki function. A Kiki function is a social event, with categories. It's significant because it can only be hosted by members of houses. Hosting a Kiki function proves Bristol ballroom scene's authenticity. The event was called the Wave Your Flag Kiki. I covered the event, taking photographs and documenting the historic moment [4].

Walkers were encouraged to wear their home country's flags or traditional costumes. Before it started, everyone was hugging each other, saying hellos. People were bubbling with excitement, talking about who was wearing what, who was walking which category. Energy in the room overflowed as the roll call began. There were icons from Bristol and beyond, alongside established judges who received standing ovations. A stand out category was 'Best Dressed', where performers wore costumes representing their cultures. There were flowing gowns with Oriental fan head pieces and parasols to represent China. An interpretation of a female Welsh National Costume, was accessorised with chandelier earrings and a stylish purse. A gorgeously sculpted dress paid tribute to Liverpool's unique culture, alongside a sign being held that read 'Scouse, Not English'. Each look that came down the runway had everyone out of their seats. It was a joyous celebration of diversity, with walkers proudly representing their cultures, in a space that celebrated and championed them.

To me, fashion and the queer community go hand in hand. LGBT+ culture has influenced fashion throughout history. A great example of Bristol's LGBT+ perspective when it comes to fashion would be the annual fashion show run by the collective, Conqueer, that highlighted Bristol's queer designers, models and stylists. It was hosted in Loco Klub, a venue made up of cavernous, brick-walled tunnels underneath Bristol's Temple Meads train station.

The show was opened by a walker using a sword to cut through fabric that blocked the runway. It was highly creative. A pair of dancers wore dresses covered in mirrors. Lights shone on them, and they danced and moved as models walked past them and ambient music played. The light refracted and danced around the room, it was gorgeous. Another moment that stuck with me was when the dancers wore huge dresses filled with smoke. They span and hit the dresses, spilling the smoke out onto the runway. Performers dressed as whimsical woodland creatures, dancing while models continued to walk the runway. I seem to remember a model being pulled by a chain as they sat on a toilet, being tugged through the gravelly floor of the venue.

People like us

When I spoke with Conqueer, they cited one collective as their influence. People Like Us, or PLU, is a queer collective created by Chris Collins. Starting as a club night, the collective has moved towards live music events as well as an annual, queer festival called PLU Summer Camp. The events were created out of Chris' love for cutting-edge electronic music. Initially reliant on their friends, for years the nights welcomed around 30 to 40 attendees. This changed when PLU was asked to run a closing party for an iconic Bristol venue – The Motorcycle Showroom, on Stokes Croft. Chris told me the venue would open well into the morning, with some of the best DJs, as rain pelted through holes in the ceiling. PLU were invited to run the closing party, which ran until around 10am. It was run alongside club night Dirty Talk, whose organisers now run Strange Brew. The event had a huge catwalk going up to the DJ booth lined with dancers. All of the resident artists in the studios upstairs created decorations. People talk about The Motorcycle Showroom closing event to this day.

After the success of the event, Chris was on the lookout for a new venue for PLU. They were offered what is now Dare To. Nobody else ran events there at the time, it was still a fully functioning gay sauna. At the time when house music was in its infancy, a lot of the black, queer DJs pioneering the genre were only booked to play by gay saunas, due to discrimination. For three years, PLU had complete exclusivity at Dare To, running parties on their rooftop terrace. A few years in, Jaye Ward also joined PLU as a resident DJ, helping to elevate the parties further. When PLU announced they were ending their club nights, I interviewed Chris about Bristol's LGBT+ history [5].

Chris explained that pre-Covid, a lot of young, queer talent was lost to London. A handful of queer parties existed, but you saw the same people at each event. After Covid, new venues like Lost Horizon and Strange Brew were created. New queer collectives popped up, and PLU continued to be held in the highest regard by the community. When Chris announced that PLU would be ending as a club night, an overwhelming amount of messages were received. People said the event changed their lives. It helped them on their own journeys of navigating their identity. PLU's club nights belonged to attendees as much as they belonged to the organisers.

Chris gave me a wonderful quote: "In my experience, most parties come to an end because no one goes anymore, and I don't want to get to that stage. It would be a really sad way for it to end, we're not there yet, so I want to go out on a high. It's challenging, because I know the last few parties will be great, and I'll ask myself why we're stopping it. But I like nice endings, and I think it's good to go out on a high."

The baton for queer nights focused on music has been picked up by people like Daisy Moon. A DJ who learned alongside esteemed DJ Shanti Celeste, Daisy started a mix series and club night called Off-Kilter. Not specifically marketed as a queer club night, it perhaps represents the future of queer events in Bristol. As a queer woman, Daisy platforms queer, non-binary and trans DJs like the unstoppable Bashkka. This has attracted a queer crowd, without shouting about it being an LGBT+ night. When Bashkka performed at Strange Brew in Bristol, she bought the eclectic beats of New York's ballroom scene together with the intoxicating basslines of Berlin's dancefloors. It was the best music I'd heard since being in some of the most renowned techno clubs in Berlin. To hear that quality of music in a queer club environment is a welcome addition to Bristol.

One thing that sticks out across Bristol's LGBT+ scene is its universal friendliness, whether it's in the ballroom scene, at a fashion show or a nightlife event. Whenever I have friends to visit, it's the first thing people comment on. You can go to an event by yourself, and people will talk to you. I think it comes from being a smaller city, but also a city with a carefree, liberal reputation.

Beyond nightlife spaces

There has been a recent movement towards socialising outside of nightlife spaces. Queer people have historically been more confined to nightlife, where their creativity and expression is free to thrive in safer spaces built by the community. However, nowadays there is more mindfulness around sobriety and protecting mental health.

Queer Hiking Bristol is a group set up by Hannah Atkinson. She originally set up the group to find queer friends to walk with. Whilst Bristol is a liberal city, heading into the surrounding countryside can be intimidating for visibly queer people. In smaller villages and towns, it might not be as comfortable to walk around holding a same-sex partner's hand. That's why it's great to have a group like Queer Hiking Bristol, so LGBT+ people can take up space unapologetically in the countryside. Over a few months, the group grew in popularity. Their weekly walks grew from a handful of people, to over 50 walkers. A weekend trip to the Peak District sold out in five minutes. Organisers link drivers with people who don't have access to a car, making hiking more accessible. Queer Hiking Bristol has provided an opportunity for the LGBT+ community to meet, socialise, and enjoy the benefits of exercise. The group is increasingly popular, now drawing in walkers from Wales and the Mendips. Hannah told me how fulfilled she felt to have created a space that people are excited to come back to.

The Phoenix Song Project, created by Kat Larabi-Tchalaia and Francis Myerscoug, offers a space for trans and non-binary people who have felt uncomfortable in traditional choirs to explore their voices in a supportive, informal setting [6]. Kat explained: "We sing songs that bring us joy as trans people. It's a community that suffers a lot, especially at the moment. If I can create a small group where people can be themselves and make music, for me, that's the goal."

Mental health is widely discussed within Bristol's LGBT+ community. This is happening against a rise in anti-queer and anti-trans rhetoric internationally. According to charity Mental Health UK, LGBT+ people are 1.5 times more likely to develop depression and anxiety disorders. Mental health support charity Changes Bristol runs an LGBT peer-support group. A lot of mental health support isn't specialised to LGBT+ people. Changes Bristol has created a space where you don't have to explain aspects of being queer. There are a lot of spaces for LGBT+ people in Bristol, but having a space centring mental health discussion is important.

A challenging process for some members of Bristol's LGBT+ community is fundraising for trans individual's gender-affirming care. This encompasses procedures that can change people's physical appearance to align with their gender identity. Current wait lists are around a decade. Serving Bristol is a supper club set up by Robbie Cottle. It is a non-profit group hosting regular dinners where all of the profits go towards a randomly-selected individual's gender-affirming care. Whilst funds raised won't cover the full costs of surgery, it's a step in the right direction for what can be a mentally draining journey. The group is part of a movement amongst Bristol's LGBT+ network to find alternative spaces to meet outside of the city's nightlife. There's a DIY, anti-establishment scene running throughout Bristol. There's often a can-do attitude, whereby the community will see an issue and think of ways in which they can contribute towards solving the issue.

The city's trans community is thriving, from House of Boussé creating spaces to platform trans performers, to the election of Kaz Self onto Bristol City Council. Councillor Self is the first person to be elected onto Bristol City Council whilst being openly trans. I had the pleasure of interviewing her, and she spoke in-depth about how excited she was to represent the city's trans community [7]. Councillor Self used to be involved with Trans Pride South West. This event is now called Trans Pride Bristol and runs annually, drawing in huge crowds to celebrate the city's trans community.

The work goes on

There is still work to be done. The community has been shaken by several attacks. In Summer 2023, a Bristol Pride Billboard was set on fire [8]. That same year a trans pride picnic was disrupted by people shooting bb-gun pellets [9]. In January 2024, a man was the victim of a homophobic attack outside Seamus O'Donnells [10]. Still at some venues you'll see same-sex couples kissing, holding hands and getting scowls from other people in the venue. Bristol's LGBT+ friendliness is growing, but we must continue working to protect and champion the queer community.

Bristol's LGBT+ scene has blossomed after the extended period of Covid lockdowns. It seems like it has rebirthed in pursuit of representation and visibility. There are clubs, events and collectives for an ever-growing array of LGBT+ community interests. Bristol is becoming more visible as a queer city, being put on the map across various LGBT+ subcultures. Bristol Pride was named 'Pride Organisation of the Year' at the Gaydio Pride Awards in 2024 [11]. You can see displays of queerness throughout the city, from couples holding hands to pride flags on buses, roads and in shop windows. Bristol's reputation as an LGBT+ friendly city is now undeniable. Long may this reputation continue. ■

ACKNOWLEDGEMENTS

I'd like to thank everyone who has helped me along this journey. David, for inviting me to my first ever queer night in Melbourne. Seni, for inspiring me to move into writing and journalism as a career. Shoutout to my amazing friends for loving me as I've learned to openly express my sexuality and discover my truest identity. Edie, my sister Ingrid, and Emma – thanks for your help in reading over this chapter. Having some extra eyes helped pull everything together. I'm eternally grateful to the LGBT+ community for trusting me to tell your stories. Without your belief in me and my writing, none of this would be possible. I want to thank any platform that I've worked with. *We Are Explorers, Stuff NZ, The Bristol Cable, Bristol24/7,* you've all played a part in bringing underrepresented LGBT+ perspectives to mainstream media. To my family and my support network, I'm so grateful for your continued support throughout every step of my career.

REFERENCES

1. Andy Leake. Art and activism mingle for queer performance night in aid of Palestine. *Bristol24/7*, 18 January 2024. Available at: https://www.bristol247.com/lgbtq/news-lgbtq/art-and-activism-mingle-for-queer-performance-night-in-aid-of-palestine/ (Accessed 31 May 2024)

2. Andy Leak. Venue responds to allegations raised by queer and trans nightlife event. *Bristol24/7*, 25 August 2023. Available at: https://www.bristol247.com/lgbtq/news-lgbtq/venue-responds-to-allegations-raised-by-queer-and-trans-nightlife-event/ (Accessed 31 May 2024)

3. Andy Leake. A look inside Bristol's blossoming ballroom scene. *Bristol24/7*, 2 May 2023. Available at: https://www.bristol247.com/lgbtq/features-lgbtq/a-look-inside-bristols-blossoming-ballroom-scene/ (Accessed 31 May 2024)

4. Andy Leake. History is made as Bristol hosts first Kiki ballroom community function. *Bristol24/7*, 19 April 2024. Available at: https://www.bristol247.com/lgbtq/features-lgbtq/history-is-made-as-bristol-hosts-first-ballroom-community-function/ (Accessed 31 May 2024)

5. Andy Leake. Celebrated queer club night announces it's ending. *Bristol 24/7*, 13 February 2024. Available at: https://www.bristol247.com/lgbtq/news-lgbtq/celebrated-queer-club-night-announces-its-ending/ (Accessed 31 May 2024)

6. Andy Leake. Helping trans and non-binary singers find their voice. *Bristol24/7*, 17 December 2023. Available at: https://www.bristol247.com/lgbtq/features-lgbtq/helping-trans-and-non-binary-singers-find-their-voice/ (Accessed 7 June 2024)

7. Andy Leake. Bristol's first female councillor to be elected while openly trans. *Bristol24/7*, 17 June 2024. Available at: https://www.bristol247.com/news-and-features/features/bristol-first-female-councillor-elected-openly-trans/ (Accessed 20 June 2024)

8. Emma Elgee. Bristol Pride billboard set alight in suspected hate crime. *BBC News*, 19 June 2023. Available at: https://www.bbc.co.uk/news/uk-england-bristol-65955843 (Accessed 31 May 2024)

9. Louisa Streeting. Police investigating hate crime after BB guns fired at Trans Pride picnic. *BristolLive*, 3 July 2023. Available at: https://www.bristolpost.co.uk/news/bristol-news/police-investigating-hate-crime-after-8569077 (Accessed 31 May 2024)

10. Bea Swallow. Homophobic attack outside Bristol pub Seamus O'Donnell's. *BBC News*, 25 January 2023. Available at: https://www.bbc.co.uk/news/uk-england-bristol-68099944 (Accessed 31 May 2024)

11. Andy Leake and Betty Woolerton. Bristol Pride named 'Pride Organisation of the year'. *Bristol24/7*, 17 February 2024. Available at: https://www.bristol247.com/lgbtq/news-lgbtq/bristol-pride-named-pride-organisation-of-the-year/ (Accessed 6 June 2024)

Watershed, Bristol. Credit: Martin Booth

Watershed gender neutral toilets. Credit: Martin Booth

Toilets are for everyone

Clare Reddington, CEO of Watershed, together with Jo Kimber and Alec Stevens, describe the importance of making the Watershed toilets welcoming and inclusive...

———

April 2022: Our toilets are for everyone – so what is the problem?

Content warning: This article refers to criticism of Watershed's toilets from gender critical campaigners.

TOILETS IN PUBLIC buildings – a place to poo, get ready to go out, hide, take a breath, check your phone, wash your hands, change your tampon. Providing clean, pleasant toilets for all is part of Watershed's public service – you can pick up menstruation products for free and you don't have to be a customer to use them – they are public toilets open to everyone (an increasing city-centre rarity).

Over the years we have had a fair amount of feedback on the shabby state of our current provision, so during lockdown we decided to forge ahead with our plans for refurbishment. Our new toilets meet the needs of loads of our users – including those wanting a speedier wee, parents, carers and people with disabilities. Our toilet strategy is to provide a range of options that suit everyone and we are excited to get moving – we are currently in the process of choosing colours, and the contractor who will deliver them.

Our current toilet provision AND our planned future toilet provision feature the following options in separate locations: gender neutral toilets with fully enclosed cubicles and sinks; toilets for men; toilets for women; single unit fully enclosed toilets; accessible toilets.

We have had lots of warm, genuine love for what we are planning:

"Watershed's toilet plans are fabulous!" However, we did not anticipate the backlash we would also face by starting a public fundraising campaign in the name of toilets. Or the time it would take to manage the correspondence.

Firstly, don't get me wrong – we love feedback. Dropping us a line with a question or a concern is really welcome – we will do our best to reply fully and we hope you will take the time to read the answer. Feedback helps us learn, improve and do better. However, a lot of the feedback on our toilets – in forums, emails, letters and on twitter – is based on inaccurate information about both our current provision and our plans for upgrade. Some of it is organised gender critical campaigning, and some of it is our own community.

The complaints started with people concerned that we had abolished single sex toilets – which we have not. They now include whether we will police who can go into the women's toilets – which we will not. Some ask reasonable questions from a place of love, some from a place of fear. Lots are nasty – they hope we end up on the sex offenders register or 'get sued to oblivion'. The backlash is not as awful as others have faced, but it takes its toll at a time when working in the culture sector is pretty tough. We answer everyone at least once and move on if it is clear we can't agree.

In a way toilet-gate has been quite useful in signalling the importance of toilets in our commitment to an inclusive welcome. It is also a lesson – as we seek to embody our values and be more open about the issues we believe in, we might not take all of our customers and audiences with us.

November 2022: Our newest toilets are finally open!

It is with great relief and joy that this week we have opened (most of) our new facilities. Situated in the top foyer of Watershed, the new toilets are bright, welcoming and a physical embodiment of our values. We have spent rather a lot of time in the last two years thinking about toilets. A surprising amount perhaps, but we have learnt how vital they are to providing an inclusive welcome.

Visitors can choose whichever toilet they feel comfortable in. The new cubicles are all completely enclosed and are for all genders. Some have a sink, some are ambulant (a bit more spacious with supports such as grab rails) and there is also a large family room (that will be open soon). Next door we have a new accessible toilet (which means we now have two) and just through the Café & Bar we still have separate male and female toilets.

With very few public toilets open in the city centre we think it's an important part of our public service to make our toilets available to everyone whether they are a customer or not. And as period poverty is increasing in the UK – anyone can access free period products in all of our toilets.

Over the years we have had a fair amount of feedback on the shabby state of our loos. Originally conceived as part of a larger capital project (to include a fourth cinema), the impact of Covid meant that we had to split the project into phases for affordability. A wrench but nevertheless a small miracle that we could proceed at all.

I have written elsewhere about some of the backlash we received in pursuit of inclusive toilets – I don't intend to go back over it – our hope is that we can all move on. In general, the love and gratitude we have received has always outweighed the concern.

From the cubicles to the signage (the final signage is yet to be installed), the design has been carefully considered – we reviewed our plans for gender inclusion with experts from Around the Toilet, and used our strategic partnership with the West of England Centre for Independent Living (WECIL) to consult on signage, colour schemes, physical access, light and noise at the beginning and end of the process. WECIL have helped us put hand dryers at wheelchair user height, advised that symbols AND words on the doors are more accessible for visually impaired people, and to use raised words rather than braille. This sort of detail is easy to miss if you aren't someone with lived experience of disability, which makes consultations with groups like WECIL essential before making changes to a building and we are grateful for their support and help.

For a talk on public conveniences recently, Helen Jaffa shared some of the ways that Watershed's toilets are used on a weekly basis including changing period products, crying, resting, having a panic attack, doing drugs, keeping warm, sleeping, washing, getting changed and getting ready to go out. Some of these are illegal, so we ask people to stop and support them to leave, but most are just very human functions and demonstrate why accessible and inclusive toilet spaces are essential.

Watershed's new toilets also now serve excellent Insta – the light is lovely and the mirrors in there are fab. It was in the comments of a toilet selfie that Sandy Mahal and I came up with the idea of a celebration of the public toilet and its many uses. This brief was more than smashed by Jo Kimber and Alec Stevens, who have collected your toilet stories into a most brilliant zine. Grab a (toilet) seat, get comfy and have a read of this moving, charming love letter to the many functions of a public loo.

Inconvenience – stories from inside Watershed's loos

Illustrations Alec Stevens, words Jo Kimber

Everything you are about to read is true and I'll start with this: everybody goes to the toilet. This isn't the place to be shy about that; we're going to get into it all, this is a roll your sleeves up, very extra long marigolds up to the elbows kind of situation. I spent a lot of time undercover in the toilets at Watershed, which yes is weird but it was for research and I learned (and smelled) a lot.

There are a lot of noises in toilets: whispers and burps and yes really delicate farts and big performative show offy ones, and sniffles and tears and giggles and plops; the rush of water running competing with the hand dryer, strains followed by moans, followed by deep relieved sighs; the rustle of clothes being pulled down then up; toilet paper endlessly being rolled around a hand or folded neatly into two, ready for the wipe; tampons being ripped out of wrappers or sanitary towels unstuck from knickers; strategic coughs to try and hide exactly what it is that's going on inside.

Toilets for some of us are places of great unease: the fear of being heard, of creating a smell so bad people actually comment on it, out loud, disgusted, or of not having the right bag and so instead having to stuff your knickers with toilet roll so you don't get your period everywhere. Or not having a body that is conducive with the space with low seats that makes the pain worse and adds to an already plethora of discomfort. Or not actually thinking you should be in that space, faced with a toilet that isn't available right now and told in no uncertain terms to just go somewhere else. Personally, I have a deep rooted crippling anxiety of toilets that flush automatically, they always seem ready to go before I am, then I'm stuck with 'damp bum' and no matter how much toilet paper I throw at it, it never feels completely dry.

But I like toilets. I like how awkward they can be and how awkward us humans can be in them. For clarity, toilets are being awkward when they won't flush the gigantic poo you've just deposited. A helpful hint I recently learned about the two flush poo rule, which is a must for public toilets (such tight pipes) where you do a little cheeky flush halfway through and then keep going, therefore not having to violate any toilet brushes or god forbid get a member of staff and tell them what you've done. I like listening to the choir of sounds they and their users make, childish melodies punctuated by the occasional wet fart and streams of pee that hit each toilet bowl at different speeds, like the woodwind and string sections of an orchestra trying to outdo one another.

I love the moment when someone realises they might have finished what they were doing before the person they came in with has finished what they were doing, which is probably (and let's get this out of the way at the beginning) a poo, or a wee, or bog bingo: a very celebrated both. Do you wait for them? Or do you slip out without saying anything? Perhaps they are already outside, wondering where the hell you are? Next time you're in the toilet I implore you to listen out for this: a drama so real, it's better than telly. The best thing is when they speak, a frantic, 'oh my god, Brenda.... are you still in here?' or a bolder, more passive aggressive, 'We're running late. I'm waiting outside'. Note the absence of a name here but don't be deceived, they know who they are. When a reply does come, I can always tell the difference between someone who is still mid-poo and someone who is aimlessly scrolling through twitter without a care in the world #whenelsedoihavetimeforthat

And once you've waded through the noise and social disquiet, I recommend allowing yourself a moment, just one little moment to fully appreciate that the seat you're warming or have warmed or may warm at some point, exists. There really aren't many in Bristol centre. Public toilets are a breather; they are places we seek out that mean we don't have to stay tethered to the safe boundary line of, 'but will we make it home in time'?

They are freedom, giving us privacy to do what we gotta do when we're out and about. This zine is a celebration and acknowledgement of that.

We hope you enjoy the stories of the people who use the loo at Watershed; a place you'll always be welcome to visit even if the only thing you need to do when you get there is an emergency poo.

Colin works as the Security Guard at Watershed most nights. He'll have held the door open for you and wished you a good evening on your way in and probably on your way out too. He does this for everyone, it's all part of the service. We wanted to know if he had any stories about the toilets at Watershed and we were under no illusions that some of them might not be very nice.

Colin knows most of the homeless folk who frequent the walkway outside of Watershed. He calls them walkway dwellers and when they come in to use the toilet, he says, 'they have a wee, sometimes a wash and sometimes, something else. The access toilet is left in a right state sometimes. Recently, two girls came in all fine and dandy but one of them did a runner, leaving her mate to get a lift to hospital via a blue light taxi; there was evidence they'd done drugs.' Have you seen the yellow box in this toilet? Perhaps you chose to ignore it or think that's an odd thing to be in the accessible toilet next to cinema one. It's a sharps bin by the way, a specially designed box with a lid that is a safe place for people to dispose of needles.

Colin also told us about a man who once fell asleep whilst on the toilet at Watershed. He gave him the tried and tested, 'Time to go fella', but it didn't work so Colin had to give him a poke with a broom handle, gently of course, whilst leaning precariously over the top of the cubicle. As the man started to stir, he thought Colin was taking photos of him and became verbally and physically aggressive. Colin spotted the man months later as he was leaving Watershed with his mum; Colin was as ever the consummate professional.

There are other stories and Colin said that sometimes it's more horror than humour. Not that many people would notice that because of the cleaners, the front of house staff team, the person that orders the loo paper, the member of staff that checks the temperature of the water, the person who deals with a blocked urinal by removing a hairball of pubes, the one that clears up the sick, the one who knocks gently on the cubicle door because they can hear someone crying, the guy who checks each cubicle each night to make sure no-one is left behind. We asked Colin if he ever felt like the gatekeeper of the toilets and, slightly offended, he said, 'no, as public, well that means all, doesn't it.'

Spy game

I have an unpredictable stomach and as much as I try to plan around it, it's often not an option and I have to sprint to wherever is nearest when my tummy is uneasy. That is often Watershed. For a long time I didn't know they were public, so I've always sneaked in, which as you can imagine when you're on the brink of ruining your trousers is no easy feat. I always pause just outside, take a breath and assess the situation, channelling my extensive spy training (I've watched at least two of the Bourne films). When you get past the box office or security, it's straight up the stairs, take a left and hope a film hasn't just finished, though I do know about the secret toilets on the other side of the bar now. Once I used the side automatic door, thinking I was clever, trying to stay low and avoid eye contact. It was absolutely pointless. At least two members of staff said hello to me and hoped I had a nice day.

Bringing Up Baby

When my daughter was a baby, I took her to cinebabies, the weekly parent and baby cinema screening at Watershed. After the film had finished, I realised I needed to change her nappy, immediately. We went to the accessible toilet with the fold down baby changing table. It was at this point I found what can only be described as an 'apoocalypse.' It was awful. My child was literally covered in their own poo and wriggling around quite happily in it. The speedy nappy change turned into an entire outfit and full body wash, I believe there were moments when we both cried. Other parents had also started knocking on the door, asking if we were ok. We were not ok. I laugh about it now but will never forget, and I often remind my daughter when we visit Watershed, the time she exploded in cinema 3.

January 2023: Watershed flushed with success at the Loo Of The Year Awards

The Loo of the Year Awards have been running since 1987 and are aimed at highlighting and improving standards of 'away from home' toilet provision across the UK. We picked up their best loo in England (Individual Business Category) award for our facilities situated in the top foyer, which opened in November 2022. Watershed were also graded Diamond for the Eco Friendly Toilet Award, awarded to entries judged to be the most environmentally friendly.

These bright and welcoming loos are some of the very few public toilets open for everyone in Bristol city centre. As part of the Awards, inspectors make unannounced visits to thousands of toilet sites to judge them, rating against 101 categories including signage and décor, fixtures and fittings, accessibility, cleanliness, overall management, and customer care.

Our toilets were designed with the goal of being one of the most inclusive and welcoming spaces in Bristol. They include floor to ceiling self-contained toilets (some with hand-washing facilities and mirrors and some that are ambulant), another accessible toilet, baby changing facilities and a large family room. Anyone can use the free period products in the toilets supplied by ethical and sustainable provider Grace & Green, whose mission is to provide access to safe and sustainable period products for all.

The design was carefully considered: our plans were reviewed by experts from Around the Toilet, and strategic partners WECIL consulted on signage, colour schemes, physical access and light and noise. The Eco Friendly Award recognises the most environmentally friendly toilet from all entry categories. Our toilets include low energy lighting, energy efficient heating, cooling and hot water systems and wall tiles and flooring made from recycled materials. As part of the opening of the new facilities in November 2022, we launched Inconvenience, a zine by Jo Kimber and Alec Stevens celebrating stories from the toilets and why access to toilets is so important. It's a great read.

Clare Reddington, Watershed CEO, said: "Toilets are such vital pieces of cultural infrastructure, that are used for many human needs. We are so proud of our award-winning toilets, which are joyfully designed to forefront comfort, access, and inclusion. Despite moments of concern from some of our community when we announced our plans they are now loved by audiences and visitors and this award is a testament to that." ∎

ACKNOWLEDGEMENTS

With grateful thanks to Clare Reddington, Alec Stevens and Jo Kimber for permission to reproduce the words and illustrations in this chapter – and to all those who shared their toilet stories.

REFERENCES

Clare Reddington. Our toilets are for everyone – so what is the problem? Watershed, 29 April 2022. Available at: https://www.watershed.co.uk/articles/our-toilets-are-everyone-so-what-problem (Accessed 5 June 2024)

Clare Reddington. Our toilets are for everyone – and now our newest toilets are finally open! Watershed, 2 November 20022. Available at: https://www.watershed.co.uk/articles/our-toilets-are-everyone-and-now-our-newest-toilets-are-finally-open (Accessed 5 June 2024)

Inconvenience – stories from inside Watershed's loos. Illustrations Alec Stevens, words Jo Kimber. Available at: https://www.watershed.co.uk/inconvenience-zine (Accessed 5 June 2024)

Watershed Flushed with Success at the Loo of the Year Awards. Watershed News. 19 January 2024. Available at: https://www.watershed.co.uk/news/watershed-flushed-success-loo-year-awards (Accessed 5 June 2024)

SEND protest 2018. Credit: Jen Smith

SEND protest placards 2018. Credit: Jen Smith

Key moments in the Bristol SEND risis 2018-2022

Jen Smith investigates issues and concerns within Bristol's SEND services, advocating for improvement and accountability...

———

ALL LOCAL AUTHORITIES in England struggled in the wake of the 2014 reforms for young people with Special Educational Needs (SEN) or Disabilities. Defenders of Bristol City Council's turbulent SEND history always point out that the city's issues are simply a reflection of this national picture. It's true that SEND funding is a national crisis, but a separate story runs parallel to this in Bristol. This story shows an ongoing crisis with poor decision making by senior council leaders, compounded by the mayoral system. Issues have been characterised by a failure to follow the Education, Health and Care Plans (EHCP) process and a historic failure to adequately resource its SEN team, leading to chaotic delays to educational provision for children and young people. A predicted crisis in specialist school places resulted in pupils failing to access education. Against this there has been protest and push back from Bristol families and political opposition. This has included legal action, complaints, campaigning and social media action for educational equity. This has been met by ferocious attempts from the Council to guard its public reputation and has led to allegations of surveillance.

The 2014 SEN reforms

The 2014 SEN reforms changed the landscape of education for children with Special Educational Needs and Disabilities (SEND) in England. The reforms saw the Children and Families Act come into law on 1 September 2014 [1].

The new system extended provision from birth to the age of 25, aiming to get the right support in place as soon as it was needed. It also aimed to bring families and children into the decision making. This extended into the co-production of services with Parent Carer Forums. These forums are funded by the Department for Education (DfE) through the charity Contact. Local forums feed back about services, co-producing policy around education, health and social care services to meet the needs of local families. Each local authority signs a Memorandum of Agreement with a constituted local forum.

The reforms saw the launch of Education, Health and Care Plans (EHCPs). This is a legal document personalised to a child's needs after an Education, Health and Care Needs Assessment (EHCNA) has taken place. It should clearly set out education, health and social care needs identified by relevant professionals. It must specify the exact provision required as well as an education setting which can meet those needs. Crucially, local authorities have a legal duty to implement the provision in the plan. The reforms also reduced assessment and plan issue times down to 20 weeks.

Parents push back

Arguably, it was a 2018 Judicial Review which kickstarted the ongoing push back against Bristol SEND failures. Three mothers set a legal precedent by taking Bristol City Council (BCC) to the High Court over £5m in cuts to SEND funding. Judge Barry Cotter QC, found the Council had acted unlawfully, ordering the cuts to be quashed [2]. It was the first legal action of its kind, putting the city on the SEND map and adding to Bristol's reputation for being a city of social justice.

A month later, Liberal Democrat Councillor Tim Kent, brought a SEND motion to Full Council [3]. It was voted through, protecting the SEND budget for a further year. An additional £2.7m in funding was also allocated after special permission was granted from the Secretary of State.

Due to the issues families were facing with EHCPs, local SEND parents set up a confidential Facebook group which quickly became an important resource for families. The peer-to-peer support helped them share experiences, resources and information. Along with national charities – Independent Provider of Special Education Advice (IPSEA) and SOS!SEN – families were finally able to understand their children's rights to education. It formed part of the push back against BCC by families who felt forced towards taking the legal steps of judicial reviews and tribunals against potentially unlawful decisions made around EHCP decisions for individual children. Further push back came in the form of questions and statements in the public forum at Council meetings.

It is the use of social media, particularly X (formerly Twitter), by families which drew the ire of BCC officers and the Mayor's Office throughout this time. Under the mayoral system, the local authority guarded its public image and reputation in the extreme.

A shortage of specialist school places for children with EHCPs was beginning to come to a head around the same time as the judicial review. In a Public Forum question at Full Council in December 2018, Mayor Marvin Rees was asked what the Council would be doing over the next five years to make sure children with an EHCP who needed specialist settings were able to access one.

Rees replied: "There is still existing capacity within Specialist Education Settings in Bristol for children and young people who have SEND with Education, Health and Care Plan and the most complex needs, for whom this is the right placement." [4]

The crisis escalates

By March 2019, the crisis had escalated. Severe delays around the assessment and issuing of EHCPs saw Councillor Tim Kent publicly question Marvin Rees [5]. Rees said that during 2018, just 24 per cent of EHCPs were issued within the statutory timescale of 20 weeks. In September 2018, Rees had promised families that the SEN team's capacity would be increased by over 100 per cent – an increase of 20 posts. This had not occurred.

It led to Bristol Independent SEND Community (BISC), now known as Bristol SEND Justice (BSJ), to write an open letter to Rees, which stated: 'When, in December 2018, we queried what was happening in relation to these 20 additional SEND case-workers, we received vague and unhelpful assurances and confirmation that no new caseworkers had yet been employed. It now appears that the commitment has been watered down such that little more than half this number of new case-workers will actually materialise.'

An article in *Bristol Live* included the full text of the letter and a response from BCC [6]. According to the Council, the SEN team had only been increased by 11 full-time members of staff and one part-time employee. The row over the 20 caseworkers continued throughout 2019.

All the while a huge backlog in EHCNAs was forming.

In June of that year, former Executive Director of People, Jacqui Jensen, took to the stage at Bristol Parent Carers annual participation event [7]. Speaking to families alongside then interim Director of Education, Alan Stubbersfield, Jensen upset families by appearing to laugh after a statement by a distraught parent who had spoken passionately about how the Bristol SEND crisis had affected her child. In footage of the day, captured by the former iteration of the Bristol Parent Carer Forum, Stubbersfield said of the caseworker row that "20 was not the right answer" because it was not going to solve the problems. Jensen added that they might have been looking for 20 caseworkers they didn't need, and that "strategically" Bristol was in a "much, much, much better place".

The same meeting saw the launch of the non-statutory Bristol Support Plan – a document setting out the needs and provision for a pupil in a similar way to that of an EHCP. The problem with these plans is that they were not legally enforceable. The plan was the idea of the Inclusion in Education Group – a group formed from the Inclusion Reference Group which had been tasked with an action plan to reduce the SEND spend that had led to the 2018 Judicial Review. The Bristol Support Plan was met with suspicion from many who believed it to be a way of reducing the number of families applying for EHCNAs [8].

Throughout this period, families were finding themselves siphoned through the First-tier Tribunal (Special Educational Needs and Disability). This legal route allows families to challenge local authority decisions, but concerns were raised that it was being used as a delaying tactic by the Council.

Families speak out

In the spring of 2019, SEND simply wasn't going away as a problem. More families were beginning to speak out publicly about their experiences.

On 30 May 2019, a national day of SEND action and campaigning took place across England. Bristol families held a protest outside of City Hall. It attracted both local and national media attention [9]. The event brought together local SEND and education campaigners for a rally on College Green. Come the afternoon, a group of protesters entered City Hall with placards. They shouted for ring-fenced SEND funding, and for Marvin Rees to come and meet with them. He did not.

All the while, a lack of specialist places and EHCP delays were causing children real trauma, resulting in them falling out of education. This was not a new problem. Bristol Learning City had released an Alternative Provider (AP) report addressing such issues in September 2015. At Bristol Schools Forum in April 2019, Stubbersfield reported that the spend on AP in Bristol was the highest of any city outside of London.

The Bristol Local Area SEND self-evaluation, June 2019, stated: 'There is poor school attendance, high persistent absence and high levels of fixed term exclusions for children with SEND.' It went on to say that for children with SEN support and EHCPs, the level of attendance and exclusions is a 'concern.' Further unease that AP was concealing a lack of school places and SEND provision in schools came in the form of a letter written in September 2019 by Bristol's Alternative Learning Provision Hub. The letter said the local authority was addressing concerns about children being left in 'long-term unregistered AP'.

Investment into SEND was approved at a Cabinet meeting in July 2019 [10]. As a result of the meeting, BCC commissioned an Independent Review of SEND data, which found several areas of failure in SEND administration, including problems with tracking individual cases through the system [11].

The difficulties families were facing with the EHCP process were not improving. At a People Scrutiny Commission meeting in July 2019, Jacqui Jensen said: "Even with all the money that we've been given, the situation around timeliness and compliance is not going to be massively improved for months." [12]

The crisis with specialist places which emerged publicly from around 2018 was not new information. In 2015, the Integrated Education and Capital Strategy (2015-2019) was published under Bristol's former Mayor, George Ferguson [13]. It found, through pupil projections modelling and needs analysis, that the 'maintained' capacity for specialist settings in Bristol was full. By 2019, there would be a shortfall of 128 specialist places in Bristol. It was a prediction that came to fruition despite Marvin Rees' assurances in 2018 that things were fine.

To tackle SEND issues, Jensen gave a presentation to Bristol Schools Forum on proposals for a system-wide transformation of Bristol's Education Provision [14]. A member of the Forum said: "It's like a four-year-old's Christmas list, with nobody to spend any money on. It's great, but it doesn't do what we need it to do. It's great having a plan, but there's no delivery there. It's just disappointment."

As the academic year wrapped up in July 2019, a cluster group of 26

Bristol Special Educational Needs Coordinators (SENCos) became the next group of people to add their voices to the crisis. They wrote an open letter to the Council expressing their alarm over 'excessive' ongoing delays to the EHCP system [15]. The letter described their colleagues in the SEN team as 'overwhelmed' with schools experiencing a 'crisis'.

By November 2019, published data for People Scrutiny Commission showed that between 1 April and 30 September 2019, no EHCP was issued within the statutory time frame [16]. December apparently presented an opportunity to BCC. A message on the council's website stated: "So that we meet the six week statutory deadline, we can process requests that we get by 26 November 2019. We'll start accepting new requests from 6 January 2020" [17]. This was a breach of statutory guidance, and was reversed after a public outcry. Councillor Tim Kent said: "Clearly the department is struggling to the point of collapse but to create a new way to ignore and break the law seems to go beyond bizarre and reach the levels of total incompetence and unacceptable and unprofessional behaviour."

Families vindicated

Bristol's long anticipated Joint SEND Inspection by Ofsted and the Care Quality Commission (CQC) took place during the latter part of 2019. As part of the inspection process, which ran between 30 September and 4 October 2019, a meeting took place at City Hall between parent carers and inspectors. Around 40 parents spoke to inspectors in a meeting that was described as a 'bloodbath' [18]. The Council's SEND provision was utterly decimated by tearful and angry parents.

The release of the final report was vindication for Bristol's SEND families [19]. Five key areas of significant weaknesses were found, forcing Bristol to address them through a Written Statement of Action (WSoA). The city would be re-inspected in due course. The five areas were:

1. The lack of accountability of leaders at all levels, including school leaders
2. The inconsistencies in the timeliness and effectiveness of the local area's arrangements for the identification and assessment of children and young people with SEND
3. The dysfunctional EHC plan process and inadequate quality of EHC plans
4. The underachievement and lack of inclusion of children and young

people with SEND, including the high rates of persistent absenteeism and fixed term exclusions

5. The fractured relationships with parents and carers, lack of co-production and variable engagement and collaboration.

Campaign group Bristol Send Justice (BSJ) immediately released a statement blaming the 'culture at the heart of strategic leadership'.

On 14 October 2019, shortly before the SEND inspection took place, Bristol had finally advertised nearly 20 EHCP related jobs for the SEN Team. The new employees would not come into post until the January of 2020 and there would still be a further delay caused by staff training.

On 3 February 2020, an extraordinary People Scrutiny Commission meeting was held at City Hall to discuss the Ofsted and CQC SEND inspection report [20]. Sally Kent of BSJ raised the critical issue of a lack of specialist school places saying: "Where are these children going to be placed? There's no school places. The bomb has gone off and everyone's quietly stepping around it."

The People Scrutiny Commission held an Evidence Day to conduct in-depth scrutiny into the local authority's performance on EHCPS. It was held as a result of the wide-ranging concerns regarding the system, including those constantly raised by Bristol families. Following the event, People Scrutiny Commission made nine recommendations for ongoing policy and service improvement [21].

Misleading communication

It wasn't long after the Evidence Day that the restrictions of the Covid-19 pandemic were imposed. It was another opportunity for Bristol to manage its EHCP backlog. In April 2020, BCC told people applying for EHCNAs that they would be filing requests without acting on them because of Coronavirus related issues. BSJ immediately contacted the Council to point out its incorrect usage of the law, asking them to stop sending 'misleading communication'.

Once again Bristol had to backtrack on its position. In a letter to the campaign group, the Council stated that the email from the SEN team was sent to the parents with the 'best intentions' to make them aware that there 'could' be a delay in meeting statutory timescales, accepting that quoting Section 4 was 'inappropriate in these circumstances' [22].

The specialist places shortage in Bristol again raised itself publicly following a report to Cabinet in September 2020 [23]. It revealed that 190 'young people' with an EHCP did not have an education setting due to a lack of specialist places, and approximately 250 more young people would also need an appropriate setting over the next 12 months [24].

Marvin Rees had said little on the subject of SEND but, when he finally addressed it, he caused outrage across the community. It started on a Facebook Live session with the mayor streamed on 12 March 2021. SEND parents had joined in the comments trying to bring the mayor's attention to difficulties they were facing. It wasn't long until parents realised their comments were being hidden from the wider public view [25]. The backlash was swift.

'Why are all the comments about SEND on this page being censored? Parents have a right to ask elected officials and candidates questions,' one parent posted. 'I can't believe that you Marvin, or whoever is monitoring this page, thinks it is acceptable to delete valid comments in this way. I am really shocked,' another said. Bristol SEND Justice's Sally Kent criticised the action on X: 'Who accesses the Mayor's account on Facebook and is it appropriate for these people to be deleting or hiding inoffensive comments on a Facebook page promoted and monitored by Bristol City Council? Does the council have a policy on this?'

In a further Facebook video on Sunday 17 March 2021, a parent succeeded in getting Rees to address SEND issues directly. Through most of his answer Rees appeared to be reading from a document. But then he put forward his own personal opinion. Rees said it was the Council's view that many SEND pupils could remain in mainstream education with 'adequate support' rather than 'segregation in specialist education' [26].

The backlash for referring to specialist education as 'segregation' was instant. Instead of apologising, Rees doubled down. He referred to specialist education being segregation for a second time in a BBC Radio Bristol interview with John Darvall. Rees told listeners that being educated in a mainstream school 'is the best option' and that attending a 'segregated school' is 'not necessarily' the best.

Rees also argued on air with a SEND parent, saying: "So first off there are not 250 children without a school place." But a statement from the Council in February had indicated: "Today in Bristol there are 250 children and young people who are eligible for specialist settings." [27]

In April 2021, rising tensions over the shortage of school places saw another visible protest held outside City Hall by the Bristol SEND Alliance.

A number of local SEND groups came together with a manifesto calling for accountability, funding and transparency around data. The protesters tied 250 flags to poles on College Green to represent each child without a school place.

Negative reputation

Bristol's reputation was to suffer again in May 2021. A report by Sir Stephen Bubb found systemic barriers against the city's autistic population. He said: "Bristol can no longer claim to be an 'autism friendly city' and should stop using this slogan." [28]

Further EHCP delays caused cross-party concern at the People Scrutiny Commission in March 2022 [29]. Figures released by BCC showed a backlog of hundreds. Conservative Councillor Mark Weston branded the situation an 'absolute nightmare'. Labour Councillor Kerry Bailes described the wait for specialist school places as 'total and utter chaos'. People Scrutiny Commission Chair Tim Kent said it was 'not acceptable'.

The city administration was becoming increasingly guarded around its negative reputation, particularly in online spaces it couldn't control. In the summer of 2022, Bristol was hit by allegations of covert online surveillance on SEND families. *The Bristolian* published a story on 19 July featuring a leaked email and other documentary evidence suggesting that BCC senior officers and the External Communications team had spied on SEND parents who had publicly criticised Bristol's SEND failure [30]. This had involved monitoring social media accounts, collating, cataloguing and sharing the results – including one person's wedding photographs [31]. The article caused a furore. The subjects of the surveillance were senior members of the city's Bristol Parent Carer Forum (BPCF).

After extensive media coverage and just one week later, BCC publicly made the decision to stop the DfE funding to the Forum [32]. This was a loss of £17,500 towards the co-production of services between SEND families and the Council. Councillor Tim Kent tweeted: "Probably one of the worst things I have seen come out of Bristol City Council in the last 10 years. Truly disgusting behaviour – the Parent Carer Forum dared to not go along with the council spin and now parents of disabled children are to suffer the council's vindictive wrath."

The events led to BCC officers conducting an internal 'fact finding report' into its own behaviour [33], which was presented to People Scrutiny Commission on 26 September 2022. The report concluded that 'no evidence has been seen that this has been on anything other than an ad hoc basis and would not amount to monitoring'.

Conservative Councillors, unhappy with the alleged surveillance, brought a motion to Full Council in October 2022 [34]. The motion, led by Councillor Geoff Gollop, called for the Mayor 'to hold a genuinely independent inquiry'. They also asked for funding to be restored to the Forum. The motion was passed.

Sufficient progress?

In October 2022, Ofsted and the CQC re-inspected Bristol. It found that 'sufficient progress' had been made towards four out of the five areas of 'significant weaknesses' [35]. It was a contentious finding for SEND parents still struggling with their children's education. The inspectors did acknowledge that BCC had not made sufficient progress addressing the 'fractured relationships with parents and carers, lack of co-production and variable engagement and collaboration'.

Deputy Mayor Councillor Asher Craig ended 2022 with an article on the Mayor's blog [36], stating: 'As a local authority we recognised that our city needed more specialist provision places back in 2021, and we made the decision to set this work in motion.' Craig's blog signified a defiance from the administration to acknowledge responsibility for Bristol's SEND failures.

It wasn't until May 2023 that Bristol backed down on the Forum funding row [37]. BCC once again recognised BPCF as their official co-production partner, allowing them to receive funding from the DfE. No independent inquiry was undertaken into the social media surveillance. The matter seemed put to bed in July 2023 by the Mayor, who responded to a written question at full council by stating that 'there had been an internal investigation and no wrong doing was found' [38].

But Bristol's SEND failures were severe enough to see an escalating High Needs budget throughout 2023. This culminated in the approval of a 'secret' application for the DfE's contentious Safety Valve programme just before the local elections in 2024 [39]. The mess left behind will impact hundreds of Bristol's children long after the city has seen the back of a mayoral administration that damaged relationships with SEND families and failed to educate their children. ■

REFERENCES

1. Department for Education, 2014. Children and Families Act 2014 PART 3 Children and young people in England with special educational needs or disabilities. Available at: https://www.legislation.gov.uk/ukpga/2014/6/contents (Accessed 2 June 2024)

2. R (on the application of (1) KE; (2) IE; and (3) CH) v Bristol City Council [2018] EWHC 2103 (Admin) Available at: https://www.bailii.org/ew/cases/EWHC/Admin/2018/2103.html (Accessed 2 June 2024)

3. Kent, T. Full Council Supplementary Information Altered Motion 2 – SEND. 11 September 2018. Available at: https://democracy.bristol.gov.uk/documents/b10418/Altered%20motion%202%20-%20SEND%20-%20to%20be%20moved%20by%20Cllr%20Kent%2011th-Sep-2018%2018.00%20Full%20Council.pdf?T=9 (Accessed 2 June 2024)

4. Rees, M. December Full Council Public Questions PQ03&04. Personal email to: J. Smith, 19 December 2018.

5. Bristol City Council Member Forum. Questions and Statements from Councillors, 18 March 2019. Available at: https://democracy.bristol.gov.uk/documents/g3196/Public%20reports%20pack%2019th-Mar-2019%2016.00%20Member%20Forum%20-%20Questions%20Statements%20from%20Councillors.pdf?T=10 (Accessed 2 June 2024)

6. Turnnidge, S. Parents of SEND pupils claim their children are still being 'failed' by council. *Bristol Live*, 16 April 2019. Available at: https://www.bristolpost.co.uk/news/bristol-news/parents-send-pupils-claim-children-2753241 (Accessed 2 June 2024)

7. Bristol Parent Carers. Participation Event 2019 – PART 3. Available at: https://www.youtube.com/watch?v=JJOAHfCnf8o&t=2270s (Accessed 2 June 2024)

8. Smith, J. Bristol SEND Support Plans Non-Statutory EHCP Launch. *Chopsy Bristol*, 21 June 2019. Available at: https://chopsybaby.com/magazine/bristol-send-support-plans-non-statutory-ehcp-launch/ (Accessed 2 June 2024)

9. Turnnidge, S. (2019) 'Live updates as parents protest in Bristol city centre', *Bristol Live*, 30 May. Available at: https://www.bristolpost.co.uk/news/bristol-news/live-updates-parents-protest-bristol-2923357 (Accessed 2 June 2024)

10. Bristol City Council, Cabinet meeting 2 July 2019. Resourcing plan for Send Function. Available at: https://democracy.bristol.gov.uk/documents/b18216/Supplement%20to%202%20July%20Cabinet%2002nd-Jul-2019%2016.00%20Cabinet.pdf?T=9 (Accessed 2 June 2024)

11. SF Independent Specialists Limited (2019) SEND Data Independent Review July 2019. Available at: https://www.bristol.gov.uk/files/documents/3611-bristol-city-council-send-data-independent-review-july-2019-final/file (Accessed 2 June 2024)

12. Jensen, J (2019) People Scrutiny Commission verbal update 18/07. Available at: https://x.com/ChopsyBristol/status/1152937594428317696 (Accessed 2 June 2024)

13. Bristol City Council (2016) The Integrated Education & Capital Strategy (2015-2019). Available at: https://www.bristol.gov.uk/files/documents/2804-school-strategy-integrated-education-and-capital-strategy-full-2015-to-2019/file (Accessed 2 June 2024)

14. Bristol Schools Forum Supplementary Agenda, 26 November, 2019. Hurley, A. System Wide SEND and Inclusion Improvement. Available at: https://democracy.bristol.gov.uk/documents/b18844/System-wide%20SEND%20and%20Inclusion%20Improvement%2026th-Nov-2019%2017.00%20Bristol%20Schools%20Forum.pdf?T=9 (Accessed 2 June 2024)

15. Bristol SEND Justice (2019) *Open Letter of 29 Sendcos*. [Facebook] 18 July. Available at: https://www.facebook.com/bristolsend/posts/pfbid02s1iab6S9u2NSUrq14jT1Kueuj8bmapfxw7VfLpNjAw42F39JDKJgoNP43JH1yCiEl (Accessed 2 June 2024)

16. Jensen, J. People Directorate's performance progress report for quarter 2, 2019/20. 28 November 2019. Available at: https://democracy.bristol.gov.uk/documents/s43505/People%20Scrutiny%20Q2%20performance.pdf (Accessed 2 June 2024)

17. Cameron, A. Bristol City Council reverses 'completely unlawful' SEND move. *BristolLive*, 10 December 2019. Available at: https://www.bristolpost.co.uk/news/bristol-news/council-reverses-unlawful-send-move-3625817 Accessed 2 June 2024.

18. thebristolblogger. Parents Send Their Regards. *The Bristolian*, 24 November 2019. Available at: https://thebristolian.net/2019/11/24/parents-send-their-regards/ (Accessed 2 June 2024)

19. Ofsted and Care Quality Commission. Joint local area SEND inspection in City of Bristol, 13 November 2019. Available at: https://www.bristol.gov.uk/files/documents/1385-ofsted-and-cqc-send-report/file (Accessed 2 June 2024)

20. Extraordinary meeting of People Scrutiny Commission, 3 February 2020. Available at: https://www.youtube.com/watch?v=FsXWbtOZPEs (Accessed 2 June 2024)

21. Bristol City Council. Special Educational Needs and Disability Evidence Day: Report of the People Scrutiny Commission. February 2020. Available at: https://democracy.bristol.gov.uk/documents/s55094/SEND%20Evidence%20Day%20-%20Report%20of%20the%20People%20Scrutiny%20Commission.pdf (Accessed 2 June 2024)

22. Smith, J. Bristol City Council Backtracks on EHCP Request Blocking but Sticks with 'Best Endeavours'. *Chopsy Bristol*, 17 April 2020. Available at: https://chopsybaby.com/magazine/wp-content/uploads/94224545_532839047420558_1991793514471489536_n.jpg (Accessed 2 June 2024)

23. Bristol City Council. SEND Sufficiency and Capital Proposals. Report to cabinet, 1 September 2020. Available at:

https://democracy.bristol.gov.uk/documents/s51731/SEND%20Sufficiency%20-%20Decision%20pathway%20 Report.pdf (Accessed 2 June 2024)

24. Cork T & Cameron A. Parents' fury as 190 children can't return to special school in Bristol next week. *Bristol Live*, 26 August 2020. Available at: https://www.bristolpost.co.uk/news/bristol-news/parents-fury-190-children-cant-4459980 (Accessed 2 June 2024)

25. Gogarty, C. Bristol mayor comes under fire amid SEND crisis. *BristolLive*, 17 March 2021. Available at: https://www. bristolpost.co.uk/news/bristol-news/bristol-mayor-comes-under-fire-5191346 (Accessed 2 June 2024)

26. Cork, T. SEND: Bristol mayor's comments on 'segregated education' anger parents. *BristolLive*, 18 March 2021. Available at: https://www.bristolpost.co.uk/news/bristol-news/send-bristol-mayors-comments-segregated-5200269 (Accessed 2 June 2024)

27. Trevena, L. 66 new special school places to be created in Bristol. *Bristol24/7*, 24 May 2021. Available at: https://www. bristol247.com/news-and-features/news/66-new-special-school-places-to-be-created-in-bristol/ (Accessed 2 June 2024)

28. Bubb, S. Building Rights. A report to the Keeping Bristol Safe Partnership Board, 2021. Available at: https://www. bristol.gov.uk/files/documents/1652-building-rights/file (Accessed 2 June 2024)

29. Smith, J. Cross Party Concern Raised over Bristol EHCP Crisis. *Chopsy Bristol*, 10 March 2022. Available at: https:// chopsybaby.com/magazine/cross-party-concern-raised-over-bristol-ehcp-crisis/ (Accessed 2 June 2024)

30. thebristolblogger. Leaked Documents: Send Parent Spy Material Revealed. *The Bristolian*, 19 July 2022. Available at: https://thebristolian.net/2022/07/19/leaked-documents-send-parent-spy-material-revealed/ (Accessed 2 June 2024)

31. Seabrook, A. Bristol City Council's surveillance of SEND parents revealed. *Bristol24/7*, 20 July 2022. Available at: https://www.bristol247.com/news-and-features/news/bristol-city-councils-surveillance-send-parents-revealed/ (Accessed 2 June 2024)

32. Seabrook, A. Bristol City Council scraps funding support for special needs charity in surveillance row. *Bristol Live*, updated 27 July 2022. Available at: https://www.bristolpost.co.uk/news/local-news/bristol-city-council-scraps-funding-7379378 (Accessed 2 June 2024)

33. Legal Services Bristol City Council. Fact-finding report – Use of social media by council staff in respect of the Bristol Parent Carer Forum. 22 August 2022. Available at: https://democracy.bristol.gov.uk/documents/s75175/SEND%20 Fact-finding%20report%20-%202.9.22_Redacted.pdf (Accessed 2 June 2024)

34. Seabrook, A. Bristol councillors vote for independent inquiry to investigate monitoring of SEND parents. *The Bristol Cable*, 19 October 2022. Available at: https://thebristolcable.org/2022/10/bristol-councillors-vote-independent-inquiry-investigate-monitoring-send-parents/ (Accessed 2 June 2024)

35. Minns P. Joint area SEND revisit in Bristol. Ofsted and Care Quality Commission, 18 November 2022. Available at: https://files.ofsted.gov.uk/v1/file/50200048 (Accessed 2 June 2024)

36. Craig, A. More specialist school places planned for Bristol. *theBristolMayor.com*, 23 December 2022. Available at: https://thebristolmayor.com/2022/12/23/send/ (Accessed 2 June 2024)

37. Postans, A. Bristol City Council SEND U-turn sees funding restored to parent carer forum. *Bristol Live*, 16 May 2023. Available at: https://www.bristolpost.co.uk/news/bristol-news/bristol-city-council-send-u-8442195 (Accessed 2 June 2024)

38. Public Document Pack, Full Council Agenda, 30 June 2023. Available at: https://democracy.bristol.gov.uk/ documents/b32406/Public%20Forum%20Responses%20Full%20Council%2011%20July%202023%2011th-Jul-2023%2018.00%20Full%20Council.pdf?T=9 (Accessed 2 June 2024)

39. Seabrook, A. Outrage at secret 'Safety Valve' bailout plan to rescue Bristol's special needs budget. *Bristol Live*, 6 March 2024. Available at: https://www.bristolpost.co.uk/news/bristol-news/outrage-secret-safety-valve-bailout-9146881 (Accessed 2 June 2024)

Disabled campaigners enter City Hall, Bristol. Credit: James Ward

Disabled people celebrate as Bristol drops the Fair and Affordable Care Policy.
Credit: Helen @PortalHaiku

Nothing about us without us!

Bristol Reclaiming Independent Living, with pro bono legal advice from Oliver Lewis and Alice Irving of Doughty Street Chambers, challenge the unfair 'Fair and Affordable Care Policy'...

———

ON 6 JUNE 2023, at a cabinet meeting of Bristol City Council, approval was given for public consultation on a draft Fair and Affordable Care Policy which caused alarm amongst Disabled people in Bristol and beyond.

"...there seems to be a strong likelihood that if the policy is adopted, you could be effectively told by the council that it will no longer support your current care arrangements – the arrangements that allow you to *live in your own home*, perhaps with your family, to go about your life with the support of the team of carers or personal assistants who may know you and your needs very well – and you may in effect need to move into an institution, into residential care. This is turning the clock back on decades of efforts to support people to live independently in the community." [1]

The proposed consultation took place between 18 September 2023 and 31 January 2024. This chapter reproduces the detailed submission from Bristol Reclaiming Independent Living (BRIL). Campaigning by BRIL and other disability rights organisations resulted in the withdrawal of the policy in February 2024. But, despite the success of the campaign, concerns remain that the Council may not have fully taken on board the voices of Disabled people.

Bristol Reclaiming Independent Living

Bristol Reclaiming Independent Living (BRIL) is a community group run by and for Disabled people, neurodivergent people, people living with chronic illness, and people who experience mental distress. Our aims are to: campaign for equality and inclusion for all Disabled people; promote the principle of 'Independent Living' for all; provide peer support.

BRIL defines Independent Living as: the right to live in the community; being free from segregation and isolation; having choice and control over our lives, on an equal basis to other people; having access to support and personal assistance that meets our needs.

BRIL welcomes the opportunity to respond to Bristol City Council's Fair and Affordable Care Policy ('the Policy') consultation. Part I has been produced by BRIL members and will address: 1. Co-production and consultation; 2. People's views; 3. Recommendations and actions. Part II is a legal submission prepared pro bono on behalf of BRIL by Oliver Lewis and Alice Irving of Doughty Street Chambers.

Part 1: Submission from BRIL members
Co-production and consultation

February 2023 was the first time anyone who might be affected by the Policy had heard about it. It was clear that the Policy had been in development for some time. The announcement came in the usual email with the paperwork for the Adult Social Care Equalities Forum. Our group were concerned that no co-production or consultation had been carried out beforehand.

Every time Bristol City Council (BCC) talk about the Policy, they say it was co-produced, or 'co-developed'. However, BRIL believe this is not the case. If we look at the Think Local Act Personal (TLAP) Ladder of co-production [2], in no way was this co-produced. Since the Policy was first announced in February 2023 there has been a national outcry, highlighted in both local and national media coverage [3-8].

BRIL has been contacted by Disabled people, Disabled People's Organisations, family carers, human rights campaigners, academics, lawyers and social workers. There is deep concern about the implications of this Policy [1]. We have had hundreds of comments on social media, with Disabled people and families concerned about the removal of the 'safety net' for anyone needing social care now or in the future.

This includes older people being discharged from hospital, working-age people with acquired impairments, young people transitioning from SEND to adult services, mental health service users/survivors, people living with chronic illness, autistic people and people with learning difficulties.

Moving on to the consultation, BRIL welcomes the extended time period, which was only extended because Disabled people challenged the time frame. However, we have major concerns over how it has been shared. It is not a meaningful consultation, as it is constructed in a way that makes responses very difficult; for example, there are no alternatives to the Policy, it is unclear, and the Easy Read version does not explain the Policy or its potential impact in full.

BRIL would like to quote a few points from the document called 'Consultation Principles' [9]:

- Engagement should begin early in policy development when the policy is still under consideration and views can genuinely be taken into account.
- Policy makers should be able to demonstrate that they have considered who needs to be consulted and ensure that the consultation captures the full range of stakeholders affected. In particular, if the policy will affect hard to reach or vulnerable groups, policy makers should take the necessary actions to engage effectively with these groups. Information should be disseminated and presented in a way likely to be accessible and useful to the stakeholders with a substantial interest in the subject matter. The choice of the form of consultation will largely depend on the issues under consideration, who needs to be consulted, and the available time and resources.
- The purpose of the consultation process should be clearly stated, as should the stage of the development that the policy has reached. Also, to avoid creating unrealistic expectations, it should be apparent what aspects of the policy being consulted on are open to change and what decisions have already been taken.

People's views

At an Open Meeting BRIL held on 5th January 2024, Disabled people from Bristol and from across England expressed serious concerns about the Policy BCC is proposing. Some of the comments were as follows:

- There is real fear coming from Disabled people and our families.
- Members of BRIL are very worried that putting what Bristol City Council is calling cost-effectiveness above what people actually need will have a major impact on the independence and quality of life of

thousands of Disabled people.

- It will set independent living for Disabled people back 40 years.
- I am worried my care will be cut and I will end up in a care home.
- Disabled people can express ourselves and we need to be treated with respect, and our lived experiences and concerns must be listened to.
- Independent living means people are able to choose to stay in their own homes and have their care needs met.
- Forcing people into care homes takes away our right to make our own choices about where and how we live.
- BCC has gone against their own 'Better Lives' policy that included reducing the number of people in residential care. It would also mean more public funds going to the private companies that own most residential care and nursing homes.
- The Policy is against our human rights to family and private life (Article 8 ECHR).
- What BCC is calling cost-effectiveness is incompatible with the Care Act 2014. This Policy goes against Wellbeing and Prevention duties in the Act.
- I am confused as to how the Council can create its own version of eligibility criteria when the Care Act 2014 already has criteria to be met.
- Assessments are being adjusted according to resources, not actual need.
- An act in law is a legal duty to adhere to the content of the act and duties towards disabled people can be protected if breached in any way.
- Local authorities are supposed to record all needs, whether met or unmet.
- It is clear from the Equality Impact Assessment (EQIA) that the policy will disproportionately impact Black, Asian and other minoritised people, older people and women. In other words, the Policy will result in discrimination against people with protected characteristics under the Equality Act 2010.
- BCC's policy goes against the recommendations of Sir Stephen Bubb's report, commissioned by BCC itself. BCC has failed to make any progress towards the recommendations, and with this Policy it is putting autistic people and people with learning difficulties at more risk.

- Autistic people and people with learning difficulties, living at home and in the community, could be put at serious risk of harm and trauma by this policy. Cutting budgets for people who need high levels of careful, person-centred, autistic sensitive and trauma informed support is likely to risk destabilisation and crisis. This undermines the national agenda to prevent institutionalisation and hospitalisation, and NHS England's 'Building the Right Support' programme following the Winterbourne View scandal.

- The Policy will hit Disabled people who have been detained under the Mental Health Act. For example, Section 117 aftercare, which aims to prevent people going back into hospital, is joint funded by the Council and the NHS. If the Council bring in an arbitrary cap on social care funding for individuals this will put this preventative support at risk, and could lead to mental health crises, hospitalisation and increased human and economic costs in the long run. There will be serious implications for the local authority and the NHS.

- The EQIA makes clear that the proposal is based on practices that are already the way the Council works. The Council's usual practices are, therefore, in breach of the Care Act and fail to deliver cost-effectiveness and value for money. The result is failure to match public money to real need, leading to misuse and management of public money that we often witness as members.

- What about the role of independent advocacy? Disabled people have a right to advocacy if they don't have family or friends to support them to deal with social services. Many Disabled people need support to understand what is happening, know their rights and to navigate social care processes so they can make their own choices and express their own views. However, advocacy services are stretched and under pressure. BCC's policy could put so much pressure on services that their right to advocacy is put at risk.

- There was a case in London (R (SG) v London Borough of Haringey – 2015) when a council didn't make sure a disabled asylum seeker had an advocate during a social care assessment. The council made the excuse there wasn't an advocate available. A judge told the council this was no excuse, scrapped the assessment and told the council to start again, causing more distress to the disabled person and more costs to the council.

- Disabled people may need legal advice and representation to challenge decisions made under this policy – but cuts to legal aid and the lack of specialist legal community care advice makes access to justice precarious. Disabled people's rights are under attack.

- What about the impact on personal assistants (PAs) and support workers? Disabled people who employ PAs are paying into the local economy, not private care companies. There are many skilled and knowledgeable PAs and support workers: skills and knowledge that will be lost.
- PAs and support workers could lose their jobs, meaning more financial pressure for them and their families, and in the long term on public services.
- The Policy will mean social workers, occupational therapists (OTs) and social care practitioners being pressured to practise and make decisions against their training, values and principles. The Policy is in contravention of the British Association of Social Workers (BASW) Code of Ethics and the International Federation of Social Workers (IFSW) Statement of Ethical Principles:
  - 'Respect for human rights and a commitment to promoting social justice are at the core of social work practice throughout the world.'
  - 'Social workers are expected to bring to the attention of their employers, policy makers, politicians and the general public situations where resources are inadequate, and/or where distribution of resources, policies and practice are oppressive, discriminatory or otherwise unfair, harmful or illegal.'

Recommendations and actions

a) The proposal should be withdrawn.

b) BRIL requests BCC to publish all submissions in this consultation.

c) BRIL and its members remain available to meet with BCC councillors and officers to discuss the Draft Policy or alternative proposals.

d) There remains deep concern for BRIL on two grounds, even if the proposal is withdrawn. Firstly, the Council has declared it believes that a small number of people receiving care above the cheapest option is unfair on the majority. Disabled people with high needs have not chosen to have high needs; it is because of what has happened in life, but is characterised as unfairly getting more than others get, yet we are most likely to end up in institutions. This is discriminatory. Disabled people must not be pitted against each other in this way. Secondly, the EQIA makes clear that the proposal is based on practices that are already the way the Council works. The Council's usual practices are, therefore, in breach of the Care Act 2014 and fail to deliver cost-effectiveness and value for money. The result is failure to match public money to real need, leading to misuse and management of public money that we often witness as members.

e) BRIL therefore believes there should be a fundamental review of the way the Council assesses needs and allocates resources. The review must ensure that resources are consistently matched to real, individual need as lived experience. The review should also be designed to satisfy the top rung of the TLAP co-production ladder.

f) Only service users have the knowledge of need as lived experience upon which the new system should be built. Representatives of all user groups and carers should be involved.

g) If the Council agrees to the review and adopts strategies that they label 'co-production', but which are clearly not, BRIL will refuse to engage and will advise other groups accordingly.

h) 'Cost-effectiveness' and 'value for money' are misused terms. Privatisation has enabled profiteer companies to make large profits from councils' adult and children's social care spending – to the detriment of Disabled people reliant on homecare; unwaged family carers trying to make up for the drop in quality of homecare; low-paid/zero-hour contract homecare workers, mainly women, who get only a fraction of the fees councils pay to care agencies; and children suffering in privatised 'care' placements.

i) As regards to children's social care, BCC spends an enormous amount on children's placements outside the city, in some cases over £600,000 for one child [10], which would be better spent supporting families with Disabled children/Disabled mothers and keeping families together. The open letter from disability organisations to BCC in November 2023 highlighted that severely Disabled mothers could be separated from children under the Policy [11]. It calls on BCC to seek increased central government funds instead.

Part 2: Legal submission prepared on behalf of BRIL

1. In April 2023 it was reported that Bristol City Council (BCC) had cut £4m from its £153m adult social care budget [12]. BCC published version 11 of its draft Fair and Affordable Care Policy ("the Draft Policy") on 21

June 2023, and the relevant Equality Impact Assessment was signed off on 30 June 2023.

2. This is one of two BRIL submissions in response to BCC's consultation on the Draft Policy and has been drafted by counsel instructed pro bono. In short, in response to questions 3-4 of the consultation survey, BRIL strongly disagrees with the Draft Policy and asks BCC to abandon efforts to adopt it.

3. BCC's overarching duty, under the Care Act 2014, is to exercise its adult social care functions in relation to individuals to promote their well-being. Well-being is broadly defined to include personal dignity; control by the individual over day-to-day life (including care and support, and the way in which it is provided); participation in work, education, training or recreation; domestic, family and personal relationships; and suitability of living accommodation (s.1(1)-(2)). The Care and Support Statutory Guidance ("the Statutory Guidance") is clear that the Act "puts wellbeing at the heart of care and support" (paragraph 1.1).

4. BCC should begin from the assumption that an individual is best-placed to judge their own well-being, and should ensure decisions about the individual are made having regard to all their individual circumstances, and is not based on unjustified assumptions (s.1(3)).

5. Central to any adult social care assessment are the outcomes the individual wishes to achieve in their day-to-day life (s.9(4)). Indeed, the first paragraph of the Statutory Guidance states that, "The core purpose of adult care and support is to help people to achieve the outcomes that matter to them in their life" (paragraph 1.1).

6. These core features of the Care Act 2014 regime are part and parcel of a deliberate paradigm shift in adult social care. As explained in the Statutory Guidance, *"The Act... signifies a shift from existing duties on local authorities to provide particular services, to the concept of 'meeting needs'... The concept of meeting needs recognises that everyone's needs are different and personal to them. Local authorities must consider how to meet each person's specific needs rather than simply considering what service they*

will fit into" (paragraph 1.9-10).

7.   Accordingly, under the Care Act 2014 there is a duty to meet an individual's eligible needs for care and support (s.18) and a non-exhaustive list of examples of how needs might be met (s.8).

8.   The Draft Policy states at paragraph 3.1 that BCC's duty is to *"try and meet all the needs that are agreed with the person".* This is a misstatement of the law in two ways.

   a.   First, if BCC has made a determination under s.13 of the Care Act 2014 that an adult has eligible needs for care and support, then pursuant to s.18 of the Act, BCC *"must"* meet that person's needs if the person meets the criteria for ordinarily residence and if they are financially eligible (s.18(1)(a)-(c)). It is not a duty to *"try".* A lack of resources is no defence to a failure to discharge a statutory duty.

   b.   Second, the Draft Policy is inaccurate with respect to a person in need of care and support who lacks capacity pursuant to s.3 of the Mental Capacity Act 2005 to make decisions about care. In these cases, a person may be able to express wishes and feelings, and these must be taken into consideration when making a best interests decision. However, the person need not, and may not be able to, *"agree"* that their needs be met in a particular way. BCC still has a duty to meet the person's needs.

9.   The Statutory Guidance explains:

   "1.18 Although not mentioned specifically in the way that wellbeing is defined, the concept of 'independent living' is a core part of the wellbeing principle. Section 1 of the Care Act includes matters such as individual's control of their day-to-day life, suitability of living accommodation, contribution to society – and crucially, requires local authorities to consider each person's views, wishes, feelings and beliefs.

   1.19 The wellbeing principle is intended to cover the key components of independent living, as expressed in the UN Convention on the Rights of People with Disabilities (in particular, Article 19 of the Convention). ***Supporting people to live as independently as possible, for as long as possible, is a guiding principle of the Care Act.*** *The language used in the*

Act is intended to be clearer, and focus on the outcomes that truly matter to people, rather than using the relatively abstract term 'independent living'." [emphasis added]

10. The UN Convention on the Rights of Persons with Disabilities (CRPD) is a treaty that is binding in international law. The UK took an active part in negotiating the CRPD, and the UK ratified it in 2010. Although it is not incorporated into English law and does not bind BCC directly, it is clear from the Statutory Guidance that local authorities must consider the CRPD when meeting a person's needs for care and support as it is part of the wellbeing principle. BCC therefore needs to take Article 19 of the CRPD into account when deciding whether to progress its Draft Policy. BRIL considers that the Draft Policy is incompatible with Article 19 of the CRPD and that it should therefore be abandoned.

11. The premise of Article 19(a) CRPD is that disabled people have equal rights to choose where and with whom to live and are *"not obliged to live in a particular living arrangement"*. The central premise of the Draft Policy is that a disabled person may be forced to live in a care home or other residential setting, because funding that would enable them to continue to live in their own home has been cut. On the face of it this would be a violation of Article 19(a) of the CRPD.

12. Article 19(b) of the CRPD sets out that disabled people should have access to a range of community support services that meet their needs, and these services should be designed in such a way as *"to prevent isolation or segregation from the community"*. Article 19 was drafted to combat the global phenomenon of institutionalisation of disabled people, and to spur efforts towards closing institutions. It was intended to ensure that each disabled person can choose where to live in the community and has access to the support and public services that enable them to make decisions about their life, friends, workplaces and transportation. In short, they should have opportunities to flourish on an equal basis with others. Again, the Draft Policy seeks to increase segregation from the community by placing people against their will in congregate care settings.

13. In 2012, Thomas Hammarberg, the then Commissioner for Human

Rights of the Council of Europe, published a report on Article 19 of the CRPD. He explained the concept of independence as a human right:

"people with disabilities may require supports to live a full life. The notion of independence is based on a social model of disability which recognizes that people are not limited in their choices because of any inherent feature or condition of the person him or herself, but by the social and physical environment in which they live. In enabling environments, things are not done to a person, but rather people are supported, just like anyone else, to make independent and autonomous (and in some cases supported) decisions." [13]

14. The UN supports the social model of disability. The UN Committee on the Rights of Persons with Disabilities ("CRPD Committee") is the body that oversees the implementation of CRPD rights in the countries that have ratified the CRPD. It consists of 18 experts in disability, drawn from around the world. It provides evidence to governments about how to interpret and implement the Convention.

15. In 2017 the CRPD Committee published General Comment No. 5, which focuses on Article 19 of the CRPD. It explains that any form of institutionalisation is contrary to Article 19 of the CRPD. It clarifies that the size of a living arrangement is irrelevant, but rather what is important is if the place of living has *"defining elements of institutions or institutionalization"*. These defining elements include:
    a. obligatory sharing of assistants with others and no or limited influence over whom one has to accept assistance from;
    b. isolation and segregation from independent life within the community;
    c. lack of control over day-to-day decisions;
    d. lack of choice over whom to live with;
    e. rigidity of routine irrespective of personal will and preferences;
    f. identical activities in the same place for a group of persons under a certain authority;
    g. a paternalistic approach in service provision;
    h. supervision of living arrangements; and
    i. usually also a disproportion in the number of persons with disabilities living in the same environment.

16. If BCC were to adopt the Draft Policy, BCC would be placing itself into the invidious position of falling short of basic international human rights law. It would be a clear signal to disabled people in the Bristol area that their own Council is knowingly breaching their rights.

Meeting needs with limited resources

17. Chapter 10 of the Statutory Guidance is concerned with care and support planning. Paragraph 10.27 permits a local authority to take into consideration its own finances and budgetary position in determining how to meet a person's eligible needs. The paragraph says that a local authority *"should not set arbitrary upper limits on the costs it is willing to pay to meet needs through certain routes – doing so would not deliver an approach that is person-centred or compatible with public law principles"*. It emphasises that the authority should take decisions on a case-by-case basis. While cost is a relevant factor in deciding between suitable alternative options for meeting needs, the Statutory Guidance says that this *"does not mean choosing the cheapest option; but the one which delivers **the outcomes desired** for the best value"* (emphasis added).

18. Elsewhere, the Statutory Guidance repeats that consideration of resources does not permit local authorities to elect the cheapest option. In relation to personal budgets, the Statutory Guidance states: *"At all times, the wishes of the person must be considered and respected. For example, the personal budget should not assume that people are forced to accept specific care options, such as moving into care homes, against their will because this is perceived to be the cheapest option"* (paragraph 11.7).

19. The Statutory Guidance maintains a focus on the outcomes an individual wishes to achieve in their day-to-day life, and on an individualised and person-centred approach to care-planning.

20. The core content of the Draft Policy at paragraphs 3.8 to 3.9 is fundamentally inconsistent with the structure and purpose of the Care Act 2014 and the Statutory Guidance. The Draft Policy states that where a care package at home would substantially exceed the affordability of residential care, BCC will move the person into residential care. Although BCC is careful to emphasise that this is not

a blanket policy, the Draft Policy states that *"exceptions are likely to be rare"*. Accordingly, the Draft Policy establishes a strong presumption that a person living at home with a substantial care package will have their funding cut. The result is that if they want their care needs to be met (which in many cases means survival), they will have to live in a residential setting.

21. BCC's Draft Policy is wholly at odds with the Care Act 2014's focus on individualised care-planning and promotion of well-being, to which the Draft Policy pays only lip service. The Draft Policy takes a cookie-cutter approach and makes resource considerations determinative (with rare exceptions only). Care planning carried out in accordance with the Draft Policy will be unlawful.

22. Moreover, the Draft Policy states at paragraph 3.12 that if the person with eligible needs under the Care Act 2014 disagrees with BCC's decision to offer a care home placement, then BCC will offer the amount of that placement in a budget that the person can use to purchase home care. This appears to be an upper limit (i.e. the cost of a care home placement) that risks falling foul of the Statutory Guidance at paragraph 10.27.

23. Compliance with the Care Act 2014 regime is necessary for BCC to avoid breaching Article 8 of the European Convention on Human Rights (ECHR), the right to respect for private and family life, home and correspondence. Like well-being, *"private life"* is a broad concept, encompassing a person's physical and psychological integrity, the right to personal development and the notion of personal autonomy. The very essence of Article 8 of the ECHR is respect for human dignity and human freedom: *McDonald v UK* at paragraphs 46-7. [14]

24. Where a public authority removes existing care or support provided to an individual, this will amount to an interference with their right to respect for their private life: see McDonald v UK at paragraphs 48-9. Such an interference will be a breach of Article 8 of the ECHR, unless it is justified as being *"in accordance with the law"* and *"necessary in a democratic society"* to achieve one of the aims specified in Article 8(2) of the ECHR. If adopted, BCC's Policy will result in decisions to

reduce funding that are not *"in accordance with"* the Care Act 2014 for the reasons set out above. Accordingly, a removal of funding to enable a person to receive care and support in their own home will likely breach Article 8 of the ECHR, which is directly enforceable in courts in England.

25. In 2017-18, the Equality and Human Rights Commission (EHRC) condemned similar policies adopted by 13 Clinical Commissioning Groups (CCGs) (now Integrated Care Boards). The EHRC sent legal letters challenging policies which in effect capped the amount of money available for NHS Continuing Healthcare, creating a risk that disabled people with high support needs would be moved from their homes into care homes against their wishes. The EHRC made clear that it was not sufficient for the policies to state that the cap would not apply in *"exceptional"* circumstances, because this did not *"allow the decision-maker properly to undertake... a full evaluation of the particular considerations in favour of provision... as required by [amongst other things] ... Article 8 of the ECHR, Article 19 of the UNCRPD, the [Public Sector Equality Duty under the Equality Act] ..."*. All 13 CCGs accepted the failings of their policies and agreed to revise them. The Chief Executive of the EHRC said at the time, *"Those who need help are individual human beings with individual circumstances which need to be taken into account."* [15]

26. Similarly, in 2018, the Ombudsman found maladministration in relation to Hertfordshire County Council after that authority refused to increase a disabled adult's care package because it would exceed the cost of a care home placement. The ombudsman held: *"While councils must always have due regard to the public purse, care provision should be based on assessed needs and where there is no evidence of appropriate assessment such remarks may be indicative of attempts to inappropriately ration limited resources."* [16]

27. For all the above reasons, while BCC can take into account resources in care planning, the Draft Policy's strong presumption in favour of care homes is inconsistent with BCC's legal obligations under the Care Act 2014.

28. BRIL acknowledges the significant financial pressures experienced by BCC and other local authorities. Recent observations of the Supreme Court are relevant here. In the case of R (Imam) v Croydon London Borough Council [17] a disabled person took their local authority (Croydon) to court for failing to secure her suitable accommodation when Croydon had a duty to do so under the Housing Act 1996. The local authority resisted the claim on the basis of severe budgetary constraints. At paragraph 56, one of the Supreme Court Justices Lord Sales stated: *"A public authority which has limited resources available for use to meet its statutory duties and to fulfil functions which are merely discretionary is obliged to give priority to using them to meet its duties."*

29. In the face of budgetary constraints, BCC is required to prioritise budgetary allocation so that it can meet its duties under the Care Act 2014.

Discrimination

30. BRIL considers that BCC has failed to comply with the Public Sector Equality Duty (PSED) under s.149 Equality Act 2010 in relation to the Draft Policy. The PSED requires BCC to have due regard to the need, amongst other things, of eliminating discrimination and advancing equality of opportunity between disabled and non-disabled persons. This includes removing or minimising disadvantages faced by disabled persons.

31. Although BCC has carried out an Equality Impact Assessment (EQIA), it is deficient for the following reasons.

32. First, BCC states the Draft Policy was adapted from a similar policy implemented by Devon County Council, concluding on this basis that *"there is evidence of other local authorities successfully implementing an approach to ensure a more consistent and fair application of social work practice when considering how we meet the needs of individuals with eligible care and support needs"*. However, there is no publicly available evidence that Devon County Council has conducted a review of its Policy, so the basis upon which BCC asserts that Devon's Policy has been *"successful"* is unclear. Further, BCC says that success is defined in terms of consistency and fairness. This cannot be the only metric to

measure "*success*" and indeed should not be the main metric. "*Success*" must at a bare minimum include whether the relevant local authority has complied with its statutory duties, including under the Care Act 2014 to ensure that a person's eligible needs are met in accordance with the well-being principle.

33. Second, although the EQIA assumes that there may be exceptions to the approach of moving a person to a care home where this is cheaper than a package of care at home, the EQIA fails to acknowledge that the Draft Policy states in terms that any exception will be "*rare*". The failure of the EQIA to consider that exceptions will be "*rare*" means it does not accurately reflect the likely impact of the Draft Policy. BRIL is concerned that BCC will think it is complying with its policy if it offers one of the 162 at-risk individuals funding that is greater than a care home placement.

34. Third, the EQIA identifies that as of 17 May 2023, 162 persons were receiving a personal budget over the rate for residential care and thus would likely be impacted by the Draft Policy. However, the EQIA does not provide a demographic breakdown of this group. This is remarkable, given that BCC knows who each of those 162 people are and has completed needs assessments in relation to each of them. Demographic data is available to BCC without the risk of identifying individuals.

35. Further, it is unsafe to assume that the demographics of this cohort will map onto the demographics of all individuals receiving care and support at home, which is the basis upon which the EQIA proceeds. For example, BRIL considers it highly likely that individuals with significant physical impairments (as opposed to those who are frail) who use a team of Personal Assistants 24/7, and those with learning disabilities and/or who are autistic who require complex and specialist support, will be overrepresented in the cohort of individuals with expensive home care packages. It also seems plausible the cohort will include a higher proportion of younger individuals, on the basis that older individuals with high levels of need are more likely to have moved into residential care already.

36. BRIL is acutely concerned that autistic persons and/or those with learning disabilities who are living with support at home will be forced to move out of their homes and away from family. They will be denied the carers that they trust, who are skilled at meeting their individual needs, and placed in a care home where they know none of the residents or staff, and where their autonomy and independence will be severely curtailed. For many people, this is an absolutely terrifying prospect. There is a very real risk that a person in these circumstances forced into residential care will display behaviours that challenge. In turn, this could lead to detention under the Mental Health Act 1983 in inappropriate mental health units. While an admission to hospital would of course save BCC money (as the NHS pays for an inpatient stay), BCC should be taking steps to prevent admissions under the Mental Health Act 1983, rather than taking steps that make such admissions more likely.

37. The lack of analysis of the actual cohort affected by the Draft Policy prevents any proper understanding of its likely equality impacts. BCC has denied civil society the opportunity to respond to the consultation using the data that BCC holds but has not published.

Access to the courts

38. BRIL anticipates that none of the 162 people who the Council has identified with home care packages costing more than a care home placement will want to move into a care home. There is likely to be a dispute between the Council and each of the 162 persons who do not agree to move into a care home.

39. BRIL asks BCC to confirm that it will inform each of these at-risk persons about local charities such as Bristol Law Centre, and law firms that could provide legal advice and representation, to challenge the decision made to cut home care funding which puts them at risk of institutionalisation.

40. BRIL anticipates that many of the people at risk may need an Independent Advocate to support them with assessments, reviews and challenging decisions. Some of the people being affected by the Policy will have learning disabilities, other cognitive impairments and/

or are autistic. Some may lack capacity to make decisions about their residence and/or care, pursuant to the Mental Capacity Act 2005. It is important that the Council allocates an Independent Mental Capacity Advocate ("IMCA") to each of these people, pursuant to BCC's duty under s.39 of the Mental Capacity Act 2005. BRIL asks that BCC confirms this will happen if the Draft Policy is passed. BRIL is aware that local advocacy providers are under pressure and are concerned that they may not have spare capacity to take on further IMCA clients, so BRIL asks BCC to explain how each of these people will have access to IMCAs and Independent Care Act Advocates (ICAAs).

41. BRIL would like BCC to clarify where the 162 people would go. Which care homes in Bristol that specialise in meeting the needs of working age disabled adults can accommodate 162 people between them?

42. BRIL also asks BCC to confirm in respect of each of the persons affected who lack capacity to make decisions about their residence and/or care, and that BCC will make an application to the Court of Protection to invite the court to decide where it is in the person's best interests to live and receive care. Again, BCC should ensure that each affected person has access to a solicitor specialising in welfare applications in the Court of Protection. BRIL asks BCC to confirm that it will not move any person who lacks capacity to make a decision about residence and/or care without first making an application to the Court of Protection.

Conclusion

43. BRIL strongly disagrees with the draft Fair and Affordable Care Policy. The presumption in favour of moving disabled people to care homes rides roughshod over BCC's obligations under the Care Act 2014 including the obligation to promote well-being and to support people to live as independently as possible, for as long as possible, and Article 8 ECHR and Article 19 CRPD. Moreover, BCC has not complied with the PSED in preparation of the Draft Policy.

44. BRIL asks BCC not to adopt the Draft Policy as it is fundamentally flawed, likely unlawful, and would cause misery to many disabled people and their family and friends in Bristol. BRIL invites BCC to confirm its decision as soon as possible, given that many disabled

people and their friends and families have suffered significant worry and distress since BCC published the Draft Policy.

Fair And Affordable Care policy withdrawn

In February 2024, the controversial policy was withdrawn. Councillor Helen Holland announced: "In discussion with the Mayor, we have now agreed that the policy will not be taken forward at this time, and that officers will work on the basis that a future policy will come forward to a future administration for a decision" [18]. In response, BRIL issued the following media statement [19].

Following the campaign against the 'Fair and Affordable Care Policy' led by Disabled people, alongside concerns shared by thousands of people across the country and in local press and national media, BRIL are pleased to announce that Bristol City Council have withdrawn their 'Fair and Affordable Care Policy'. However, while we welcome the Council's decisions to withdraw the policy, to set up an inquiry, we remain concerned.

In the letter to the Chair of the Bristol Disability Equality Commission, Councillor Helen Holland made the following three points on behalf of the Council:

The first is that everyone recognises that the financial crisis facing not just Bristol City Council Adult Social Care but every Adult Social Care department in England is not of the Council's own making. It is a result of chronic underfunding of Adult Social Care due to central government austerity over the years.

The council is setting up an inquiry into how to build a system to fairly allocate Adult Social Care funding within the agreed budget to meet the diverse needs of the population. To be co-produced with the relevant interested parties.

The third is the range of views that I have heard clearly expressed during the Fair and Affordable Care consultation. I particularly note the strong concerns that some Disabled People in our city and nationally have raised. I am keenly aware of the worries that the consultation has provoked for some people regarding their personal circumstances.

BRIL would like to make the following statement in response:

Disabled people are not to blame for financial crisis or for austerity. While we recognise the harm caused by 14 years of government cuts to local authorities, councils must still make choices with communities, and decisions that are both lawful and in the interests of people they aim to serve.

To begin with an aim to *'allocate Adult Social Care funding within the agreed budget'* suggests that Bristol City Council may not have fully taken on board the concerns of Disabled people, or the advice of our legal counsel. We believe that allocation of support based on budgets, rather than need, may lead to unlawful decisions contrary to The Care Act 2014. We wish to work in true coproduction with the Council, and not to be brought back to the situation we were in before the policy was withdrawn.

An inquiry where the terms are already set is not co-production. The inquiry must be independent and be genuinely co-produced with Disabled people and our organisations, and include the voices and experiences of the most marginalised people and communities.

The decision to produce a report in October 2024 risks passing responsibility onto whoever has overall control after the local and national elections. This will only add to the worries of Disabled people and families.

Nothing about us without us! ■

ACKNOWLEDGEMENTS

Thanks are due to Mark Williams of Bristol Reclaiming Independent Living, and Oliver Lewis of Doughty Street Chambers, for permission to reproduce the statements in this chapter.

REFERENCES

1. Lucy Series. Fair? Affordable? Care? *The Small Places*, 10 November 2023. https://thesmallplaces.wordpress.com/2023/11/10/fair-affordable-care/

2. Think Local Act Personal – Ladder of co-production (13 January 2021). Posted by Patient-Safety-Learning, 29 March 2022. https://www.pslhub.org/learn/patient-engagement/think-local-act-personal ladder-of-co-production-13-january-2021-r6495/

3. John Pring. Fears over 'catastrophic' policy that could force disabled people into care homes. *Disability News Service*, 23 February 2023. https://www.disabilitynewsservice.com/fears-over-catastrophic-Policy-that could-force-disabled-people-into-care-homes/

4. Disabled people in Bristol could be moved to care homes to save council money. *itvX*, 28 December 2023. https://www.itv.com/news/westcountry/2023-12-28/

5. Jasmine Ketibuah-Foley. Disabled residents fear care consultation has been missed. *BBC News*, 20 January 2023. https://www.bbc.co.uk/news/uk-england-bristol-67993985

6. Tristan Cork. Disabled people in Bristol have 'no idea' they could be forced out of their homes by policy change. *Bristol Post*, 21 December 2023. https://www.bristolpost.co.uk/news/bristol-news/disabled-people-bristol-no idea-8988590

7. Social care cuts 'serve spreadsheets not communities'. Sarah Kennelly. *Local Government Chronicle*, 17 January 2024. https://www.lgcplus.com/services/health-and-care/social-care-cuts-serve-spreadsheets-not-communities-17-01-2024/

8. Frances Ryan. Think of this: a plan to 'warehouse' disabled people. What kind of nation is Britain becoming? *The Guardian*, 25 January 2024. https://www.theguardian.com/commentisfree/2024/jan/25/warehouse-disabled-people-bristol-city-council

9. https://assets.publishing.service.gov.uk/government/uploads/system/uploads/attachment_data/file/255180/Consultation-Principles-Oct-2013.pdf

10. Alex Turner. More children in care are being housed outside Bristol as Covid fallout bites. *The Bristol Cable*, 16 September 2021. https://thebristolcable.org/2021/09/more-children-in-care-place-outside-bristol-as-covid-fallout-bites/

11. Bristol: Stop the proposed "Fair and Affordable Care" policy. winvisibleblog 28 November 2023. https://winvisible.org/2023/11/28/bristol-stop-the-proposed-fair-and-affordable-care-policy/

12. Tristan Cork. Disabled people 'terrified' new council policy will see them put in residential care. *BristolLive*, 5 April 2023

13. Thomas Hammarberg. The right of people with disabilities to live independently and be included in the community. Council of Europe Publishing, Strasbourg, 2012.

14. (2015) 60 EHRR 1

15. Equality and Human Rights Commission. NHS u-turns on discriminatory policies. 31 May 2018. https://www.equalityhumanrights.com/nhs-u-turns-discriminatory-policies

16. https://webarchive.nationalarchives.gov.uk/ukgwa/20230504171644/https://www.lgo.org.uk/decisions/adult-care-services/safeguarding/16-017-084#point1

17. [2023] UKSC 45; [2023] 3 WLR 1178

18. Bristol Council withdraw disability care policy. *BBC News*, 8 February 2024. https://www.bbc.co.uk/news/uk-england-bristol-68231455

19. Media Statement in response to Bristol City Council's withdrawal of the proposed 'Fair and Affordable Care' policy. Bristol Reclaiming Independent Living, 7 February 2024.

Placards from a Black Lives Matter protest in Bristol. Credit: Robert Browne

B-Bond warehouse has been identified as the site for a cultural, educational and visitor experience, focusing on the Transatlantic Trafficking of Enslaved Africans. Credit: Robert Browne

Atonement and reparations

Recent achievements of the reparations movement in Bristol are documented in an article by Priyanka Raval, an Atonement and Reparation motion passed by Bristol City Council, and the announcement of new initiatives...

———

2020: Bristol activists spearhead the call for reparations for the legacy and current damage of slavery and colonialism

BLACK LIVES MATTER (BLM) campaigns rage around the world: a demand for radical changes to the status quo, a cry for racial equality. The movement may have started in the US, but protests in the UK have been instrumental in shining a light on racism at home. Racial profiling, police brutality, stop-and-search and racial pay gaps are just some of the conversation topics once more brought to the table. Meanwhile, institutions up and down the country are interrogating issues of diversity and representation within their structures.

The typically youth-led, US-originated, Black Lives Matter movement of hashtags and marches have dominated the spotlight. But due credit must also be paid to the reparations campaigners – a typically older demographic, coordinating a much longer-running operation with organised demands. Typically, they identify less as 'Black', but 'African heritage' and accordingly they say that the Black experience must be understood in terms of the historical and enduring crimes committed against the African continent. They advocate for a meaningful enquiry into the crimes – past and continuing – so that they can properly be addressed and compensated.

In recent weeks, in the wake of the toppling of Edward Colston's statue at the hands of BLM protestors [2], the topic of reparations has hit Bristol City Hall.

What are reparations?

In 1833 the Slavery Abolition Act signalled the gradual abolition of slavery in most parts of the British Empire. A few years later the Slave Compensation Act 1837 was passed. It did not, as you might assume, provide compensation to formerly enslaved people, but instead to the slave owners for their losses of land, property and people. In fact, that compensation – to the tune of roughly £20 million of public money, equivalent to about £16 billion today – was one of the conditions that were needed for the abolition to be accepted. Research by the Centre for the Study of the Legacies of British Slave-ownership [3] at University College London, revealed that a staggering 46,000 Britons received compensation under this act. People who were trafficked from the African continent and enslaved received nothing.

A dictionary definition of 'reparations' is: "the action of making amends for a wrong one has done, by providing payment or other assistance to those who have been wronged". But there is also a legal framework for reparations enshrined in international law [4], which affirms victims' rights to "equal and effective access to justice, adequate, effective and prompt reparation for harm suffered, and access to relevant information concerning violations and reparations". Governments and heads of state have often expressed regret for slavery, without directly apologising – because that could, inconveniently, open up the case for states having to make serious amends for their colonial pasts.

Esther Stanford-Xosei, a lawyer, historian and prolific reparations activist, argues that reparation means restoring the victim "to the original situation before the gross violation was committed". For African-heritage people, that means asking, what would Africa have been like had its people never been kidnapped and enslaved? What would the world look like if this exploitation and dispossession of a people had not occurred?

Returning to such a position takes far more than money. Professor Chinweizu from the Pan-Afrikan Reparations Coalition in Europe – a grassroots alliance of organisations, groups and campaigns working to amplify voices of African communities – argued, back in 1993, that the financial component of reparations is "not even one percent of what reparation is about" [5].

Reparation is mostly about "making repairs" – psychological, cultural, organisational, social, institutional, technological, economic, political and educational – "repairs of every type we need in order to recreate sustainable Black societies," Chinweizu said. How, then, might this look in practice?

Reclaiming our history

It means recognising that the aftermath of slavery and enduring racist practices have psychological impacts. Afrophobia for example, or Post Traumatic Slave syndrome [6] and feeling ashamed of black skin and features. Compensating for this could mean building independent institutions of education, healthcare, spirituality and culture. Or, providing culturally appropriate medical and social care, and programmes of recovery, with a focus on decolonising people's mindset – repairing a sense of identity.

"A big part of our campaigning is recognising we are Afrikans," says Esther Stanford-Xosei. "Recognise our right to exist and to call ourselves and to name ourselves and to reclaim and reconstruct that history, that culture, that heritage and inheritance that is denied to some of us."

The transatlantic slave trade was not only the trafficking of a people – it sparked a paradigm shift in agriculture, health, arts and commerce. The experience is understood as a genocide, or the Swahili word 'Maangamizi', because of its twofold definition. Genocide includes the destruction of the national pattern of the oppressed group, and then the imposition of the national pattern of the oppressor. Due to various colonial occupations by Western nations, many African countries now speak in non-indigenous languages and follow foreign religions.

Stanford-Xosei calls for "global cognitive justice" – which means acknowledging and restoring the indigenous Afrikan system of knowledge. Even spelling Afrika with a 'k' – a reminder that the hard-sounding 'c', which did not historically exist linguistically in most of the continent, is a legacy of colonial translation – symbolises that this would be a restoration of language, spirituality and philosophy, music, art and symbolism.

Bringing structural change

As well as the internal work, structural changes also constitute reparations. This could include state-issued official apologies, criminal prosecutions and truth-seeking, commemorative events, and the development of museums and monuments honouring Black history. Another key demand of the reparations campaign in the UK is the establishment of the All Party Parliamentary Commission of Inquiry for Truth and Reparatory Justice.

George Floyd's murder on a Minneapolis street at the hands of a white police officer has led to a fresh reflection on how institutional racism remains in certain sectors of our society. The deconstruction of privilege, including via reparations, is the only way to undo the social inequities experienced by Black communities – and to achieve true racial equality in society, which would properly address the historical injustices. For more on that, let's now hear from Bristol-based campaigners.

Jendayi Serwah: Seizing the moment in Bristol

Jendayi Serwah is a reparations activist, community organiser, educator, consultant of the Black South West Network, vice-chair of the Stop the Maangamizi campaign and co-founder of the John Lynch Education Forum.

I think it's unfortunate that it takes the death of an Afrikan man, in the States, in broad daylight, on camera, uncontested, to really bring attention to the UK that Afrikan-heritage lives are being snuffed out every day all around the world. The recent events have been an opportunity for Afrikan-heritage people to express their anger, their voice, their frustrations. For our young people, it's a moment to galvanise and organise themselves; to reflect on their position in this society and think, what changes do they want to see. They are organising not necessarily under the banner of Black Lives Matter; they are just realising that self-determination is part of the solution to the problem.

So, I see this moment as an opportunity for us to build whatever structures that we need to develop in order to have more power and voice in Bristol. It's not just about police brutality and not it's not just about the police. There are many ways our people are brutalised all around the world by state and non-state forces and this is what our young people – and everyone – needs to understand and get to grips with.

The Afrikan ConneXions Consortium was established in 2016 after Marvin Rees became the Mayor. His One City Plan stated his desire and ambitions to work towards sharing power and making Bristol an inclusive city. So we got together as six organisations – St Pauls Carnival, Black South West Network (BSWN), Bristol Black Carers, Bristol Somali Resource Centre, Malcolm X Centre and Ujima Radio – who had wide constituencies of membership of the Afrikan-heritage communities to lobby and influence and elevate our voices in city affairs beyond tokenism. So it's not just about being a black face in a white space.

The Stop the Maangamizi campaign is about saying to people: you need to stop the harm, so we can begin to repair the damage. So it's not just the school-to-prison pipeline, it's not just our over-representation in the mental health institutions, it's not just our excessive sentencing and over-criminalisation, it's not just the disproportionate exclusions our young people face in schools... We are saying these things are not isolated events; they come from a history of dehumanisation and disenfranchisement of a people.

So we are saying, let's stop the harm and start repairing. Let's start a dialogue through the establishment of an All Party Parliamentary Commission of Inquiry into Truth and Reparatory Justice, but also through building mechanisms, like people's assemblies, in our own communities, so we can set up our own mechanisms to hold the state, corporations and other institutions that have soft and hard power as a result of empire, accountable.

Komoomutjiua Hangero: What could reparatory justice look like in practice?

Meet Komoomutjiua Hangero from the Stop the Maangamizi: We Charge Ecocide and Genocide campaign in Bristol.

Protests are good. It's a method of demanding justice. They get people hyped up and that is a valuable means of campaigning – but after getting people on the street, what is the plan? I applaud, as we all must, the people who sacrifice their time and liberty by getting statues rid of in that manner. It's commendable, they achieved what years of talk did not. But it's not challenging the structure that kept the statue there for so long. Of course, there is room for both methods, but we have been oppressed for the best part of 600 years. When oppression is institutionalised, a statue is tokenistic. We need to organise ourselves and make concrete plans and galvanise a power base in the community. Without that, it won't make a dent.

...But what would reparatory justice look like in this country? We need space, autonomous spaces to thrive. We are misunderstood as a people. We need to uphold our culture and embed it in our institutions. We believe in 'Ubuntu' – it means "I am because we are. We are, therefore I am." It means I want my people to flourish – if I look at them, and see myself.

Instead of centralised governments imposing their will on us, we would return to our roots, bring back our institutions and empower them... Would this result in a more segregated society, you say? We are already segregated! And no, I believe it will help us integrate rather than segregate. When you have your own spaces, it provides a degree of respect from people, it permits people to be proud of where they are from, and most importantly it gives a sense of belonging. Then, you can open up to society, rather than society imposing itself on you. The lack of space creates more misunderstanding about what people stand for. Now, we only have the illusion of inclusion.

We need land and autonomy wherever we are, backed by power from the continent. For us to repair, we need to get every aspect back of the livelihoods we've lost – land so we can have a home, education and health – and money will come last. Living here is hard – you are always torn between multiple identities, but that can only flourish in an environment which is authentic to you, and here that is more difficult.

Cleo Lake on taking the fight to Bristol

July 2020 has been a busy month for former Lord Mayor and Green party councillor, Cleo Lake. On Tuesday 7 July, Lake submitted a motion to Mayor Marvin Rees to write to the prime minister, Boris Johnson, asking "that the UK government immediately establishes an All-Party Parliamentary Commission of Inquiry for Truth & Reparatory Justice to acknowledge, apologise and instigate reparations for the Transatlantic Traffic in Enslaved Africans" [7].

"The motion wasn't heard, but that was down to a technical thing," Lake explains. "My last option was to put forward questions to the Mayor. I asked him to write to the Government to set up the Inquiry and also for equity for our black-led institutions in the city." He said he would consider it, she tells me. Meanwhile, Lake is fully intent on keeping up the pressure.

Lake spoke at the All Black Lives Matter gathering on 12 July in Eastville Park. She used her speech to highlight the link between BLM and reparations. In our interview, I asked her about the relationship between the two movements, were they competing or complementary?

Cleo Lake tells me she does want to see a coming together of the movements. "They both have a part to play, but I do see a disconnect between some of the young people involved in BLM and the reparations activists – such as the ones you've already spoken to. For one thing, I'm not as clear about what their demands are, whereas in the reparations campaign the demands are fully listed. Also, it is a bit frustrating that these grassroots movements have attracted very little support in the mainstream and virtually no funding while doing a hell of a lot of work. Some of these new BLM movements can attract millions."

Keeping up the pressure

In July 2020, Cleo Lake had submitted a question to Bristol City Council Members Forum asking Mayor Marvin Rees to write to the Prime Minister requesting an All-Party Parliamentary Commission of Inquiry for Truth and Reparatory Justice.

The Mayor replied: "For an issue as significant as this I suggest it would have been better to have brought a group of people together to discuss the ins and outs of it. The theatre of an unrepresentative Full Council doesn't serve this issue. I would have suggested that the best way to progress an issue about this would have been to book in to have a chat with me about it sometime over the past four years to discuss what reparations means. I would be glad to look at your draft of a letter and we can discuss it [8]."

In September 2020, Cleo Lake again submitted a reparations motion to Full Council but the Labour, Conservative and Liberal Democrat groups were unwilling to extend the meeting to allow a debate on the motion. Lake said: "There were over 130 statements and questions in support of the motion – for many people today was the first time they had ever attended or submitted a question or statement to a council meeting. They will be disappointed that it has been blocked from being discussed today. I can promise everyone that lobbied the council over this issue that we will keep pushing it up the council agenda [9]."

This determination won through and, at an Extraordinary Full Council Meeting on 2 March 2021, Bristol became the first UK core city to back the campaign for reparations [10]. Councillor Cleo Lake moved the following motion, which was seconded by Deputy Mayor Councillor Asher Craig.

2021: Atonement and Reparation for Bristol's role in the Transatlantic Traffic in Enslaved Afrikans

Differences in power manifest in asymmetrical access – a privilege which continues to run along racial lines. To re-imagine race equality, we have to be mindful of the past and how inequalities continue to manifest. We should reflect on how racial inequalities are embedded in the current economic system. Afrikan heritage people and communities systematically have poorer economic outcomes. Unless these systemic failures and their drivers and sources are identified and addressed, we are in danger of replicating them in any attempt to design a fair and resilient economy.

Historical attempts to disenfranchise these communities have resulted in the disproportionate health, economic and policing impacts experienced today. Alternative solutions and spaces are therefore needed, spaces which do not seek to privilege certain groups over others but seek to centre these voices, change the template, and create alternative solutions and spaces for Afrikan heritage people to thrive.

'Reparations' is a legal term defined by the United Nations (UN) which calls for 'holistic repair'. Our city and our country need a 'process of repair' to re-examine the reality and impact of Afrikan enslavement and its ongoing impact on communities today. As outlined by the UN, reparations should be holistic and can include many initiatives including public apologies, social justice initiatives, education, cultural projects, commemorative ceremonies and affirmative action. Nobody has the answers as to exactly what reparations should look like – that's why what we are calling for is a process of repair which hears from many of the voices in our communities that have been impacted and are often not heard.

Full Council believes...

1. It must be a priority for Bristol to actively acknowledge this history and actively seek to bring about reconciliation and reparations by lending and leading its voice as an institution towards remedial holistic reparations and action towards the legacies that continue to plague contemporary life for descendants of the Afrikan Caribbean enslaved. The continuation of harm and discrimination manifests itself in but is not limited to: over representation in the mental health system; discrimination within the criminal justice system; poverty and disadvantage.

2. The International Decade for People of Afrikan Descent, proclaimed by UN General Assembly resolution 68/237 and to be observed from 2015 to 2024, provides a solid framework for the United Nations, Member States, civil society and all other relevant actors to join

together with people of Afrikan descent and take effective measures for the implementation of the programme of activities in the spirit of recognition, justice and development. Such a process is long overdue in Bristol.

3. Reparations are necessary for achieving social justice, as racism and racial hierarchy continues to be a key driver of the divisions that have undermined the efforts to identify the common cause and build the united voice against other drivers of social hierarchy and injustice such as class and sexism.

Full Council resolves...

To call on councillors, the Mayor or other appropriate council agency to:

1. Write to the Speakers of both Houses of the UK Parliament, Chair of the Commons' Women and Equalities Committee, and Chair of the Commons' Home Affairs Committee to express Bristol City Council's view that they should consider establishing, and seeking UK Government support for, an All-Party Parliamentary Commission of Inquiry. The purpose of this unprecedented commission would be to work on the scope of how reparations may be delivered and may also include for example raising concerns about how tax payers were until 2015 paying back compensation paid to enslavers.

2. Support Afrikan Heritage Community (AHC) organisations in Bristol to galvanise support for the emerging Bristol AHC led 'Reparations Plan' from, and in collaboration with, wider stakeholders including institutions, city strategic leaders, corporate leaders, key strategic programmes/initiatives and cross-party politicians.

3. Implement Community Wealth Creation strategies that support and encourage community wealth building to produce more sustainable equitable growth whilst alleviating systemic poverty. The social economy, civil society and community wealth are the key to fair employment and equitable growth. The community wealth building model of economic development is emerging in our cities and communities offering real, on-the-ground solutions to localities and regions battered by successive waves of extraction, disinvestment,

displacement, and disempowerment. If the source of racial injustice in the twenty-first century is the economic injustice or domination of the global economy established in the seventeenth century, then a more just economy is the only way to sustainably achieve racial justice.

4. Recognise that reparative justice should be driven by Afrikan Heritage Communities experiences, voices and perspectives to ensure that advocacy messages not only reflect but also respond to the real needs of the community in order to recognise inequalities.

2024: Launch of reparation initiatives

Three years after the atonement and reparation motion was passed, the Bristol Legacy Foundation announced several city-wide reparatory justice initiatives [11]. Bristol City Council published the following press release:

> Today (15 March 2024), Bristol Legacy Foundation (BLF) officially launched its work, looking at Bristol's history, racial justice and the future for African heritage communities in our city. As part of today's launch event at M Shed, BLF announced their vision to home a cultural, educational and visitor experience, dedicated to the Transatlantic Trafficking of Enslaved Africans (TTEA) in bonded warehouse B Bond. Attendees heard from the working groups of the four projects established to assist the city in exploring its legacy of the TTEA:
>
> **Memorialisation**: Creating a national and international monument in Bristol to honour the victims of enslavement.
> **Story House**: Establishing a museum or Story House chronicling the history, lives, and futures of those affected by enslavement.
> **Reparatory Justice**: Building an African Heritage Centre of Excellence and Pan African Community Education Complex, along with a land-based initiative (Zenzele Village).
> **Partnerships, Investments and Resources**: Focuses on building partnerships, finding investments and resource support for the Bristol Legacy Foundation's activities related to memorialisation and the museum/storyhouse.
>
> Bristol City Council has made a commitment with BLF to support

the aims of these projects and explore ways to deliver them together for the bicentenary of the Slavery Abolition Act (1833) in 2033. ∎

ACKNOWLEDGEMENTS

Thanks are due to the Bristol activists who campaign for atonement and reparation, Priyanka Raval and *The Bristol Cable* for permission to reproduce text from the article first published in July 2020, and Bristol City Council legal services for permission to reproduce text from the Atonement and Reparations motion.

REFERENCES

1. Priyanka Raval. Bristol activists spearhead the call for reparations for the legacy and current damage of slavery and colonialism. *The Bristol Cable*, 30 July 2020. Available at: https://thebristolcable.org/2020/07/bristol-activists-spearhead-the-call-for-reparations/ (Accessed 22 May 2024)
2. Priyankal Raval. Colston statue toppled during Bristol's Black Lives Matter protest. *The Bristol Cable*, 7 June 2020. Available at: https://thebristolcable.org/2020/06/colston-statue-toppled-during-bristols-black-lives-matter-protest/ (Accessed 22 May 2024)
3. Study of the Legacies of British Slave-ownership. University College London. Available at: https://www.ucl.ac.uk/lbs/ (Accessed 22 May 2024)
4. Basic Principles and Guidelines on the Right to a Remedy and Reparation for Victims of Gross Violations of International Human Rights Law and Serious Violations of International Humanitarian Law: resolution/adopted by the General Assembly. UN General Assembly 21 March 2006. Accessible at: https://www.refworld.org/legal/resolution/unga/2006/en/12095 (Accessed 22 May 2024)
5. Reparations and A New Global Order: A Comparative Overview by Professor Chinweizu A paper read at the second Plenary Session of the First Pan-African Conference on Reparations, Abuja, Nigeria, April 27, 1993. Available at: https://ncobra.org/resources/pdf/Chinweizu-ReparationsandANewGlobalOrder1.pdf (Accessed 22 May 2024)
6. Dr Joy DeGruy. Post Traumatic Slave Syndrome. Available at: https://www.joydegruy.com/post-traumatic-slave-syndrome (Accessed 22 May 2024)
7. Call for Bristol slavery reparations goes 'unheard', says councillor. *BBC News*, 9 July 2020. Available at: https://www.bbc.co.uk/news/uk-england-bristol-53339526 (Accessed 22 May 2024)
8. Question from Councillor Cleo Lake. Bristol City Council Member Forum, 7 July 2020. Available at: https://democracy.bristol.gov.uk/documents/s50624/FC%20answers%20July%2020%20FINAL%202.pdf (Accessed 30 June 2024)
9. Amanda Cameron. British slave trade reparations debate at Bristol City Council postponed again. *BristolLive*, 9 September 2020. Available at: https://www.bristolpost.co.uk/news/bristol-news/british-slave-trade-reparations-debate-4500382 (Accessed 30 June 2024)
10. Bristol council passes slave trade reparations motion. *BBC News*, 2 March 2021. Available at: https://www.bbc.co.uk/news/uk-england-bristol-56258320 (Accessed 22 May 2024)
11. Bristol City Council. Bristol Legacy Foundation launches city-wide reparatory justice initiatives. 15 March 2024. Available at: https://news.bristol.gov.uk/press-releases/1d1b7df5-2e2e-4162-b76c-b916a644d40d/bristol-legacy-foundation-launches-city-wide-reparatory-justice-initiatives (Accessed 22 May 2024)

Community
Campaigning

Ursa the Bear welcomed people to Bristol from the roof of the men's toilets in the Bearpit roundabout. Credit: *Bristol24/7*

Campaigners outside City Hall, Bristol. Credit: *Bristol24/7*

Ursa The Bear lives on

Richard Jones, a former member of the Bearpit Improvement Group and a director of the People's Republic of Stokes Croft, recalls the battle to save Ursa The Bear and the broader politics of the Bearpit experiment...

———

BRISTOL'S FIRST ELECTED mayor George Ferguson unveiled the statue of Ursa the Bear in the Bearpit on 10 May 2013. Ferguson's successor, Marvin Rees and the Labour group on Bristol City Council oversaw her removal six years later. The loss of Ursa sparked a public protest and effectively signalled the end of the Bearpit experiment that had achieved so much before being derailed.

Chris Chalkley, founder of The People's Republic of Stokes Croft (PRSC) and a member of the Bearpit Improvement Group (BIG) worked with artist Jamie Gillman to create Ursa in the yard at PRSC's Jamaica Street headquarters [1]. It took almost a year of trial and error to create the 12-foot-tall geometric statue.

Gillman admits that at one point Ursa looked more like a gopher than a bear, but eventually she took shape. A structural engineer gave the go-ahead for Ursa to be erected, on a 4-foot-tall base on top of the gents' toilets in the Bearpit. Steel rods were welded into place to support her (Ursa was subject to annual safety inspections) and Bristol had a striking, popular symbol of community activism.

Chalkley says: "What made Ursa The Bear special is that she was a significant sculpture that occupied an unloved space in the public domain. Made largely from scrap wood, she represented the idea of bottom-up change."

On Friday 10 May 2013, Mayor Ferguson unveiled Ursa on the roof of the men's toilets in the Bearpit [2]. A joint initiative between PRSC and BIG, the sculpture reinforced the notion of Stokes Croft and the Bearpit as an outdoor gallery, and was funded by a grant from Arts Council England. The Ambling Band and others performed at the unveiling and the Art Container hosted an exhibition of work by Jamie Gillman.

In the beginning

The Bearpit Improvement Group (BIG) was formed in 2010 under Henry Shaftoe, former urban-design professor at the University of the West of England. It consisted of nine elected directors and members. The volunteer group was the UK's first Community Action Group and was granted semi-autonomy in managing the Bearpit as a Community Action Zone. Its remit was to create a 'welcoming, safe, diverse and inclusive environment' in an unloved and neglected public space.

A Bristol City Council cabinet report in July 2012 indicated "there has long been an aspiration to improve the public realm of St James Barton Roundabout" and "with an understanding of the lively and creative cultural mix in the area, the Bear-pit Improvement Group wants to build a space that is better suited to imaginative community uses" [3,4].

Meanwhile, the Bearpit Improvement Group suggested "the toilet block roofs offer a possible site for installation of large sculptures which would be visible from inside the Bearpit as well as from the highway and pavements outside" [5].

BIG's formation was partly inspired by the grassroots regeneration in nearby Stokes Croft where The People's Republic of Stokes Croft had used radical art to better the area – painting the streets with politically evoking graffiti, improving the space visually under a DIY anti-establishment ethos, to 'shame the council' into caring for the formerly impoverished area.

BIG was a success. PRSC brought in a 1979 Bristol VR bus. The iconic green double-decker was delivered to Dan Paton's yard in St Werburgh's where it was converted into a cafe before being craned into the Bearpit. Containers were converted into a take-away coffee bar and a fruit shop.

The Cube was erected to display political and other messages – an alternative billboard for the city. Another container was converted into a performance space and Sara Venn and her team from the Incredible Edible charity transformed the gardens into an inner-city wildlife sanctuary, working with a range of community projects as well as engaging with the homeless 'residents' of the Bearpit.

There were regular outdoor art exhibitions, markets, music and theatre performances and more.

Things fall apart

I joined BIG a couple of years before things fell apart in 2017 – although things were starting to go wrong then. Essentially, the model of the Bearpit traders paying rent to BIG, which would then be reinvested in making the Bearpit a better place, didn't work. Despite their best efforts, the traders never made enough money to pay the rent.

Bristol City Council and Bristol Waste seemed to make matters worse. Remarkably, our liaison person within the Council was a senior traffic and transport manager who knew a lot about roundabouts and a lot less about working with community activists.

Things hit a particular low in November 2017 when Bristol Waste removed an artwork board from the Bearpit after a complaint was received from Tory councillor Mark Weston that it was 'offensive' [6]. The art was part of the Journey to Justice exhibition, an international campaign inspired by Dr Martin Luther King and the US Civil Rights movement.

The board in question celebrated the role of Walter Ayles in fighting for social justice and, in particular, his role as a leading campaigner against the First World War. Ayles was a Bristol councillor before the First World War and was sent to prison for his opposition to it. Soon after his release he was elected MP for Bristol North.

The information for the board was researched by Journey to Justice trustee and Bristol Co-ordinator Dr Madge Dresser (a Senior Research Fellow at UWE and Honorary Professor of History at the University of Bristol) and by Colin Thomas author of *Slaughter No Remedy: The Life and Times of Walter Ayles, Bristol Conscientious Objector* [7]. The board was created by artist Bo Lanyon who worked with the Creative Youth Network to inspire their work in the Bearpit. Dr Paul Stephenson OBE, one of the leaders of the 1963 Bristol Bus Boycott, was a patron of Journey to Justice.

But that didn't stop Bristol Waste removing the artwork [8]. When the incident was reported in the press, the managing director of Bristol Waste made an apology saying: "We were asked to remove this artwork and acted in good faith to do so. We now accept this decision was not the right one. We will reinstate it and apologise to all concerned." Nevertheless, it was becoming apparent that Ursa and her radical values were living on borrowed time.

D-Day for Ursa

In March 2018, Bristol City Council 'took back control' of the Bearpit [9]. Deputy Mayor, Asher Craig, said: "we cannot ignore the unacceptable anti-social behaviour that has taken place recently, so it is necessary for us to take action and take back full control of the area. We need to ensure that this space is providing a safe and positive environment that people across the city can enjoy."

BIG, and the following year PRSC, were ordered to remove everything they had brought in and built there. Ursa was arguably Bristol's best-loved and most creative piece of public art of recent times, and a 'Save Our Bear' petition, demanding Mayor Rees allowed Ursa to stay in the Bearpit, was set up in October 2018.

The petition reached 2,000 signatures in just two days, and went on to achieve more than the 3,500 Bristol signatures required to force the full council to consider saving Ursa [10]. Many of the people who signed that petition sent messages saying how much Ursa meant to them; gave them a sense of place, pride and identity. Some parents said they had made up special songs with their children to sing when they passed Ursa.

Caitlin Telfer had joined the Bearpit Improvement Group after completing her dissertation *Cultural Activism and the Reconfiguring of Public Space and Identity in the Bearpit, Bristol* at University College London in 2016 [11]. Surrounded by Ursa supporters, she made the opening speech at City Hall:

"In taking back the space, this Council took back the responsibility for ensuring that the good things that happened under the Bearpit Improvement Group were built upon. However, since this has happened, you, our council, have spent vast amounts of public money on ineffective anti-graffiti paint, and torn down without notice the alternative advertising boards. In my research, the street art and alternative ideas on The Cube were widely seen as what made the Bearpit interesting. This council appears intent on removing both.

"There has been a clear deterioration in the Bearpit since the council took back the license, with it fast looking like it once did – a dead space. With the traders vacating, and nobody to organise events, markets or performance, the 'eyes on the street' that once made the Bearpit more welcoming, have disappeared. Anti-social behaviour has risen and the only response has been Public Space Protection Orders which only moves problematic behaviour into another public space.

"So now this council has issued notices to the Bearpit Improvement Group (which no longer exists) and PRSC to remove ALL structures at huge cost to the group that funded them – PRSC. It would seem that this council wishes to send out the message that community action will be thwarted, and punished.

"The amount of support rallied for this petition in such a short time clearly shows how strongly Bristolians care about the cultural future of our city. We ask that the notices to remove the Bear and other community structures, many of which have been publicly funded, be withdrawn, and that this petition is referred to the Mayor. In the interests of public accountability. We also ask, which councillor and/or officers authorised these notices and why?

"We appeal to the council to recognise the value of alternative cultural spaces in the city, and to work actively with community to retain what it is that makes our city so special."

Labour's response was led by Cllr Mark Brain (Hartcliffe) who said: "I struggle to find why someone would bring a petition on a model of a bear... It just seems to me that domestic violence, child poverty and homelessness are far more suitable topics in this chamber... I thought it was a pretty mediocre piece of art in the first place. It would look very nice in Wilmott Park in Hartcliffe. I am sure the locals would enjoy interacting with it... This should not have been a debate in this chamber."

But his dismissive views were not shared by speakers from other parties.

Cllr Matthew Melias (Conservative, Avonmouth and Lawrence Weston) said: "People like this artwork. This is a good piece of art. People have come to see the bear as iconic of the city."

Cllr Paula O'Rourke (Green, Clifton) argued: "I cannot believe that you would say it's not popular. In the *Naked Guide to Bristol*, it is regarded as the foremost statue in the city [12]. I used to go to the Bearpit a lot during 2016 when there were restaurants there and you could get your food at lunchtime. I am in despair at what you see happening there now. Something needs to be made better but I go back to my point which is that whoever is just deciding that you can get rid of this really great symbol of what people love in the city, really makes me question what all the other decisions are being made behind that. I remember when I first came to Bristol in 2013, and the first thing I saw when I was coming down and driving into the city for the first time was the bear. And I was making a decision about where I was going to relocate. I wanted to come somewhere that was different, inclusive, edgy, had a great variety of interesting people and that's one of the things that I thought I saw."

Cllr Mark Wright (Liberal Democrat, Hotwells and Harbourside) argued: "We don't have to be vindictive about this. We don't need to throw the baby out with the bathwater. We in the Liberal Democrat group think the bear has become iconic in the area and we don't think anything is gained by getting rid of the artwork. This petition shows a good deal of support for Ursa. So I will conclude by appealing to the Mayor and his team for a bit of compromise here, so that Ursa can be kept and integrated into the exciting new plans for the area."

But Deputy Mayor Asher Craig was adamant: "Whilst none of us doubt that the Bearpit Improvement Group had good intentions, the problems here must now be tackled through a different approach. Safety cannot be compromised for sentiment. Thousands of people who signed the petition clearly share our enthusiasm for St James Barton roundabout. Bristolians' number one priority for this space is public safety. So after listening to the city we took back control. If, as we continue to listen to the city, it becomes clear that there is overwhelming support for the bear staying, then I am sure that the owners will consider donating it to Bristol. The council does not own the statue."

The following day, former members of the Bearpit Improvement Group and the Peoples Republic of Stokes Croft issued a statement [13], asserting: "We are deeply disappointed that the Labour group did not respond to the substance of the petition. In her justification of the order to remove Ursa the Bear and the community infrastructure, deputy mayor Asher Craig referred to several incidents, at least two of which (occupation and arson in the closed toilets) happened after Bristol City Council 'took back control' in early 2018 (and none of which involved the structures referred to in the petition)."

Ursa leaves the Bearpit

In 2024, five years after that Full Council debate, Caitlin Telfer reflects: "Ursa represented difference, creativity and community. She welcomed people arriving in Bristol with her (made from recycled materials) arms. She was and continues to be a symbol that people have adopted to represent Bristol – that's quite something. Ursa also became symbolic of a movement of creative community activism in the Bearpit. She came down when that activism was excluded from the Bearpit. I think that's what she would have wanted. I don't think she would have wanted to stay."

The Council may claim that Ursa was excluded from the general order to remove all items belonging to BIG and PRSC from the Bearpit, but it was clear to the community activists that the Mayor's Office and the Labour group did not share the values Ursa represented. Chris Chalkley says: "When, finally, the Bearpit experiment was crushed, we took the decision to remove the bear ourselves. For the bear to remain under such circumstances would have been a travesty."

So, in September 2019, a team from PRSC dismantled Ursa and took her back to her birthplace in the Jamaica Street yard. Her removal was reported in the local press: "It was a poignant moment for the artist who created Ursa the bear as he buckled on a harness to begin dismantling the sculpture on Thursday morning. For six years, the black and white sculpture has looked over the Bearpit, becoming one of Bristol's most loved landmarks featuring on mugs, postcards, prints and murals."[14]

Ursa lives on

After 'rescuing' her from the council-run vision of the Bearpit (hanging baskets and anti-graffiti paint), PRSC received various offers to rehome Ursa. The most realistic offer was made by Dennis Stinchcombe MBE of Broad Plain Riverside Youth Project by the side of the M32. The plan was for Ursa to overlook traffic entering the city. It was an attractive proposition for various reasons. Dennis, a veteran and highly respected youth worker, was someone PRSC could work with, and the position was almost as prominent as the Bearpit, so that Ursa would still be a Welcome to Bristol symbol.

Unfortunately, once freed of her supports, some of the recycled wood was found to have rotted and only Ursa's head remained fully intact. The reality was that Ursa would need to be completely rebuilt, and that would take time and money. PRSC had been financially and emotionally battered by the Bearpit experience. Chris Chalkley had diverted funds into the project when the BIG financial model failed, and felt vilified by the establishment in return. There simply wasn't enough energy or funding to rebuild Ursa.

Ursa's head made a few appearances at community activist events and displays, but would otherwise have been hidden from public view. Then, an unlikely ally appeared in the shape of Bristol Bears. Tom Tainton, then Head of Communications at the rugby club and now its Chief Operating Officer, got in touch asking if Ursa could be resurrected at the club's training ground in Abbots Leigh. I picked up the email from Tom expressing interest in Ursa becoming a symbol of Bristol Bears and sent the following reply:

Hello Tom,

I've recently joined the Board of the People's Republic of Stokes Croft and I've picked up Bristol Bears' interest in Ursa Bear from Lisa Furness, who you have been in touch with.

As I am sure you are aware, the situation regarding the future of Ursa is complicated with Mayor Marvin Rees and Cllr Asher Craig demanding the bear is removed and then seeming to change their minds when they realised how unpopular this would make them.

Initially the council was working with PRSC to look at alternative sites, but they have failed to respond to correspondence for the last month or so. Therefore, we are unclear about their intentions. So we are looking at all options for the future of Ursa including your interest.

Ursa represents several values which we would want to maintain wherever she ends up.
1. She's female.
2. She represents grassroots activism.
3. She represents community, equality and free thinking.

So it would be inappropriate if Ursa were to become a corporate symbol because she's also a raging Leftie.

Tainton explained that the club's values, and those of its award-winning Community Foundation, are around inspiring community through rugby success. Part of this is a commitment from all players and staff to deliver hundreds of hours of voluntary work throughout the season. That includes Sunday evenings volunteering at soup kitchens, an annual day where the squad take litter pickers out in central Bristol, as well as many school and community centre visits.

There was even talk of two Ursas being erected at the Ashton Gate ground – a bit like the old Twin Towers at Wembley. Sadly, that was not possible, but instead Bristol Bears worked with Jamie Gillman for Ursa to be the main image on the 2023-24 season away shirt [15].

Speaking on Bears TV at the launch of the shirt, first team prop forward, Bristolian Yann Thomas said: "With the Bear being on the shirt this season, it's a massive honour for us and what the city represents for us."

Fellow Bristolian Amber Reed, who won the Women's World Cup with England in 2014 and is the Bears Women co-captain, said: "I used to see her there every day standing proud when I drove past on my way to training. Every time you pull on a Bears shirt it's special, but to have something synonymous with the city, and travel the land and have that little reminder and that feeling of home, is something pretty cool."

The Bristol Bears shirts quickly sold out and fans will continue to wear them for years to come. Benoit Bennett, a PRSC director and member of the crew who dismantled Ursa and brought her home to safety, said: "We have been exploring various ways she can be brought back to life and it's beautiful to see her coming back into the world."

Ursa and her values live on. ■

REFERENCES

1. https://prsc.org.uk (Accessed 3 June 2024)
2. St James Barton Pedestrian/Cycle Improvements. Bristol City Council Cabinet, 4 July 2012. Available at: https://democracy.bristol.gov.uk/Data/Cabinet/201207041800/Agenda/0704_8.pdf (Accessed 3 June 2024)
3. www.bearpitimprovementgroup.co.uk (Accessed 3 June 2024)
4. Bearpit Improvement Group. The Bearpit: A New Way Forward Proposals to improve an under-used City Centre public space. Available at: https://democracy.bristol.gov.uk/Data/Cabinet/201207041800/Agenda/0704_8.pdf (Accessed 3 June 2024)
5. Bristol 'Bearpit' sculpture marks area's regeneration. BBC News, 10 May 2013. Available at: https://www.bbc.co.uk/news/uk-england-bristol-22477673 (Accessed 3 June 2024)
6. Tristan Cork. Fury as 'offensive' artwork on Bristol's conscientious objector is removed ahead of Remembrance Day parade. *BristolLive*, 9 November 2017. Available at: https://www.bristolpost.co.uk/news/bristol-news/fury-offensive-artwork-bristols-conscientious-753870 (Accessed 3 June 2024)
7. Colin Thomas. *Slaughter No Remedy: The Life and Times of Walter Ayles, Bristol Conscientious Objector* Bristol Radical History Group, 2017.
8. Michael Young. 'Offensive' artwork in Bristol Bearpit about conscientious objector reinstated after being torn down. Bristol Live, 10 November 2017. Available at: https://www.bristolpost.co.uk/news/bristol-news/offensive-artwork-bristol-bearpit-conscientious-759774 (Accessed 3 June 2024)
9. Bristol City Council takes back control of Bearpit. Ellie Pipe. *Bristol 24/7*, 13 March 2018. Available at: https://www.bristol247.com/news-and-features/news/bristol-city-council-takes-back-control-bearpit/ (Accessed 3 June 2024)
10. Bristol City Council. Full Council 15 January 2019. Available at: Full Council Tuesday, 15th January, 2019 2.00 pm (youtube.com) (Accessed 3 June 2024)
11. Caitlin Telfer. *Cultural Activism and the Reconfiguring of Public Space and Identity in the Bearpit, Bristol.* Dissertation undertaken at University College London, 2016. Available at: https://prsc.org.uk/wp-content/uploads/2019/02/Cultural-Activism-in-The-Bearpit-Caitlin-Telfer-.pdf (Accessed 3 June 2024)

12.   The Naked Guide to Bristol, 2019. Tangent Books.

13.   Benoit Bennett. There is no place in political debate for this kind of threat. *Bristol24/7*, 17 January 2019. Available at: https://www.bristol247.com/opinion/your-say/there-is-no-place-in-political-debate-for-this-kind-of-personal-threat/ (Accessed 3 June 2024)

14.   Ellie Pipe. End of an era as bearpit bear dismantled. *Bristol24/7*, 26 September 2019. Available at: https://www.bristol247.com/news-and-features/news/end-of-an-era-as-bearpit-bear-dismantled/ (Accessed 3 June 2024)

15.   The story of the strip: Ursa the Bear! Bears Foundation, 6 September 2023. Available at: https://www.bristolbearsrugby.com/bristol-bears-men/the-story-of-the-strip-ursa-the-bear/ (Accessed 3 June 2024)

Mandy Sharman of Bristol Boaters Community Association has lived on boat in the harbour for more than a decade. Pictured here with her daughter Primrose. Credit: Martin Booth, *Bristol24/7*

Boats in Bristol Harbour. Credit: Martin Booth, *Bristol24/7*

Navigating the waters: the fight for justice in Bristol Harbour

George Colwey, a campaigner with Bristol Boaters Community Association, describes the ongoing campaign for representation and justice by a group of boat-dwelling Bristolians...

––––

QUALITY, AFFORDABLE AND secure housing has become increasingly rare in Bristol. Having bounced between short-term lets and poor-quality housing, my perspective on housing approaching my 30s was jaded. I found a route into home ownership by a stroke of luck, being presented with an opportunity to buy a cheap boat in Bristol harbour. The seller explained the longstanding unofficial arrangement regarding living on board. At that time in 2020, only eight residential licences were provided in the harbour, the rest being leisure or commercial licences. He assured me all I had to do was tell the Harbour Authority that I would adhere to a vague bye-law stating I would not reside on board more than 14 nights in a period, without actually defining the duration of that period. This was the tenuous start to my life on the water.

Upon moving onboard, I found that, despite the layers of secrecy, there existed an open and supportive community of boat dwellers in the heart of Bristol. Being new to boat life, every day presented a new challenge to overcome. Where do I take rubbish? Where do I empty my waste tank? Why is this critical looking piece of hardware leaking? Thankfully my neighbours were always willing to lend an oar and I was soon invited to join a community group set up by my neighbour across the water, Amanda Sharman better known as Mandy.

Mandy lives with her partner John and their two young children and

I soon found out that, having lived under this fragile arrangement for eight years at the time, Mandy wanted security and safety for her young family. The Bristol Boaters Community Association (BBCA) was set up with a mission to represent the interests of our underground community of boaters and to create a legitimate path for those residing in the harbour to gain residential status.

The first meeting I attended was held on the John-Sebastion lightship, a beautiful old boat with a lighthouse on the deck and a club-house for the Bristol Cruising Club, who at that time managed the Bathurst Basin on behalf of Bristol City Council (BCC). During this meeting, I was made aware of a new proposal from BCC called 'The Harbour Review'.

The Harbour Review and the formation of the Bristol Boaters Community Association

The Harbour Review was first proposed back in 2018. Its purpose was facilitating Bristol Harbour changing from a Municipal Port (managed by the local authority) to a Trust Port (independent from the local authority). One justification for this was cost saving. A BCC presentation, entitled 'Bristol City Docks Review Project', indicated: "Trust ports have better financial performance than LA managed ports and it is an aspiration of the DfT." [1]

To become a Trust Port, harbour authorities are required to become cost neutral. The Harbour Review was therefore in part an attempt to analyse the financial status of Bristol harbour and identify means of increasing revenue streams. According to the Department for Transport, one key aspect of successful Trust Ports is building a relationship with stakeholders: "6.3 Major Trust Ports invest considerable time and effort in developing and maintaining relationships with their wide range of stakeholders. This is an essential aspect of the trust port model and lies at the core of what trust ports should be seeking to achieve." [2]

It therefore made sense that an emphasis on building stakeholder relationships formed an integral part of the planned Harbour Review. In 15 documents published by BCC between 2018 and 2022, there is mention of consultation with stakeholders, and several acknowledgements that this consultation should be conducted before the conclusion of the review. The Bristol City Docks Review Project presentation also stated that the 'fees and charges' work stream would include public engagement and consultation.

The BBCA formed in 2019, with Mandy and others believing that the consultation presented boaters with an opportunity to have their voices heard. Mandy and others wanted live aboard licences and recognised rights of tenure to be on the table. The next few years saw the BBCA establish itself as a proactive group with regular meetings, litter picking schemes, safety training projects and more. The pre-existing relationship of mutual aid among boat dwellers went some way to enabling this new relationship to form easily; there was a mutual concern in protecting the rights and interests of boat dwellers and their families. This is reflected in the BBCA's membership numbers rising to 152 by the end of January 2023.

While our campaign has seen significant losses, the victories and opportunities we have accrued are in no small part down to the early work of Mandy and other BBCA founders. This grassroots organising gave us a foundation upon which we were able to respond to events quickly, which proved invaluable; this included building a record of correspondence and publications related to the Harbour Review which I have structured much of this chapter around.

The early campaign for representation

Since its formation, the BBCA has engaged with the authorities wherever possible, to establish its interest in helping to facilitate the promised consultation. Mandy even had direct correspondence with Mayor Marvin Rees. In an email on 26 April 2021, he stated:

"It is positive that you have formed a group to represent those people living on boats in the harbour. As you say this can help improve communications between the council and I would like to continue this dialogue. As I am sure you are aware, we are approaching an election in two weeks, but should I be re-elected to office I would of course meet and discuss further. In the meantime it is important that you have been able to talk with the harbourmaster about operational issues – these shared spaces are under increased pressure during the pandemic and as we return from lockdown and so their management is a real challenge. The situation for many communities through the pandemic has been especially difficult and I can imagine the boat community has had specific issues too. Longer term the harbour review is an important opportunity to make sure that the harbour continues to be a vibrant place to live, a thriving economy and financially sustainable. We hope to be able to work with you and other harbour users and local residents on it." [3]

Mandy says following this email she "felt hopeful that we had a chance to talk to those in power" and the BBCA were encouraged to continue building their campaign for representation.

BBCA arranged election hustings during this period, on 28 April 2021 via Zoom. The intention was to provide the harbour community with an opportunity to question candidates, including Labour councillor Kye Dudd who sat on Mayor Rees' cabinet. It was at this meeting that I caught my first indication that BCC might not be quite as enthused about our stakeholder group as Mayor Rees had previously indicated. Kye Dudd encouraged attendees to pursue individual claims rather than acting as a group. Looking back, I wonder why he would do this.

By Summer 2022, Marvin Rees was re-elected and communication between his office and the Harbour Authority with the BBCA had ceased. The idea that the promised consultation may not happen seemed increasingly possible. Even though the BBCA were repeatedly asking for updates, nobody in BCC would disclose information about when the consultation would take place. The BBCA took the decision to conduct its own consultation with members.

Since 2019, the main focus of the BBCA's member meetings was to update the community on consultation developments, and to record concerns of members in relation to the review. The BBCA working group compiled a survey, led by member Molly Petts, consisting of over 100 questions reflecting members' concerns, in an effort to quantify and relay them to BCC when an opportunity arose. Live aboard licences and fee increases were integral to the survey.

Precaution was taken to ensure the survey was anonymous in order to allay fears held by boat dwellers of being outed as operating outside of the terms of their licence. These fears were justified; many people had children and had built their livelihoods in the locale of the harbour, working in dockside businesses. The Harbour Master had considerable power in relation to the removal of vessels from the harbour, through the role's associated byelaws [4].

Emails were sent, flyers were printed and posted by BBCA volunteers, and many a conversation was had, stressing anonymity and our intended use of the data. We received 100 responses and assembled the data into graphs. We were now able to demonstrate that there were just under 80 respondents interested in acquiring live aboard rights.

Following the survey, the authorities continued to fail to communicate with us. To speculate with hindsight, this stonewalling may have been due to an internal decision to drop the consultation, believing that by not recognising our organisation's viability, consultation may not have been statutorily required. Furthermore, there would be no legal obligation to conduct an Equalities Impact Assessment (EQIA) including boat dwellers. BCC's website regarding EQIAs states: "Our assessments have to be based on good evidence which includes listening to the views of the people who are likely to be affected." [5]

Resentment was building within the community by this point. Having been strung along for four years, and having spent an excessive amount of time voluntarily conducting work that was due to be conducted by the council, there was a feeling that this survey simply had to pay off. It came as a devastating blow, therefore, when Molly stumbled upon an agenda item entitled 'Bristol City Docks-Fees and Charges Review' for the forthcoming cabinet meeting on 24 January 2023 [6].

The road to judicial review

Item 21, Bristol City Docks – Fees and Charges Review, scheduled to be approved by cabinet on 24 January 2023, proposed increases of up to 177% for boat licences [7], and was being rushed through cabinet with the increases scheduled to take effect in May 2023, three months after the BBCA caught wind of the proposal. To put this increase into perspective, Mandy was previously paying £2,600 per year for a 20-metre long vessel; this would go up to £6,500. The announcement of the Fees and Charges schedule indicated that the review had been concluded, and yet we had not been consulted.

It was clear that our campaign had to react. What followed was a months-long crash course in community campaigning, culminating in a legal case that none of us had asked for.

We held an emergency meeting at the John Sebastion with record turnout on 31 January 2023. People were distraught, there were more than a few tears. The general feeling was one of betrayal. The many who were cautious at first about engaging with the campaign now saw the importance of speaking out, and that the council would likely steamroll our community if we didn't act.

Green councillor Ani Stafford-Townsend, who had attended our hustings and subsequent BBCA meetings, provided us with the information required for submitting a petition to the council. We had to raise 3,500 signatures and submit it seven days before the next full council meeting on 14 March 2023. We launched a petition asking for the mayor to withdraw the policy until we were consulted.

Alongside running the petition, I became the BBCA's media liaison. A community which formerly survived by maintaining secrecy, suddenly had to morph into a public facing campaign group within three weeks. *The Bristol Cable* promptly put out a short article on the day we launched the petition [8]. Other media outlets across the city soon picked up on the story, with the headline figure of 177% council fee increase being easy for readers to sympathise with. Mandy and others were interviewed on local radio and ITV [9].

We also found campaign support with organisations such as Citizens UK, the National Bargee and Travellers Association, and ACORN the union. Fiona Meldrum of Citizens UK helped us identify some key strategies in the weeks leading up to the petition deadline. One of these was to get letters of support from community representatives. We received letters from Sam Williams, Head Teacher of Redcliffe Nursery where several boat-dwelling children attended, and from Reverend Kat Campion-Spall of the harbourside parishes, who wrote: "We urge the council, the Harbour Master and the Director of the Harbour Review to meet with the harbour community before introducing these fees, undertake the proper assessment and ensure those who reside in Bristol Harbour will not be deeply affected by any proposed changes." [10]

The traction of our campaign had made its way back to the Mayor's office, with Marvin Rees releasing a statement on his blog, the day before the cabinet meeting on 24 January 2023, where he wrote: "Boat users failing to comply with the license system and treating a leisure permit as a residential privilege are abusing the system and damaging the city's ability to manage the harbour for all... The harbour is owned by the city for the city. We must ensure it is managed effectively for all, not for a privileged few." [11]

Our petition had gained in excess of 4000 signatures [12] but we were informed that, because not enough of those signatories had entered a Bristol postcode, it would not be scheduled for a full council debate. (We nevertheless submitted the petition and it was eventually presented to full council, without debate, by Councillor Ani Stafford-Townsend on 14 March 2023.)

On 24 January 2023, members of BBCA assembled outside City Hall with an array of placards, waiting to go in and face Mayor Rees and his cabinet. The feeling was one of exhaustion and doom. We had worked overtime these past three weeks, scrambling to organise and establish on what basis we might be able to claim our long-fought-for consultation as our right.

BBCA members made speeches in defence of our community: "I found out today from a website that the mayor has put up that I am abusing the system and damaging the city's ability to manage the harbour for all, not for the privileged few. Yesterday I was planning for my family's future. Today I am vulnerable." [13]

Some of these speeches were subsequently clipped and used in reports on BBC Radio Bristol, reported on in the local papers, and even led to national coverage from the BBC and ITV West. We had made our voices heard on that day. But ultimately, enabled by the mayoral system, it was a done deal and the Bristol City Docks Fees and Charges Review was approved by cabinet.

Our attendance in city hall on 24 January caused a stir. In a phone call with a BCC informant, Amanda was told that internal representatives of both Stand Against Racism and Inequality (SARI) and BCC's Gypsy Roma and Traveller (GRT) Service were alerted to the absence of an EQIA which acknowledged the presence of boat dwellers within the harbour. It was established at a meeting of SARI Voices Group back in October 2020 that boat dwellers were classed as GRT and therefore considered a protected group.

In light of this significant oversight being brought to the surface, GRT services coordinator Ian Bowen was able to arrange two engagement sessions between the BBCA and the Harbour Authority beginning on 15 February 2023. During these sessions, we managed to get the Harbour Authority to commit to offering 70 live-aboard licences. We were unaware at this point that those licences would be charged at the same rate as residential but would offer no material improvements against the leisure licences outside of the right to stay on board all year round. For example, today, a number of live-aboard licensees do not even have access to water or electricity or safe access to their vessel. Despite these shortfalls, this was the biggest win of our campaign to date and offered a glimmer of hope during an otherwise dark period.

The judicial review

Simultaneous to the engagement sessions with the Harbour Authority, the BBCA were quietly building a legal case. This was championed by retired lawyer and BBCA member Bernie Rowe. We found a solicitor called Keith Lomax, as suggested by Pamela Smith of the NBTA, to assemble our pre-action letter for judicial review.

We knew that as soon as BCC caught wind of our lawsuit, they might cease negotiations. But, in order to launch a judicial review, the legal procedure dictated that we had to submit our pre-action letter by 16 March 2023. This gave us a window of roughly one month within which we needed to get the council to commit to providing as much as possible before a potential end to negotiation. We submitted our pre-action letter including our 15 examples of the council promising to conduct, or referring to, a consultation and we received a response from BCC's legal department which stated: "The claim is resisted in full."

The road to judicial review was gruelling, with a focus on fundraising through more media engagement alongside more enjoyable fundraising events. We launched our fundraiser through Crowdjustice; a crowdfunding model which specialises in legal pursuits. I assisted our solicitor, Keith Lomax, and our Lawyer, Stephen Cottle, in acquiring as much material as possible and contributing in some small way towards the construction of our legal argument.

We were relying on law regarding consultation which states that a public body has a duty to consult based on four circumstances: statutory duty to consult; a promise to consult; an established practice of consultation, and; a failure to consult would lead to conspicuous unfairness [14]. We were relying on the second of these circumstances. We brought forward the previously mentioned 15 documents in which BCC referred to, or stated outright, that there will be a stakeholder consultation associated with the Harbour Review.

While building our case for judicial review, in June 2023, the Harbour Authority issued the new licences. These hastily written documents were full of errors and contained clauses as ludicrous as banning dancing on deck and as devastating as banning outright the use of wood burners and diesel heaters on board harbour vessels. Whilst I generally agree with the premise behind new fuel burning policies for environmental reasons, imposing them on a community with scarce access to electricity and no viable alternatives, under duress of losing their licence, is reckless. I wrote about this particular issue in detail in an article for *The Bristol Cable* [15].

On 4 October 2023 in court, the judge, Justice Jay, after careful consideration and a 3-hour trial, failed to see that any of our examples represented an "unambiguous promise" to consult, and he denied our application for judicial review.

We interpreted the behaviour of the council's legal department during this case as intimidatory. They repeatedly threw huge numbers around regarding legal costs, including their lawyer on the day attempting to charge us £5,000 for simply turning up. Thankfully, the judge was sympathetic to our status as a community group and we walked away owing BCC £12,500 in legal damages.

The aftermath

The case was closed and the council had won. We were now due to pay the increased fees retrospectively. We had certainly lost the battle but maybe not the war.

It is easy to lose sight of progress made when a campaign revolves around events as consequential and final as a court case against a government body. Morale is a vital aspect of any enduring grassroots campaign. Institutions as powerful as the government and the courts have, in the abstract, limitless resources to throw at a campaign. Citizens do not, and we rely on mutual support as a primary resource, with help from organisations designed to facilitate campaigns being important. A fight like ours, as a relatively small group can be taxing, and keeping morale high is important to avoid burnout, loss of willpower and ultimately the failure of a campaign. One key aspect of keeping morale high is to take stock of your achievements however small. For the BBCA, these achievements are as follows:

- Reputation: we have built a public-facing presence as a formerly underground and marginalised community and have established that we will fight back.
- Recognition: we are now recognised as an official stakeholder group by Bristol City Council.
- Housing security: though still incomplete and inadequate, we at least have live aboard licences where none existed before.
- Legal rights: we are now recognised as a protected group; this means among other things, that we have to be included in the city's

statutory obligation to conduct an accommodation needs assessment periodically.

- Alliances: through our campaign, we reached out and found organisations willing to help both locally and nationally, and maintain a relationship with those organisations to date.
- Knowledge: throughout this process we have learned a significant amount about power, law and advocacy. We have used this knowledge to support parallel campaigns including the *Bristol Allotmenteers Resist!* Campaign, and a campaign by Spike Island residents.

As a recognised stakeholder group, the Harbour Authority is now required to meet with us quarterly, giving us a framework within which we can continue our campaign to improve our community's outlook. As Bristol shifts to a new post-mayoral system, we have a small seat at the table. Compared to the former arrangement, this is a huge win.

Through campaigning, we have learned more about our roles as citizens within the political framework. We have witnessed the powerful prioritising capital over people, using loose interpretations of law to save money, disregarding the impact on normal people's lives. Mayor Rees' expressed early desire to work alongside our community rings hollow today: 'the harbour review is an important opportunity to make sure that the harbour continues to be a vibrant place to live, a thriving economy and financially sustainable. We hope to be able to work with you and other harbour users and local residents on it.' [3]

This was either untrue or he changed his intention without notifying those affected. Either way, this is reflective of the mayor's political legacy, favouring the closed door over the open forum. Maybe the post-mayoral system will be slower, but maybe some things should be. ∎

ACKNOWLEDGEMENTS
Many thanks to Amanda Sharman for your support in writing this chapter and your determination in leading our community, and to the BBCA working group for all your committed hard work throughout this campaign: John Sharman, Ben Ewing, Phoebe Ewing, Maria, Molly Petts, Trevor, Mike, Tina, Jonny, Mark, Helen Wakeham, Carl, Bernie Rowe. Thanks to all the BBCA members who showed up and rallied around when we needed it. Thanks to Keith Lomax and Stephen Cottrell for your commitment to justice and your openness to representing boat dwellers.

My parents Deborah and Jonathan for your continued support and Alexi my partner for the same. Priyanka Raval, Max Walsh, Tony Gosling and *The Bristol Cable* for your assistance in navigating the press and your fair coverage. Fiona Meldrum for your considered guidance. Thanks to our 4000+ signatories for taking the time to show your support. Thanks to Cllrs Ani Stafford-Townsend and Patrick McAllister for facilitating the submission of our petition, and demonstrating what sincere engagement looks like. Thanks to Bristol Cruising Club for hosting our meetings and providing a community hub, and to Gareth for your solid fundraising support. Thanks to all the staff in the Harbour Authority who are helpful and supportive in keeping our community safe.

REFERENCES

1. Bristol City Council. Bristol City Docks Review Project. Presentation to BCC Growth and Regeneration Scrutiny Commission, 29 November 2018. Available at: https://democracy.bristol.gov.uk/documents/s27419/Bristol%20City%20Docks%20Review%20Project%20Slides.pdf (Accessed: 20 May 2024).
2. Trust Port Study Key Findings and Recommendations. Department for Transport, May 2016. Available at: https://assets.publishing.service.gov.uk/media/5a80e1caed915d74e6230fc0/trust-port-study-key-findings-and-recommendations.pdf (Accessed: 20 May 2024).
3. Marvin Rees. Email correspondence to Amanda Sharman, 26 April 2021.
4. Bristol City Council. Bristol City Docks Bye-laws 2009. Available at: https://www.bristol.gov.uk/files/documents/874-city-docks-byelaws/file (Accessed: 20 May 2024).
5. Bristol City Council. Equalities impact assessments. www.bristol.gov.uk. Available at: https://www.bristol.gov.uk/council-and-mayor/policies-plans-and-strategies/equality-diversity-and-cohesion-policies/equalities-impact-assessments (Accessed: 20 May 2024).
6. Bristol City Council. Decision Pathway Report. Bristol City Docks-Fees and Charges Review. 24 January 2023. Available at: https://democracy.bristol.gov.uk/documents/s79910/CABINET%20REPORT%20Increase%20of%20Fees%20and%20Charges.%20Docks%20and%20Harbours%20FINAL.pdf (Accessed: 20 May 2024)
7. Ella Hambly and Christopher Mace. Bristol Harbour boaters and businesses fear mooring price hikes. *BBC News*, 23 January 2023. Available at: https://www.bbc.co.uk/news/uk-england-bristol-64365952 (Accessed 20 May 2024)
8. Liz Mizon. This week in Bristol: Harbour dwellers face massive fee hikes. *The Bristol Cable*, 20 January 2023. Available at: https://thebristolcable.org/2023/01/this-week-in-bristol-harbour-dwellers-face-massive-fee-hikes/ (Accessed 20 May 2024)
9. Max Walsh. Bristol harbour fee hikes could force boat-dwellers and businesses to sell. 13 February 2023. Available at: https://www.itv.com/news/westcountry/2023-02-10/harbour-fee-hikes-could-force-boat-dwellers-and-businesses-to-sell (Accessed 20 May 2024)
10. Rev'd Kat Campion-Spall. Copy of objection to dock fees review. Bristol Harbourside Churches. Available at: https://www.bristol247.com/wp-content/uploads/2023/03/Copy-of-Objection-to-Dock-Fees-Review-from-Bristol-Harbourside-Churches.pdf (Accessed 20 May 2024)
11. Marvin Rees. Making harbour fees ship shape and Bristol fashion. *thebristolmayor.com* 23 January 2923. Available at: https://thebristolmayor.com/2023/01/23/bristol-harbour-fees/ (Accessed 20 May 2024)
12. George Cowley. Save Bristol Harbour community – ask the City Council to give us our Democratic process. *Change.org* 20 January 2023. Available at: https://www.change.org/p/save-bristol-harbour-community-from-reckless-city-council-give-us-our-democratic-process (Accessed 20 May 2024)
13. Alex Seabrook. Marvin Rees heckled by boaters over harbour fees hike. *Bristol24/7.* 26 January 2023. Available at: https://www.bristol247.com/news-and-features/news/marvin-rees-heckled-by-boaters-over-harbour-fee-hike/ (Accessed 20 May 2024)
14. R (Plantagenet Alliance Ltd) v Secretary of State for Justice and others. (2014) EWHC 1662. Available at: https://www.judiciary.uk/wp-content/uploads/2014/07/richard-3rd-judgment-.pdf (Accessed 20 May 2024)
15. George Colwey. Bristol Harbour boat dwellers face harsh winter as council bans stoves. *The Bristol Cable*, 26 July 2023. Available at: https://thebristolcable.org/2023/07/bristol-harbour-boat-dwellers-face-harsh-winter-council-bans-stoves/ (Accessed 20 May 2024)

An online petition, objecting to Bristol City Council's planned changes to allotment rules and rent, gained thousands of signatures.
Credit: Martin Booth, Bristol24/7

Members of Bristol Allotmenteers Resist protesting outside City Hall, Bristol.
Credit: Robert Browne

Bristol allotmenteers resist

Holly Wyatt, a campaigner with Bristol Allotmenteers Resist, describes her experience of the campaign, the potential impact of changes to allotment rules and fees, and the value of these spaces for our city...

———

IN DECEMBER 2023, Bristol City Council (BCC) launched a consultation around proposed changes to allotment rules, additional fees and rent increases, which was due to run from 11 December until 22 January. The first many of us heard of these proposals arrived in the form of a very unexpected email from the Council's Allotment Office, and it took a while to grasp the full scope of these proposals. There were to be plot rent increases on varying scales, additional water charges, transitional arrangements, new supplementary charges, and proposed rule changes. The consultation having been planned to coincide with the Christmas period was concerning in terms of ensuring maximum engagement with allotment tenants, and the contents of the consultation itself were confusing.

We reached out to our wonderful site rep, Lizzie, to see if she had any further information, but unfortunately our message was the first she knew about these proposals. The Council had not thought to engage with her and her fellow site reps when formulating these plans: to utilise their combined wisdom and experience to ensure they were well-received by the wider allotment community. They had not even considered the prudence of forewarning those who would ultimately be responsible for policing these new rules should they come into effect. Despite her nearly 20 years of experience as a site rep, Lizzie simply received the same standard email that we had.

After speaking with Lizzie, my wife Sal and I began delving into these proposals more thoroughly as well as discussing them with our allotment neighbours. These proposals covered far more than I can possibly unpack in this piece, but the main areas of concern surrounded the following:

- All trees to be removed from plots except permitted fruit trees: limited to three per plot.
- Large play equipment to be removed from plots.
- Joint tenancies no longer allowed, with joint tenants needing to decide who would be the named tenant and the other having to register as a co-worker (at an additional cost).
- Discontinuing of temporary helpers.
- All glass on plots to be removed and replaced with twin walled plastic.
- Additional charges: covering everything from co-worker registration to applying for permission for sheds, greenhouses, fruit cages, cold frames and ponds to keeping chickens and bees.
- Charges to hold events, with no details as to how this would be calculated.
- Huge rent increases, which would see most plots over-doubling in price and with the highest rent increase being a whopping 492%!
- Introduction of combined water charges: adding an additional charge for water on top of rent prices for tenants on sites with access to water.

To address concerns that these proposals would make allotments less accessible, the Council also announced plans to extend the eligibility of their current 50% rent reduction scheme to those in receipt of Universal Credit and pensions, which personally I welcomed as a positive. However, it is worth noting that under these proposals, this 50% reduction would still leave many rent prices higher than the current full price rents for those eligible.

Sal and I completed the Council's online consultation on the evening that it was launched, but were hugely worried about what these proposals could mean for us. After taking on our first allotment plot in Bedminster back in 2017 we were bitten by the allotment-bug almost instantly and poured hours of hard work and devotion into transforming our overgrown, unloved scrap of land into our food-growing paradise. We installed two mini-ponds which almost instantly became home to frogs and newts, we had birds nesting in the trees around us, and saw evidence that our site was home to badgers when our sweetcorn disappeared – just as it was ready to harvest! We would catch glimpses of foxes from time to time, enjoyed the constant fluttering of butterflies and buzzing of bees, sat fascinatedly watching bats darting around in the twilight, and were amazed to see the family of buzzards living in the trees next to our site who would occasionally fly overhead.

With allotment popularity much lower then than now, we were able to take on a second plot shortly afterwards which was double the size and required complete transformation as well. We started keeping chickens and got to know lots of the other tenants on site at community events such as our annual charity bat walk. I joined a bee club at our site's community farm to learn more about beekeeping, and the allotments became an integral part of our lives. As a low-income household they helped us stretch our money further by reducing our expenditure on food; whilst at the same time increasing our activity levels and offering enormous benefits to our mental health.

However, in the face of these proposals from the Council, we faced the genuine risk of losing all of this. Where we had already been struggling financially but just about getting by, the pandemic had decimated our business and the cost-of-living crisis had pushed things even further. The huge increase in rents proposed by the Council had us discussing which of our two plots would be the priority for us to keep. These proposals could see all our hard work and investment (because developing plots and growing food isn't free) swept away, and we were both devastated by the Council's heavy-handed approach to these spaces which mean so much to so many.

Creating a campaign

I felt sure we would not be the only ones in this heartbreaking position, and I was also confident that others would be similarly horrified by the environmental impact of these proposals. Not knowing what else to do at that stage, I set up an online petition the following day simply in the hopes of raising awareness of the Council's plans; and to my surprise it quickly gained traction [1]. Soon comments started appearing from fellow allotment holders, highlighting the enormous mental health benefits allotments have and the potentially devastating impact of the Council's proposals on our city's wildlife, ecology and environment. People highlighted the need for allotments to remain accessible for everyone, and spoke of their own concerns around how they would continue to afford the plots they had not only come to love but also to rely on as part of their food supply.

In the coming days I began to seek media engagement to further raise awareness of this consultation, and we were fortunate enough to receive really positive engagement from several news outlets. We also had a link shared with us to a newly formed WhatsApp group called Bristol Allotmenteers Resist (BAR), and on joining I was immediately reassured that we were not alone in our efforts. Others had also engaged with media, were petitioning councillors and MPs, and had responded to the Council's consultation in droves. This WhatsApp group quickly grew to almost 600 people, and a meeting was planned for early January 2024 to formulate an action plan.

Despite torrential rain, this meeting was incredibly well-attended; and even against the negative backdrop which had brought us together, it was hugely positive to see the passion in the room for protecting our allotment sites [2]. Alongside an interesting and informative lineup of speakers which had been organised, there was time for general discussion around the impact of these proposals; and attendees were encouraged to respond to the consultation, sign and share the petition, lobby their local councillors and MPs, and to lobby Marvin Rees (Mayor) and Cllr Ellie King (Cabinet Member for Public Health and Communities).

With this meeting BAR had well and truly been established, and with the creation of a campaign and admin coordination subgroup, Sal and I quickly got to know a wonderful group of people who were equally passionate about all things allotment. BAR was fortunate enough to benefit from artists creating stunning logos and artwork for posters as well as people with a whole host of talents, gifts, and aptitudes; from social media and event-organising experience, to administrative and factual analysis skills. A flourishing community quickly formed, with individuals taking on tasks which they felt were best suited to them and offering as much or as little time as they could to the campaign. A BAR Core Group was set up separately to the main WhatsApp group, with representation from each of the subgroups; to allow for any necessary discussions which needed to be held aside from the media and political individuals who we knew had joined the main discussion groups. There was one further face-to-face meeting arranged for those who wanted to be involved in the BAR Core Group, before regular online meetings became a chance to catch up on what others had been doing and to formulate proposals for action.

Interesting facts started to emerge from BAR's wonderful volunteers, who had been scrutinising these proposals and the evidence behind them more closely. The widely varying percentages for rent increases ranged from just 7% to a whopping 492% depending on plot size. The evidence to support the Council's claims that the allotment service currently ran at huge subsidisation from other areas was noticeably lacking, with the last available financial year's figures (2021/2022) showing only a shortfall of £5,412 between income and expenditure. Requests for the last financial year's figures only returned the answer from the Council that these figures weren't available; and yet, despite their apparent unavailability, they had somehow formed the cornerstone of the supposed need for the scale of these rent increases.

In mid-January, the Council announced it was extending the closing date of the consultation to 31 January 2024 in response to the volume of feedback they'd received around it having been launched to coincide with the Christmas period. It was clear from this that the Council had come under far more pressure over these proposals than they had expected, and had been unable to withstand criticism that the consultation's timing had not allowed for maximum engagement. Many tenants had still not received any notification of these proposals either via email or letter, and whilst some allotment sites had had Council posters attached to their gates advertising the consultation, many more had not.

The momentum of this strength of feeling led to a protest planned to coincide with the next Allotment Forum meeting. I felt nervous about this as Sal and I walked towards City Hall on the day of the protest, placards (and bongos) in hand – hoping that we wouldn't be the only ones there. We weren't disappointed! Over 200 people attended, with a wonderful array of props – the human-sized stuffed carrot being a personal favourite – and some fantastic slogans plastered across banners and placards. 'Keep off the glass', 'trees and bees not sky-high fees', 'growing your own shouldn't cost the earth' and 'resistance is fertile' were some that stick with me. With Sal merrily setting a rhythm on the bongos, a loud proud crowd of angry allotmenteers all joined in the chant of 'BCC, get your hands off our plots'!

The Council responds

We had a live interview with ITV News outside City Hall, and Councillor Ellie King was asked to comment. In her interview she responded to criticism over the rent rises by saying: "People have got 15 months between now and then in order to adapt to that new change". This justification – that anyone in poverty, living below the breadline, on low incomes or generally struggling financially during a cost-of-living crisis – had 15 months to rectify their finances in response to this surge in rents only further highlighted the lack of awareness the Council had over how significant these rent rises were; and how disproportionately they would impact those who could most benefit from accessing space to grow their own food.

During the Allotment Forum meeting, attendees posed some incredibly valid and interesting questions and statements. A question from Ruth Hecht around whether or not an Equality Impact Assessment (EQIA) had been completed had to be asked multiple times before an answer was obtained in the negative, with the surprising answer that this would only be completed after the closure of the consultation. Two votes tabled by Stephen Pill – 'this Forum believes that the non-involvement of site reps in drafting new rules which they will necessarily be involved in administering is a major process failure' and 'this forum believes that there has been a major process failure in the rents/fees consultation and that it needs to be re-run, if not extended' – received almost unanimous support, but interestingly were not recorded in the Allotment Forum minutes despite the votes, by show of hand, having been actively counted by the meeting chair and with Stephen kindly providing them with a written version to ensure accurate wording.

Under mounting pressure, the Council proposed to hold a workshop around the new rules which was planned for 5 February. A priority list was announced to decide how the 40 spaces available would be filled: with site reps first, then working down through other groups with tenants last. This priority list completely excluded engagement from those on the waiting list who would have been most affected by the proposed supplementary charges and would also have ensured limited representation from those most affected by the financial implications of rent increases; as site reps receive either discounted or rent-free plots. It is also worth noting that there is no formal process for how site reps are selected, with many never having been elected by the allotment tenants on their site but rather having put themselves forward for this role. Our own site rep is a phenomenal asset to our site, who I would absolutely elect for the role given the opportunity, but democratically it would be hard to argue that this often-unelected group of people alone had a mandate to represent the interests of the entire Bristol allotment community.

I emailed to complain about this proposal, as did others; and as the consultation came to a close the Council announced that actually they would not go ahead with this workshop after all. Instead, on 6 February, I received an email from the Allotment Officer announcing that, after a high level of response to the consultation, the Council had decided to postpone the introduction of the proposed rule changes and additional fees to allow more time to consider this feedback. This felt like a huge victory. The potential impact on wildlife, site communities, individuals who needed helpers to enable them to continue accessing their plots, and the mounting cost of additional charges new tenants would have faced were postponed with the suggestion of a more collaborative approach for the future. With over 3,000 responses received to their consultation, over 100 emails sent to them directly from both individuals and organisations, and our online petition nearing 6,000 signatures, the Council had been forced to make a concession.

Of course, this was only part of the battle. On 14 February, Councillor Ellie King released an open letter confirming the changes to tenancy rules, fees and additional charges were not being taken forward; but that the Council was still considering the consultation feedback around the proposed allotment rents and combined water charges [3]. BAR quickly began to discuss how to proceed from this point, as we knew the timeline for these proposals to be passed would see them brought to the next Cabinet meeting on 5 March for sign off.

A second protest

The proposal of a second protest was adopted, and planned for the Sunday before the cabinet meeting to allow for maximum attendance. Additionally, BAR organised the installation of a campaign billboard, complete with stunning artwork by Rosanna Morris, which couldn't have summed up the beauty and inclusivity of modern allotmenting any better.

At the cabinet meeting itself, our item sat at 16 in a packed agenda; and this lent itself as a good opportunity for observation prior to any of us being able to read out the questions and statements we had submitted in advance. Perhaps naively on my part, I had never realised the extent of power our mayoral system afforded to the one person in that role; and I must confess I found the whole thing remarkably interesting. Proposals were not voted upon or scrutinised by cross-party debate; and there was seemingly no meaningful way for controversial proposals to be halted or blocked by anyone, other than the elected mayor.

Unsurprisingly, but incredibly sadly, Mayor Marvin Rees supported Councillor Ellie King's proposal and the allotment rent increases and combined water charges were passed at cabinet. Despite 78% of respondents to the Council's own consultation either disagreeing or strongly disagreeing with these proposals, and the score of passionate statements and questions submitted to cabinet from allotment tenants, these rent increases were approved.

Statements around the potential impact of these rent increases met with Councillor Ellie King's response: "In reality a lot of these are the price of a coffee a week – these shouldn't be the barriers that you're suggesting they are." A statement on behalf of 14 community allotment projects and groups highlighting the risk of closure they would face – despite the huge benefits they offer to the people of Bristol including a sense of community, mental and physical health benefits, reduced need for SEND provision and drug and alcohol support – received the response: "I don't have the luxury of just catering for what is a gated community" [4]. The only positive concessions to these proposals had been to introduce these changes over two years instead of one, and to give tenants the ability to pay quarterly or monthly in addition to the current annual system.

Of course, as a group and as individuals, BAR were hugely disappointed that these rent increases had still gone ahead in their proposed format with absolutely no revision in line with the consultation feedback. The figures presented in the Decision Pathway Report submitted to cabinet were unclear, with projected expenditure on items such as 'buildings and infrastructure' exceeding previous expenditure on the same items several times over; yet with no explanation as to how these figures had been arrived at. The Council's claims that the allotment service was hugely subsidised by other areas were not evidenced by the previous five years' financial figures, and the explanation for the scale of these rent increases – and the disparity between percentage increases across different plot sizes – was still completely unclear.

The petition debate

We had decided not to submit our online petition to the cabinet meeting as we'd been advised that this could result in the mayor simply noting it in the minutes. Instead, we submitted it for debate at the next Full Council meeting on 12 March 2024. At the time of submission to Democratic Services, the petition had received a total of 6,414 signatures (although it has since exceeded this) with 3,965 verified as being from Bristol residents. This met the required threshold for debate at Full Council, and I was given five minutes to present it before responses were provided by each of the political parties.

These responses were incredibly interesting, with many of these councillors sharing contact they had had from their constituents around these proposals. The proposed rule changes came under strong criticism, with Councillor Mark Weston (Conservative) asserting: "Don't give an order you know won't be obeyed. If we give all these rules out, the allotment reps aren't going to enforce them."

There was concern expressed around the damage done to relationships with allotment tenants during this process, and the lack of engagement with allotment tenants and community groups when formulating them; with Councillor Jos Clark (Liberal Democrat) calling this "a textbook example of how not to work with, or communicate with, local residents."

The lack of evidence supplied to justify these proposals, and the confusing figures presented, were another theme of criticism; with Councillor Gary Hopkins (Knowle Community Party) highlighting "the lack of detail in terms of the assertions on how much things were going to cost. Having sat on the Scrutiny Commission and asked the questions – the answers just weren't there."

Councillor Martin Fodor (Green Party) also spoke to the value of our allotments, and listed many of the failings in this process. As such, he announced that he had "called in this decision to revisit the process that was so flawed" [4]. This was a significant development, and one which required five signatures from councillors across at least two political parties. The Call-In Sub Committee would be able to scrutinise the process, but not the actual content of the proposals.

Councillor Ellie King responded on behalf of Labour, as did Marvin Rees in his capacity as Mayor. Additionally, as myself and the wonderful group of BAR members who had come along for support left the public gallery, we were met by Ellie King and Marvin Rees out in the lobby. This was completely unexpected and felt like a significant choice on their behalf: to step out of a still ongoing Full Council meeting explicitly to speak with us. Initially I spoke with Ellie King whilst others engaged with

Marvin Rees; but as he returned to the meeting shortly afterwards, we, as a small group, had a further discussion with Ellie King.

It became clear that her personal passion very much sat around community food growing, and she indicated that she was open to a more collaborative approach to the future of our city's allotment sites. We discussed our concerns around the impact of these rent increases in further detail and, whilst the conversation did not result in an immediate reversal of the plans, the fact that both she and the mayor had felt compelled to come out to talk with us suggested that this had evoked a far greater public response than they had ever anticipated.

The decision is deferred

The Call-In Sub Committee met on 27 March 2024. Just hours beforehand, the committee members received an email from Councillor Ellie King offering to defer the decision on rent increases until after the local elections in May 2024 [6]. This was publicly announced and agreed in at the meeting. Ellie King stated: "I believe in the decision taken, which was evidence-led and undertaken in good faith. This is an opportunity to embrace the collaborative potential of the committee system, and to enable cross-party members to take ownership of the policy."

Looking to the future

I hope that our allotment sites continue to thrive. They are no more 'gated communities' than any other facility or service which requires payment to access; including the recently renovated Bristol Beacon, to which the Council contributed many millions of pounds of tax-payers' money [7], and which is necessarily only accessible to those with sufficient disposable income to afford performance tickets. In contrast, allotments provide produce for many beyond those who grow on them with surplus produce donated to food banks as well as to family, friends, neighbours and colleagues. They provide space for community groups, orchards and farms; and offer opportunities for people of all ages, economic backgrounds, ethnicities, nationalities, genders, sexualities and beliefs to come together with shared passions and interests that transcend so many of the barriers we find in our normal lives.

Community projects on our allotment sites often run with no involvement, support or funding from the Council; and to consider them as 'gated communities' with no benefit to the wider city completely ignores the fantastic environmental and ecological spaces that allotments have become. They contribute positively to our climate, and support an absolutely enormous array of native wildlife which increasingly face significant habitat loss and subsequent reduction in numbers in our modern world. All of this is not even provided to our city for free – allotment holders actually pay for the privilege of providing these benefits. They are thriving, vibrant spaces which are a phenomenal asset to our city.

On a final, personal note: having poured so much love and hard work into our two plots, we will do everything we can to try and meet the costs of any rent increases despite the cost-of-living crisis. Unfortunately, we're not in a financial situation where we can simply cut out that weekly cup of coffee suggested by Councillor Ellie King – items like this are already luxuries that we can't routinely afford, and for us it would be a case of sacrificing money from more mundane things such as food, fuel or heating. I hope with all sincerity that we, and others, are not forced off the land we love. This land is already ours – the Council are only caretakers of it on our behalf – and I hope that our allotments remain accessible to everyone in our city who wants to experience the pleasure of planting a seed, watching it grow, and bringing home produce in abundance. ∎

ACKNOWLEDGEMENTS

I'd like to acknowledge everyone who has been part of this campaign – your efforts have been incredible!

REFERENCES

1. *Change.org*. Objections to Bristol City Council's changes to allotment rules and rent. https://www.change.org/p/objections-to-bristol-city-council-s-changes-to-allotment-rules-and-rent (Accessed 19 May 2024)

2. Mia Vines. Allotmenteers to protest over 'draconian' new rules. *Bristol24/7*, 20 January 2024. https://www.bristol247.com/news-and-features/news/allotmenteers-to-protest-over-draconian- new-rules/ (Accessed 19 May 2024)

3. Ellie Pipe. Partial U-turn over controversial changes to allotments. *Bristol24/7*, 7 February 2024. https://www.bristol247.com/news-and-features/news/partial-u-turn-over-controversial-changes-allotments/ (Accessed 19 May 2024)

4. Martin Booth. Allotments said to be 'gated communities' as price rises approved. *Bristol24/7*, 6 March 2024. https://www.bristol247.com/news-and-features/news/allotments-gated-communities-price-rises-approved/ (Accessed 19 May 2024)

5. Alex Seabrook and Ellie Pipe. Greens 'call in' controversial allotments decision. *Bristol24/7*, 18 March 2024. https://www.bristol247.com/news-and-features/news/greens-call-in-controversial-allotments-decision/ (Accessed 19 May 2024)

6. Alex Seabrook. Allotment rent rises to be revisited after May elections as scrutiny session breaks down. *BristolLive*, 28 March 2024. https://www.bristolpost.co.uk/news/bristol-news/allotment-rent-rises-revisited-after-9195361 (Accessed 19 May 2024)

7. Adam Postans. How the Bristol Beacon refurbishment spiralled into a costly fiasco. *BristolLive*, 27 December 2023. https://www.bristolpost.co.uk/news/bristol-news/how-bristol-beacon-refurbishment-spiralled-8987144 (Accessed 19 May 2024)

Local residents line up at the fence erected around Stoke Lodge Playing Fields by Cotham School. Credit: Geoff Causton

The community's application for Village Green status was successful but remains under threat. Credit: Martin Booth, *Bristol24/7*

We Love Stoke Lodge: Defending access to open space

Helen Powell, together with Emma Burgess, is part of the voice of We Love Stoke Lodge, backed by a community standing firm to protect Stoke Lodge for future generations...

─────

THIS IS A chapter about a fence, how that fence brought a community together, and what it taught us about how 'stuff gets done'. Over six years of defending open public access to Stoke Lodge Playing Fields, our rollercoaster journey has taken us to the Local Government Ombudsman, the Information Commissioner's Office (ICO) and the High Court. Rather than answer our freedom of information requests, Bristol City Council officers have declared us vexatious on numerous occasions and been told by the ICO that we are not.

Now, finally, having won registered village green status for Stoke Lodge, the Council is standing with us to defend that registration in litigation brought by Cotham School – but only after a member of the Executive spent thousands of pounds trying to do the opposite, despite legal and constitutional restrictions on executive interference with the decisions of a regulatory committee.

So it's not really so much about a fence, after all. It's about the law and how people try to manipulate it; it's about how decisions get made behind the scenes and 'justified' in public; and it's about the strength of a community that decided it was up for the fight.

Origin story

We Love Stoke Lodge (WLSL) was born on 14 May 2018. By way of backstory, there had already been an application for Town or Village Green (TVG) status for Stoke Lodge Playing Fields. If you don't know Stoke Lodge, it's 23 acres of historic parkland, wrapping around a Grade II listed building that is Bristol City Council's Adult Learning Centre. It's been used as playing fields for various schools since the 1960s even though it's not particularly ideal for that purpose – it slopes from east to west, with a drop of around 10 metres overall, and has many mature parkland trees including two in the middle of the upper and lower playing field areas. It's been well-used and much-loved by the local community for decades. In 2010, Bristol City Council (BCC) ran a consultation on whether the land should be fenced off for sports use and received such a resounding 'no' that it promised to drop any such proposals 'once and for all', with the land remaining open for shared use by the community 'as of right' [1].

So what changed? Cotham School had been using Stoke Lodge Playing Fields for sports lessons since 2000, although mostly letting the University of Bristol use the fields and doing lessons at Coombe Dingle Sports Complex instead. In September 2011 the school converted to academy status and was given a 125-year lease of the facilities they had been using as a local authority maintained school, at a 'peppercorn' (nil) rent. But BCC made some changes to the standard Department for Education lease in this case – it said that Cotham School's rights to use Stoke Lodge would be 'subject to all existing rights and use of the Property, including use by the community'. In recognition of the public use of the land, BCC agreed to reduce the school's maintenance obligation and indemnified the school for any costs to do with the protected trees and listed boundary walls around the estate [2].

At that time, a TVG application (referred to here as TVG1) was already in place, and it moved slowly. There was a public inquiry in mid-2016, and the inspector appointed to hear the evidence eventually recommended that the application should be rejected because of two or three Avon County Council signs that were put up in the 1980s [3]. TVG registration depends on showing 20 years of 'as of right' use, and the period for TVG1 stretched back to 1991. Avon was abolished in 1996, and the inspector thought the signs stopped local use being 'as of right' at least until BCC took over. But in December 2016 BCC's Public Rights of Way and Greens (PROWG) Committee disagreed – they didn't think there were enough signs or that the Council had ever intended to stop people using the land. They decided to register Stoke Lodge as a TVG. Cotham School launched a judicial review, and the High Court ruled in May 2018 that the minutes of the PROWG Committee did not show how they had properly reached that decision and did not explain their reasons [4].

A community gathers

So here we are, back where we started in May 2018. Local community members (Save Stoke Lodge Parkland or SSLP) had supported the TVG1 application for seven years, through a public inquiry and a judicial review. Now Cotham School was talking about proposals to fence the land off.

Fresh energy was needed, and the campaign took to social media for the first time. The WLSL Facebook group was started and grew rapidly. Our MP Darren Jones got involved, offering to talk to BCC, Ofsted and the Department for Education to work out whether the school's claim that it needed a fence to meet safeguarding requirements was justified. He was quickly able to conclude from their replies that it wasn't.

We were a community coming together to protect our last local green space. We were confident that the Council, having protected community use in the school's lease, would keep Cotham School's ambitions in check. We believed, since the land was protected as the curtilage of a listed building, that Cotham School could not put up a 1.6km long, 2m high perimeter fence without planning permission. Darren Jones offered to host mediation sessions and we brought along a raft of proposals to help meet the school's concerns about dogs and about pupils absconding, confident that a compromise could be agreed. We had no idea what was coming.

The first mediation meeting was on 20 July 2018. Although we talked about our compromise proposals, and the school's representatives said they would go away and consider them, it's fair to say that we didn't get a good vibe. That feeling solidified when, on 24 July, the school took down the old Avon signs and put up new ones calling the land 'Cotham School Playing Field' (no mention of Stoke Lodge) and asserting that anyone on the land was trespassing and liable to prosecution. Quietly, quietly, we started putting together a new TVG application – one that would run from 1998 when Avon County Council no longer existed and BCC was in charge. We hoped we might not need it, but we wanted to be ready just in case.

The second mediation meeting was on 14 September 2018, where Cotham School's 'lead governor on Stoke Lodge' indicated that we would only be invited as stakeholders to discuss the design of their fence if we deleted our Facebook group and ceased campaigning, including the submission of FOI requests. In a letter to local residents on 18 September, Darren Jones described the tone from Cotham School as 'more focussed on power play instead of conciliation' [5]. But our power was this – when those of us in the meeting realised how Cotham School's representatives were behaving, we messaged a group waiting outside. The message? Go ahead, submit the second TVG application. TVG2 was under way.

Things done in secret...

So now we had two things in our favour – a TVG application in process and (we believed) the land protected by curtilage status. Until, that is, we discovered that the same Cotham School governor had private meetings in August 2018 with BCC's Head of Development Management and its new Head of Paid Service. Among Cotham School's objectives was a request to consider whether the playing fields could be considered to be outside the curtilage of Stoke Lodge house. Suddenly, a week after our TVG2 application was submitted, BCC reversed its position and decided that the land was not protected after all. Cotham School was told it only required 'landlord consent' and could put up a fence without making a planning application.

Why was the U-turn needed? The school's planning consultant had written a letter claiming that having to make a planning application for the fence would be 'pivotal and devastating' for the school. Just think about that – if having to go through proper process would be pivotal and devastating, that surely suggests the application is unlikely to succeed. But apparently BCC officers took it as a signal that the curtilage status needed to change, to fix Cotham School's 'problem'.

Once we found out about all this, we challenged the Council's U-turn, of course. One of the issues in the ensuing Local Government Ombudsman's investigation was whether BCC gave Cotham School its decision before or after seeking advice from a barrister on curtilage status. Ultimately the Ombudsman concluded that the Council gave the decision in early November – but two years later, following an investigation by the Information Commissioner's Office, BCC was forced to disclose key emails that were not made available to the Ombudsman. Those emails show that Cotham School was informed of BCC's new decision on curtilage and planning permission at a meeting on 21 September, and only after that meeting did officers seek external legal advice. The emails eventually disclosed include the Head of Development Management telling the Head of Paid Service on 24 September 2018 that:

'Due to the sensitivity of this decision, I have asked for a Counsel's Opinion in order to confirm that we have a robust position in the event of the inevitable legal challenge brought by local residents. Please note that this information is highly sensitive and we agreed with the school that we would not release this information before the Counsel's Opinion had been received.' [6]

You see, they knew how controversial this was and even that a legal challenge was 'inevitable'. But they went ahead anyway.

Officers initially said that Cotham School would need landlord consent over design issues, because the lease requires landlord consent to new structures – but then backflipped on this too. This led to a notorious moment at Full Council in which the elected Mayor, Marvin Rees, said that the Council had no control over Cotham School's actions because a 1.6km long by 2m high fence, concreted into the ground, was not "a structure" [7]. Derisive laughter from the public gallery did not go down well – but 'the fence is not a structure' is a phrase that still gets quoted. The result of this early executive involvement with a planning matter was that Cotham School was allowed to erect the fence it wanted, with no planning control whatsoever.

By the end of 2018 we were a lot less naive than when we started. Now we knew: the rules can be changed in backroom meetings if you know the right people, and just because there's a statutory duty to disclose information does not mean you will get the disclosure you're entitled to – even if you're the Local Government Ombudsman.

We were learning – the hard way. Over time, we did get some illuminating information through FOI requests [8], including emails from the usual Cotham School governor to BCC officers:

27 September 2018: "I thought we agreed we would have a joint press statement? Cotham is keen to show we are working together at last and not give the community a chink to pop at."

9 November 2018: "We note that this application [about one of the signs installed on 24 July] has been called in to be considered

at a Planning Committee... are you going to agree to his request? It does not seem quite right. If you do we might usefully consider which committee this goes to? ... it may be better to delay until the community have been told we are going back."

Cotham School was in the position of a developer, with its project being led by someone with experience of how things get done. The school's lead governor on Stoke Lodge had experience of working at director level for a number of councils, including Bristol. This isn't how you or I, the ordinary resident, would address BCC's Head of Development Management. The tone is very much 'Cotham School and BCC against the community', with confidence that this would be acceptable to the Council. It was only at the end of November that news began to filter out to the community that BCC had U-turned on curtilage status and washed its hands of landlord control. We were on our own.

What goes up must come down

Cotham School's diggers rolled onto Stoke Lodge on 14 January 2019. For a week we held them at bay, insisting that Council officers could not allow digging to go ahead in the root zones of the protected trees all around the perimeter of the site without specific permission [9]. But officers insisted that permitted development trumped Tree Preservation Orders – a stance they maintained until the fence was completed, and then finally admitted that they were wrong to the Bristol Tree Forum [10].

The diggers were accompanied by police, summoned by the school's facilities manager who arrived with a firm expectation of trouble. Officers seemed rather surprised to be greeted not by rioters but by local people determined to protect trees and wildlife. And so began two months of a long cold winter, protecting our trees while Cotham School's contractors dug hole after hole and poured in concrete to fix metal posts to exclude us from the land. The most painful moments? We had marked out exclusion zones with tape and paint lines at the appropriate distance from a badger sett and our oldest veteran oak tree, but Cotham School's contractors drove the fenceline through those marked zones. We gathered over 4,000 Bristolian signatures on a petition, talking about tree and wildlife protection and the lack of accessible entrances in the new fence [11]. This would normally be sufficient to trigger a debate at Full Council but the Monitoring Officer ruled that it could not be heard because we had threatened legal action about the U-turn on curtilage status [12].

But still, our TVG was in process – and TVG2 was joined in July 2019, for technical reasons, by another application, TVG3. Both Cotham School and BCC seemed to be doing all they could to block the applications at every stage, but one advantage of constant delays was the time it gave us to research – hundreds of hours in Bristol Records Office combing through old committee minutes, and in the Reference Library searching through old newspapers. With time and research, and through FOI requests, we built our case.

And then – 2020. Lockdown for us meant lockout – Cotham School locked all the gates in its perimeter fence, confining our community to narrow, overgrown and slippery walkways outside the fence – just when we most needed our local space [13]. Attitudes hardened. We no longer had expectations of anything but hostility from the school.

But still, it came as a surprise to discover that a representative of Cotham School had contacted one of the legal officers dealing with our TVG applications to express the wish that our applications should be 'kicked into the long grass' [14]. The thing is, disclosure of information is slow. We didn't discover this until a year after it happened. Backroom chats were clearly still the order of the day.

Vexing requests

It was at around this time, in mid-2021, that the Council decided we were vexatious. FOI requests to do with Stoke Lodge were considered a burden and were to be routinely refused. That caught the attention of *Private Eye* magazine, which has followed the ins and outs of the Stoke Lodge saga for several years [15].

Again, these things take time, but the Information Commissioner issued a decision notice in August 2022 which stated:

> 54. It is understandable that members of a group, or groups which seek to protect Stoke Lodge, and public access to the site, may have various reasons to contact the council acting in its different capacities. Those reasons will often have a value and purpose which outweigh the council's generalised reasons for refusing the request.
> 55. The Commissioner also does not consider that the effect of receiving the requests would be a significant burden upon an

authority the size of the council when compared to the value and purpose behind the requests for information. [16]

TVG endgame

Finally, after far too much money spent on far too many submissions trying to get the inspector to look properly at our evidence, we arrived at the PROWG Committee meeting on 28 June 2023. By now there were essentially two factual issues for councillors to decide. Were two or three signs enough, on a 23-acre site with dozens of entrances, to communicate an objection to public use of the land? And did 'everyone know' that there was an objection to use, because of the 2016 public inquiry?

Councillors engaged with hundreds of pages of reports and evidence, and considered every detail in a long and tense meeting, supported by a leading barrister who was brought in to make sure the decision-making process was secure. And they voted 6:1, cross-party, to register Stoke Lodge as a TVG! An incredible, wonderful result [17].

Cotham School launched litigation more or less immediately – two different cases, in fact. One was a judicial review of the committee's decision, which was started and immediately put on pause. The other case asks the court to look at the evidence afresh and decide whether the test for TVG status is met. In this claim, Cotham School listed BCC as a defendant in two capacities – as Commons Registration Authority (CRA) and as landowner. BCC officers decided they would be neutral on behalf of the CRA, and would side with the school on behalf of BCC as landowner. In their capacity as landowner, officers even decided they wanted to switch sides and become a claimant alongside Cotham School, continuing the claim on their behalf if the school withdrew. Officers had apparently forgotten that BCC has a constitution and has to work within it – TVG decisions are fully delegated to the PROWG Committee.

In January 2024, the cross-party PROWG Committee stood as one against this attempt by officers – apparently acting on the instructions of 'the Executive' (although to date officers have refused to say who gave the orders) – to overturn their lawful decision [18]. They were also clear that the CRA's barrister must robustly defend the decision of the PROWG Committee. Committee members insisted that the decision of elected councillors must be respected. In the dying days of the elected mayoral regime, members of the PROWG Committee took a stand for the constitution and for local democracy. It was a model of what cross-party committee decision-making could be.

When the High Court ruled on court procedures, the judge told BCC that 'it's not possible for Bristol City Council to be splitting itself somehow, amoeba-like, into two different bodies' to argue opposing points of view against itself [19]. It could not 'suck and blow' at the same time; it must be one defendant in the case. And, since a decision by a regulatory committee is the decision of the Council, the case now looked very different. Cotham School and BCC officers had planned for it to be Cotham School *and* BCC vs BCC (neutral) and the community. But now it would be Cotham School vs two active defendants – BCC and the community. The High Court also ruled that Cotham School had made a mistake assuming it could get costs protection, vastly increasing its costs and risk.

As we go to print, the school is no longer pursuing its judicial review application but is continuing with its (much more expensive) Section 14 application, to ask the court to re-examine the case for TVG registration for Stoke Lodge. The trial has been listed for late January 2025.

We're close to coming full circle. We've always known that Cotham School can hold sports lessons on Stoke Lodge TVG, just as other schools use shared public access playing fields. Once the litigation is behind us, we hope the school will come back to Stoke Lodge and do just that in this safe, beautiful and unfenced parkland, and that we can move beyond all the controversy of the last few years into a new period of peaceful co-existence that will be enjoyed for generations to come.

Lessons learned

So, six years on, and with the prize of the TVG achieved (though still being challenged by the school), what have we learned?

Firstly, some hard lessons about how influence gets exercised behind the scenes to get decisions made. Apparently, if you know the right people, you don't have to automatically accept rules you don't like. You can demand a meeting with senior officers and persuade them to reconsider decisions. That's not an opportunity that's open to most of us – in fact our experience has been that once a decision has been made, officers will hunker down on it even in the face of clear evidence that it's wrong. And this is something we hope will change with the new committee system of governance – with less centralised political power, should come more scrutiny of decision-making.

Transparency, in the form of FOI disclosure, isn't always as transparent as you might think. Sometimes the game is about running the clock down against you. And sometimes that will work – for example when you've got a time-limited opportunity to ask the Local Government Ombudsman to review what happened, and you don't have the information when you need it (as happened to us). But again, with less centralised political power perhaps we will see a less defensive attitude to transparency. That would be a real win, because transparency brings trust.

Active, informed and in-touch local councillors are absolutely invaluable, and when councillors stand together on matters of principle they are a force to be reckoned with. We are so grateful to the many local councillors who have supported us along the way, as well as our MP. This makes us truly hopeful for the future governance of our city.

Human stories are powerful motivators. For us, Stoke Lodge is not a commodity with development and commercialisation potential. We have folk who get up to see the sunrise and the foxes with their cubs early in the morning, or watch the bats at night. Our community includes people who learned to walk here again after a stroke, or grieved the loss of a child under the big Turkey oaks, or ran their way through cancer treatment on these fields. We know grandparents who taught their children to fly kites and ride bikes here, and who are now teaching their grandchildren too. And we remember the friends who started the journey with us, but didn't live to see the end. The fight for Stoke Lodge has made us a community in a way that we weren't before, and has linked us to other campaign groups across the city. If we had to do it again, we would.

And most of all: when a community comes together to fight for a cause that's dear to their hearts, that's an amazing and hugely powerful thing. We are all kinds of people with different skills and backgrounds and abilities – everyone brings something to the table and contributes to the cause, whether they realise it or not. What we do today can make a lasting difference for those who come after us and for our city. ∎

ACKNOWLEDGEMENTS
With thanks to everyone who has supported and encouraged SSLP and WLSL through the years, especially our lionesses (you know who you are).

REFERENCES

1. BCC Cabinet. 27 January 2011 Revenue Budget 2011/12 page 43; letter from Cabinet Member, 13 September 2010. Available at: https://www.stokelodgetvg.co.uk/media/1019/v114-neighbourhood-partnership-minutes-15th-septembr-2010.pdf (Accessed 25 May 2024)

2. Lease between Cotham School and BCC dated 31 August 2011. Available at: https://bristoltreeforum.org/wp-content/uploads/2019/12/cothams-lease-of-stoke-lodge-land.pdf (Accessed 25 May 2024)

3. Application by Mr David Mayer to register land known as Stoke Lodge Playing Field, Shirehampton Road, Bristol as a new Town or Village Green. Inspector's report, 14 October 2016. Available at: https://www.bristol.gov.uk/files/documents/3468-inspectors-report/file (Accessed 25 May 2024)

4. R(Cotham School) v BCC [2018] EWHC 1022 (Admin). Available at: https://cornerstonebarristers.com/wp-content/uploads/old/cotham-judgment_.pdf (Accessed 25 May 2024)

5. It's just about the signs. *We Love Stoke Lodge blog*. 28 June 2023. Available at: https://welovestokelodge.blog/category/signs/ (Accessed 25 May 2024)

6. The 2010 Cabinet Briefing Note – what came next? It could be you... *We Love Stoke Lodge blog*. 18 May 2023. Available at: https://welovestokelodge.blog/2023/05/18/the-2010-cabinet-briefing-note-what-came-next-it-could-be-you/ (Accessed 25 May 2024)

7. Adam Postans. Stoke Lodge campaigners demand to see council's legal advice that 'gagged' them. *BristolLive*, 21 March 2019. Available at: https://www.bristolpost.co.uk/news/bristol-news/stoke-lodge-campaigners-demand-see-2671115 (Accessed 25 May 2024)

8. BCC/Cotham: too cosy for comfort? *We Love Stoke Lodge blog*. 13 June 2023. Available at: https://welovestokelodge.blog/2023/06/13/bcc-cotham-too-cosy-for-comfort/ (Accessed 25 May 2024)

9. Tristan Cork. Police called to Stoke Lodge as people try to stop fence being built. *BristolLive*, 15 January 2019. Available at: https://www.bristolpost.co.uk/news/bristol-news/live-cotham-school-fence-protest-2426124 (Accessed 25 May 2024)

10. Government guidance states: 'The cutting of roots... is potentially damaging and so, in the Secretary of State's view, requires the LPA's consent'. Department for Communities and Local Government. Tree Preservation Orders: A Guide to the Law and Good Practice. Available at: https://assets.publishing.service.gov.uk/media/5a790b1d40f0b679c0a08161/tposguide.pdf (Accessed 25 May 2024)

11. We Love Stoke Lodge. Sense Not Fence – let's find aternatives to fencing at Stoke Lodge. 38Degrees petition. Available at: https://you.38degrees.org.uk/petitions/sense-not-fence-let-s-find-alternatives-to-fencing-at-stoke-lodge (Accessed 25 May 2024)

12. Adam Postans. Claims Stoke Lodge campaigners have been 'gagged'. *Bristol24/7*, 21 March 2019. Available at: https://www.bristol247.com/news-and-features/news/claims-stoke-lodge-campaigners-have-been-gagged/ (Accessed 25 May 2024)

13. Kate Wilson. Campaigners demand school unlocks playing fields during coronavirus lockdown. *BristolLive*, 26 March 2020. Available at: https://www.bristolpost.co.uk/news/bristol-news/campaigners-demand-school-unlocks-playing-3984202 (Accessed 25 May 2024)

14. What's the story with TVG2 and 3? *We Love Stoke Lodge blog*, 1 June 2023. Available at: https://welovestokelodge.blog/2023/06/01/whats-the-story-with-tvg2-and-3/ (Accessed 25 May 2024)

15. Private Eye retrospective 1: FOIs. *We Love Stoke Lodge blog*, 2 June 2023. Available at: https://welovestokelodge.blog/2023/06/02/private-eye-retrospective-1-fois/ (Accessed 25 May 2024)

16. ICO reference: IC-127328-V0W6. Available at: https://ico.org.uk/media/action-weve-taken/decision-notices/2022/4021510/ic-127328-v0w6.pdf (Accessed 25 May 2024)

17. Tess de la Mare & Alex Seabrook. School must share Stoke Lodge playing field with community. *BBC News*, 29 June 2023. Available at: https://www.bbc.co.uk/news/uk-england-bristol-66053352 (Accessed 25 May 2024)

18. Ellie Pipe. Councillors challenge council over Stoke Lodge stance. *Bristol24/7*, 13 February 2024. Available at: https://www.bristol247.com/news-and-features/news/councillors-challenge-council-over-stoke-lodge-stance/ (Accessed 25 May 2024)

19. Tristan Cork. Judge taking on Stoke Lodge saga has little time for council identity crisis. *Bristol Live*, 24 January 2024. Available at: https://www.bristolpost.co.uk/news/bristol-news/judge-taking-stoke-lodge-saga-9056020 (Accessed 25 May 2024)

George Cook explores the nature rich land of Yew Tree Farm. Credit: George Cook

Drastic clearance to the mature hedgerow where protected dormice had been recorded caused outrage from local people and nature lovers. Credit: Danica Priest

Yew Tree Farm SNCI

George Cook, a Bristol-based wildlife photographer and naturalist currently working at Avon Wildlife Trust, describes his love of Yew Tree Farm and the heart-breaking prospect of its nature-rich land being lost to housing development and the crematorium expansion...

———

FOR OVER THREE years I was lucky enough to live nearby to Yew Tree Farm in south Bristol. Throughout the course of the COVID-19 pandemic, I was just a short walk from this last working farm within the city boundary, and a site with such value for nature and wildlife it was designated a Site of Nature Conservation Interest (SNCI). As a birdwatcher and wildlife photographer, the access to this nature-friendly farm provided a lifeline during a very stressful and anxious time, and provided a place to briefly escape the worries of the pandemic and enjoy the nature on my doorstep.

The farm's unique mix of habitats make this a special place to see and photograph wildlife. There are grasslands, meadows, scrub, woodland, large hedgerows and a stream called Colliter's brook which runs along the bottom of the farm – all of which, provide food and shelter for a remarkably high number of species. I spent many evenings watching swallows swoop over the meadows, bats dart between the treetops. I carefully followed butterflies with my camera as they flapped amongst the wildflowers, and enjoyed many hours looking out across the wonderful views over the city. I felt so lucky to have access to such a nature-rich site so near to home and proud to live in Bristol, a city that valued its green spaces and wildlife. However, this wonderful place is now facing multiple threats. On its southern side, there is a threat of a housing development and, on the other end of the farm, Bristol City Council plans to expand the neighbouring cemetery and crematorium into the site. This special place, valued by wildlife and people all across the city, is now at risk.

Discovering the farm

It was just a few weeks into lockdown when I first discovered Yew Tree Farm. I hadn't long moved to Bedminster in South Bristol and as part of my daily exercise I was slowly beginning to explore my local area. And when I say slowly, I mean slowly. Just a week before the national lockdown was announced I had surgery on my knee, so I was carefully limping around my neighbourhood on crutches.

Most of these walks involved me shuffling up and down nearby streets and the estate I was living on. However, on one of these walks I managed to hop all the way to the end of the estate. This was the furthest I had come on my crutches and instead of turning back I decided to take a turn underneath the railway line. As I emerged from under the bridge, I found myself in one of the fields at Yew Tree Farm. In front of me spread a lush grass field surrounded by mature trees and hedgerows in blossom. The sounds of the vehicles and industry of the estate were replaced with singing blackbirds and song thrush. The sudden contrast between the loud urban environment and this nature-rich scene had me shocked and I was filled with the excitement of having a local green space to explore when I was finally off my crutches.

This was just one of many visits to the farm and the surrounding area over the new few years. As my leg got stronger and I abandoned my crutches, I would return to the farm again and again with my binoculars and camera. Exploring the farm and discovering the wonderful wildlife that lived there was soon something that filled most of my free time. One May morning, my partner and I ventured out before sunrise to listen to the dawn chorus and, with most cars still off the road, we were able to enjoy a symphony of unspoilt bird song the likes of which probably won't be experienced again within the city boundaries. When I was back at work post-surgery, as soon as the workday was finished I would head over to the farm thinking about the kestrels, rabbits, goldfinch and grey wagtails that were waiting for me.

After a spring and summer of exploring the farm almost every day, it was soon clear to me why this site had been granted its SNCI status. The amount of different bird species I discovered on the site was fantastic. I regularly enjoyed watching soaring buzzards hunting over the fields, skylarks singing as they rose towards the heavens, kingfishers were nesting along the banks of the brook, green woodpeckers laughed from the woodlands, dippers were spotted in the stream, and it's one of the few sites in the region where I was able to glimpse bullfinches and siskin. Although birds are my favourite, the place was also home to rabbits, foxes, hedgehogs, badgers, bees, butterflies, and there was a time when I almost stepped directly on top of a sleepy slowworm!

I had been exploring the farm fields for a few months before I met the farmer who worked and lived at Yew Tree Farm, Catherine Withers. Our first interaction embarrassingly involved her telling me to please stick to the footpaths. After I apologised and explained I had just wandered off the path to try to photograph starlings, and she saw my camera and binoculars, we were soon talking in depth about the farm and the wildlife that lives there. It was quickly apparent that she had a love for nature and had a deep care for the land and all that lived there. This was also the first time I heard about the threats facing the farm as Catherine explained the risk of the housing development and the crematorium expansion that threatened the very field we stood in.

Over the following months, I would share some of my wildlife sightings and photos with Catherine. Occasionally I would receive exciting messages such as 'Barn owl!' which would result in my dropping whatever I was doing and rushing over there with my camera. Although I missed it on that occasion, on one evening walk on a cold February evening I got a glimpse of that unmistakable, magically white owl. After this briefest of glimpses, I returned every night for over a week. I was just about to give up hope before my efforts were rewarded and she returned. Barn owls are one of my favourites and I simply couldn't believe I was able to enjoy the mystical barn owl hunting on my local patch just a couple of miles out of the city centre.

Threats to the farm and its wildlife

Having fallen in love with Yew Tree Farm, the thoughts of this land being lost to housing development, or the crematorium expansion, was heartbreaking. However, at the back of my mind I was convinced that a green, progressive city such as Bristol wouldn't allow such an important nature-rich space and a designated Site of Nature Conservation Interest be lost. After all, wasn't this was the city that was first to declare both a climate emergency in 2018 [1], and an ecological emergency in 2020 [2]? Bristol was also the UK's first city to be named European Green Capital in 2015 [3]. If Bristol couldn't protect its valuable green spaces, where could?

Interest in the site was then picked up by the BBC who were wanting to tell Catherine's story on Countryfile [4]. I was honoured to be asked to also be involved in the filming and share my experiences of the farm and its wildlife and why I thought it should be saved. Getting to show presenter Charlotte Smith and a camera crew around the site I had spent the last year exploring felt surreal. I showed them around the meadows, the wide hedgerows, the stream and even got to show some of my photographs. When it got to the end of my short segment, Charlotte and I were sat on a fallen tree by the stream when we started talking about the threats to the farm. She said: "It does occur to me sitting here, because we're so near transport links, industrial estate, housing that logically this area makes sense to develop, to put housing on."

I replied: "I know there is a need for housing but, on personal level, having a place like this to come and to enjoy the birds is really important. But also on a wider scale, Bristol was the first city to declare a climate emergency, they also declared an ecological emergency, and I think developing a site like this that helps tackle both of these issues would be a step backwards. It's a really exciting place that can grow food, look after wildlife and provide green space for people to enjoy and help their mental health."

Almost 18 months after the BBC Countryfile episode aired, Bristol City Council were going to decide on whether to go ahead with their crematorium expansion. Before the decision was made, I wrote a blog piece on behalf of Avon Wildlife Trust entitled 'Bristol City Council's commitment to nature's recovery being tested!' in September 2023 explaining to readers why the site was important and encouraging people to get involved by letting the council know their thoughts [5]. In this piece I argued that any decision to damage this SNCI would be against their own goals and targets. The council had stated in their One City Ecological Emergency Action Plan that nature would be "embedded into all council decisions" to address the drastic declines in nature and wildlife across the city [6]. They also had an ambitious goal of having 30% of Bristol's land managed for the benefit of nature. How could the council hope of achieving this target and live up to their own goals if they were willing to encroach on sites that they themselves had designated important for nature, such as SNCIs? I quoted Ian Barrett, CEO of Avon Wildlife Trust, from an earlier interview by BBC Radio 4 about the farm when he stated that Yew Tree Farm was "an immensely rich wildlife habitat supporting a wide range of species including plants, bats and birds that are increasingly scarce in surrounding areas. It is vitally important that Sites of Nature Conservation Interest are protected through the planning system, and even more so in cases such as Yew Tree Farm where the current wildlife value is so high."

Later in this blog, I also argued that the value of the Yew Tree Farm SNCI extended beyond the individual site as it was an important part of the wider landscape, linking up the city with the wider countryside. The approach to restoring nature set out in government strategies is based on the Lawton Report of 2010 'Making space for nature' [7]. This report states that if wildlife is to recover, thrive and adapt to our ever-changing world we need more sites that are bigger, better and connected. The larger the site is, the better protected it is from so called 'edge effects' of being adjacent to land that might be using pesticides or disturbance might occur. Bigger sites can also support larger populations and therefore they are better protected from disease or bad weather conditions losing the species from the site altogether. Connected sites allow species to move freely across the landscape and therefore are also less at risk at being lost. Development and encroachment into to the Yew Tree Farm SNCI will inevitably reduce its size, quality and reduce the connectivity of habitats across the city.

Despite the objections from Avon Wildlife Trust, and a lot of push back from the local community and the people of Bristol, in November 2023, the decision was made by the council to go ahead with their proposals to expand South Bristol Cemetery and Crematorium into the SNCI [8]. It was extremely disappointing to hear about their decision and heart-breaking to think about the section of the site that would be impacted. It was this field that I had spent many summer evenings in that part of the farm watching swallows and swifts feeding over the meadows and large flocks of starlings being scared off by the local sparrowhawk. Starlings are one of many birds that have already nearly been lost from the city with a decline of 96%. They used to gather in large numbers and murmurate on a winters evening over Temple Meads station. Imagine waiting for your train home on a cold January evening and being able to enjoy the twirling, dancing clouds of starlings from your platform.

We have already lost so much of our wildlife in this country and here we are still making decisions to negatively impact what little we have left. Just a few months earlier, the landmark State of Nature report had been released which detailed the current state of wildlife in the UK [9]. As you might imagine, its main findings made for troubling reading. According to this report, the most comprehensive of its kind compiling data gathered from thousands of surveyors monitoring thousands of species, 1 in 6 species in the UK are at risk of extinction. How can we hope of reversing this drastic trend when even sites that are designated for nature such as the Yew Tree Farm SNCI are not safe?

In a response to the Council's decision, I wrote in early December 2023: "Avon Wildlife Trust stands to protect wildlife and the habitats it depends on. Considering planning proposals on a case-by-case basis doesn't work for protecting ecosystems. It is imperative that decision-makers understand the cumulative impact of planning decisions. To successfully deliver Bristol's Ecological Emergency Action Plan, our authorities have a duty to look strategically at their policies and operations to assess what action they can take to further the conservation and enhancement of biodiversity, including regard to the relevant Local Nature Recovery Strategies. We share the concern expressed by Planning Committee Chair that last night's decision is part of a wider picture of encroachment on designated Sites of Nature Conservation Interest across the region. If we cannot protect this SNCI then what is stopping development on others across the city? It is a slippery slope and with wildlife in rapid free fall, there isn't much slope left" [10].

Unfortunately, as mentioned earlier, the crematorium expansion wasn't the only threat to the farm. In early 2024, contractors were called out to the southern field at risk of housing development and they carried out some drastic hedgerow clearance where protected dormice had been recorded which rightly caused outrage from local people and was reported by lots of local media [11].

In a piece responding to this, I said: "This particular hedgerow at Yew Tree Farm SNCI was designated, it was home to legally protected dormice, had been promised to be protected by local councillors and was even the site of the discovery of a potentially new species of grass fly unknown to science. And yet it still wasn't enough. If this hedgerow wasn't safe, what hope is there for any hedgerow anywhere?" I continued "Dormice have suffered huge declines in recent years with their population falling by 70% since the year 2000. Last week we saw how this happens. Piece by piece their habitat is slowly removed, degraded, fragmented and removed. The species and habitats that we all love and try to protect are being destroyed in front of our eyes" [12].

The story continues

Since I moved to North Bristol, I sadly don't get to visit Yew Tree Farm as often. I miss being able to step out of my door and within a few minutes be able to escape into the fields and get lost in the calm of nature. I often think back to my early lockdown walks on crutches walking through meadows of cowslips and knapweed as grasshoppers and butterflies disturb from around me. I was lucky to have access to such as space. People who live closer to green spaces have been found to live longer and feel happier [13]. Access to nature has also been shown to help people recover quicker from surgery [14]. I like to think that the farm helped me recover physically and mentally during this time when I was able to explore it so regularly. I hope one day, I might be able to move back near to the farm and it will still be there to enjoy.

The story of Yew Tree Farm isn't finished. Catherine, locals and nature-loving Bristolians are still fighting to protect the farm. Although it has regularly been filled with disappointing decisions and upsetting news, this has also shown me that there are people out there who do love and care about nature. Bristol is still a city full of compassionate wildlife champions who want to do their best to protect nature and their local green spaces. Whether they are creating or signing petitions, attending council meetings, joining Facebook groups, sharing social media posts or recording wildlife, people have rallied behind Catherine and her farm, and I still hope and believe that when people come together, wonderful things can happen and sites that are important to us can be saved. ∎

REFERENCES

1. Ellie Pipe. Bristol declares climate emergency and pledges to become carbon neutral by 2030. *Bristol24/7*, 14 November 2018. Available at: https://www.bristol247.com/news-and-features/news/bristol-declares-climate-emergency-and-pledges-to-become-carbon-neutral-by-2030/ (Accessed 14 June 2024)
2. Steven Morris. Bristol declares ecological emergency over loss of wildlife. *The Guardian*, 4 February 2020. Available at: https://www.theguardian.com/uk-news/2020/feb/04/bristol-declares-ecological-emergency-over-loss-of-wildlife (Accessed 14 June 2024)
3. Bristol becomes European Green Capital 2015. *BBC News*, 8 December 2014. Available at: https://www.bbc.co.uk/news/uk-england-bristol-30376460 (Accessed 14 June 2024)
4. Martin Booth. Countryfile broadcasts from Yew Tree Farm as its future remains uncertain. *Bristol24/7*, 16 January 2022. Available at: https://www.bristol247.com/news-and-features/news/countryfile-broadcasts-from-yew-tree-farm-as-its-future-remains-uncertain/ (Accessed 14 June 2024)
5. George Cook. Bristol City Councils commitment to nature's recovery being tested! Available at: https://www.avonwildlifetrust.org.uk/blog/george-cook/bristol-city-councils-commitment-natures-recovery-being-tested (Accessed 14 June 2024)
6. Martin Booth. Ecological emergency action plan 'to ensure nature embedded into all council decisions'. *Bristol 24/7*, 1 September 2021. Available at: https://www.bristol247.com/news-and-features/news/ecological-emergency-action-plan-to-ensure-nature-embedded-into-all-council-decisions/ (Accessed 14 June 2024)
7. 'Making space for nature': a review of England's wildlife sites. Department for Environment, Food and Rural Affairs,

24 September 2010.

8. Martin Booth. Cemetery given permission to expand onto Bristol's last working farm. *Bristol24/7*, 29 November 2023. Available at: https://www.bristol247.com/news-and-features/news/crematorium-given-permission-expand-bristol-last-working-farm/ (Accessed 18 June 2024)

9. State of Nature. State of Nature partnership, 2023. Available at: https://stateofnature.org.uk/wp-content/uploads/2023/09/TP25999-State-of-Nature-main-report_2023_FULL-DOC-v12.pdf (Accessed 18 June 2024)

10. George Cook. Our Response to the Crematorium expansion into Yew Tree Farm SNCI. Avon Wildlife Trust, December 2023. Available at: https://www.avonwildlifetrust.org.uk/news/our-response-crematorium-expansion-yew-tree-farm-snci (Accessed 18 June 2024)

11. Martin Booth. 'Wanton vindictive destruction' at Yew Tree Farm. *Bristol 24/7*, 23 February 2024. Available at: https://www.bristol247.com/news-and-features/news/wanton-vindictive-destruction-yew-tree-farm/ (Accessed 18 June 2024)

12. George Cook. Dormice at Yew Tree Farm SNCI. Avon Wildlife Trust. Available at: https://www.avonwildlifetrust.org.uk/blog/george-cook/dormice-yew-tree-farm-snci (Accessed 18 June 2024)

13. Natural England. Enhancing England's urban green spaces. Natural England, 30 September 2020. Available at: https://naturalengland.blog.gov.uk/2020/09/30/enhancing-englands-urban-green-spaces/ (Accessed 18 June 2024)

14. Donovan GH, Gatziolis D, Douwes J. Relationship between exposure to the natural environment and recovery from hip or knee arthroplasty: a New Zealand retrospective cohort study. *BMJ Open* 2019;9:e029522. Available at: https://bmjopen.bmj.com/content/bmjopen/9/9/e029522.full.pdf (Accessed 18 June 2024

Bristol residents were shocked to find this beautiful willow chainsawed during National Tree Week in 2022. The tree provided joy to hundreds of people walking to and from Temple Meads each day. Bristol City Council permitted itself to do this through an opaque planning process. That this could happen shows an incredibly regressive attitude to trees and urban design within the Council. Credit: Mark Ashdown

Around 80 important trees on the Baltic Wharf Caravan site are earmarked for removal by Goram Homes, a subsidiary of Bristol Holding Ltd which is wholly owned by Bristol City Council. This part of Bristol has very low tree canopy cover. In September 2021, inspired by women in India who threw their arms around trees to protect forests from being destroyed, more than 70 women "married" the trees in a ceremony carried out by a celebrant.
Credit: Peter Herridge, *Bristol24/7*

Saving Bristol's urban trees

Vassili Papastavrou, founder of Bristol Tree Forum, describes a long-standing struggle to improve the fate of Bristol's urban trees...

SPACE IS ALWAYS a limited commodity in cities and Bristol is no exception. Decisions about how we allocate this space fundamentally shape the character of our city. For example, with so much public urban space dominated by the motor car, we need to claw back that space for uses that benefit local communities. The foresight of previous policy makers has given us a city which benefits from tree-lined streets, important trees in gardens and generous green spaces. The challenge now is to preserve that legacy and build on it for future generations. In the battle for space, Bristol's urban trees need advocates and strong policies in order to protect them. Yet, over the last two decades we have seen the loss of green spaces, especially in south Bristol, and an inexorable removal of important urban trees, particularly in the centre of Bristol. This needs to change.

What have urban trees ever done for us?

The large scale planting of street trees by the Victorians all over Britain shows that they appreciated the value of urban trees. In Bristol, the predominant species are London planes and limes – both large-form street trees with the potential to reach a height of 10 metres or more. The species were chosen because of their resistance to pollution and resilience to the hard knocks of a tough urban environment. In the competition for space, they don't take up much because their branches and crowns can be managed so that they start well-above the height of pedestrians, shop window displays and even high-sided vehicles.

The next major event was the advent of Dutch elm disease which dramatically changed our tree-scape. In response, a major initiative –

Plant a Tree in '73 – was born and 4,000 large-form trees were planted along major and minor roads. One example is the trees planted outside the Arnolfini, then a desolate part of the unloved docks. If you measure the diameter at breast height of these trees you will quickly be able to spot other trees, all of which are a similar size, resulting from Plant a Tree in '73. The plantings were a collaboration between Frank Kelf, a Bristol City Council officer, Bristol Civic Society and other community organisations. I organised a reunion of those involved and got to meet Frank, by then long-retired. He was a bit of a maverick who had transformed Bristol more than any single individual over that period [1, 2].

The Victorians (and the Plant a Tree in '73 gang) may never have anticipated one key legacy of their urban trees. In the age of the climate emergency, they keep us cool. In that respect they are irreplaceable because, in the timescale that we need their cooling effect, there simply isn't the time to grow replacements. The tarmac and roofs in our cities store and radiate heat which means that city centres can be 10°C hotter than the surrounding countryside. This phenomenon is known as the urban heat island effect. In July 2022 Bristol hit 35.2°C prompting concerns that, with temperatures set to increase, the city would become unliveable, particularly inner city areas such as St Pauls which already has relatively low tree cover [3]. Research has shown that when cities become hotter than usual there are extra deaths: 66,000 heat-related deaths occurred in Europe during the hot summer of 2022 [4]. Quite simply, by keeping cities cooler, urban trees save lives.

Urban trees provide many other benefits. In addition to bringing biodiversity into our streets, they alleviate flooding by improving ground penetration and slowing rainwater run-off. They combat pollution by absorbing particulates and noxious combustion products from diesel and petrol engines. Trees have an important aesthetic value and improve mental health. Go into any city and you will find more trees in the most affluent areas. This is certainly true in Bristol where the areas with the greatest social deprivation have the fewest trees.

Size matters

Not all trees are equal. The bigger the tree, the greater the benefits it provides. And in an urban environment, larger street trees are more likely to survive everyday knocks from vans and cars. Yet in Bristol we are planting very few large-form long-lived street trees. Instead, the species chosen include amelanchier, rowan and flowering cherries. These are all relatively short-lived trees that will never become large. It would take perhaps 50 rowans to provide the shade of one mature London plane. In my area of Bristol (Redland) in 2022 there was not a single street tree planting site for a large-form tree, and large trees that are lost have been replaced by small short-lived species.

In recent times there have been two major highways interventions that have resulted in the planting of large-form street trees, along Bath Road and Whiteladies Road. In both cases the trees were planted along the middle of the roads, thus avoiding the services which tend to run beneath pavements. We need many more such schemes. Some 10 years ago the Bristol Tree Forum suggested that we "put the avenue into Filton Avenue" to counter the lack of trees in this less affluent area of Bristol. But at that stage, despite good press coverage, council officers were uninterested in taking the proposal further. There have been no other large-scale street tree proposals since.

So why the nervousness to plant large-form street trees, despite their obvious benefits? One reason is house insurance companies. Insurance companies may say how concerned they are about the climate emergency and what good things they are doing, but they contribute to climate change by forcing the removal of urban trees. In February 2024 Haringey Tree Protectors, fighting against the removal of a landmark plane, took the battle to the annual conference of the Association of British Insurers [5]. Dressing up as condemned trees and shrubs, and faceless insurers, they demonstrated outside the meeting.

Bristol, like London, has many Victorian houses with inadequate foundations built on clay. When cracks start appearing, the tree gets the blame and the insurance company then puts pressure on the council to remove it or face paying huge sums of money. This is a complex subject that I can only touch on here but there are other options such as underpinning and root barriers. The London Tree Officers Association developed a Joint Mitigation Protocol in conjunction with several insurers that provides a sensible process for dealing with subsidence issues [6]. The value of the tree is determined and more valuable trees require better evidence before they are felled.

Bristol City Council, to its credit, is increasingly taking a robust approach to defending existing trees. However, the threat of insurance claims *is* having a chilling effect on the planting of new street trees. An additional concern that we have heard is the maintenance that large-form street trees may require through pollarding. But trees we plant now won't require maintenance of this kind for at least the next 40 years and it is in this period that we will desperately need more shade. By not planting large-form street trees now, Bristol City Council is depriving future generations of the opportunity for shade. In my opinion, they will not thank us for this.

Not all councils behave in this way. During a visit to Seaford near Brighton over Easter 2024 I saw a street where the existing trees, having succumbed to Dutch elm disease, had been replaced with a mixture of disease-resistant elms, limes and field maple; all large-form trees.

Bristol Tree Forum

In 2008, a controversy regarding the removal of large numbers of trees (mainly street trees) over a very short period led to the establishment of the Bristol Tree Forum (BTF), initially with support and engagement from Bristol City Council (BCC) which for a time provided the secretariat and meeting venues. As a community group, the aims of BTF initially were (and mostly still are) to:

- protect and enhance our urban trees in streets, parks, gardens and all open spaces;
- encourage BCC to ensure the replacement of trees that have been (and continue to be) removed;
- establish sufficient funding to ensure the retention of mature trees in our city and slow the present rate of felling;
- establish sufficient funding for the planting of new urban trees;
- maintain then increase the urban canopy cover;
- work with BCC to plan for 'climate proofing' our city in accordance with predicted urban temperature increases in the next 20 years;
- argue for a formulaic approach to ensure that Bristol achieves a sustainable balance between the built form/hard surface and tree canopy cover;
- provide a mechanism for open consultation on urban trees issues between local community groups, interested professional bodies and several BCC Departments;
- promote greater understanding of the values of amenity trees and stay up-to-date with current thinking, policy and research.

An important additional task is commenting on planning applications, large and small. In short BTF tries to prevent the removal of important urban trees on development sites. Additionally, BTF has established a network of 'tree champions' who work within their local communities and provide advice and support for trees in their own area.

Starting in 2020, BTF has organised the big tree giveaway of native trees for people to plant themselves, and has given away more than 10,000 trees [7]. We have a comprehensive website covering current tree issues and providing information and advice, as well as publishing regular blogs on a variety of subjects, some more technical than others [8]. There are tutorials for those that want to get involved in commenting on planning applications and a variety of other practical information. Our sister site, Trees of Bristol, has mapped nearly all of Bristol's significant trees with further information on individual trees where this is available [9]. The individual tree information is available if you stand by the tree in question with your smartphone. The site is searchable and analyses can be conducted, for example, to find the distribution of particular species of tree and tree canopy cover in the various Bristol wards. This site is unique in the UK.

Since BTF was set up, we have provided advice to local campaigners trying to save trees in Bristol and other parts of the country. Some of these campaigns have been won and others lost. In the case of Sheffield, although a huge number of trees were felled in a bitter argument with the city council, the arguments have largely been won and a mechanism adopted to ensure proper collaboration with the Sheffield Tree Action Group before trees are felled in the future. The Lowcock Inquiry which concluded in 2023, provided some closure [10]. But, although Sheffield is an extreme example, there are instances in which other local authorities, including Bristol, wield their power to remove trees in a similar way.

One Tree per Child

If there is a present-day Frank Kelf in Bristol, it is John Atkinson who runs Bristol's One Tree per Child programme [11]. The achievements of his team are somewhat different, mainly focusing on planting within existing green spaces and engaging with local community groups and school children. All of which is done very well. A whole generation of school children is being introduced to the values of trees in an engaging and thoughtful way, for John is a teacher himself. If trees are planted with the involvement of local communities, they are more likely to be valued and to survive. According to Bristol City Council's website approximately 6,000 trees are planted each year with around 90,000 trees planted since 2014.

Rabbit in the headlights

Perhaps the most important role of BTF is to encourage community engagement in tree management decisions. In a paper, published by the *Arboricultural Journal*, I argue that there are inhabitants in the urban forest and there are many advantages in allowing them to become involved in urban tree issues [12].

Yet many important decisions on urban trees are made by council officers entirely on their own. Often they don't even seem to consult each other. I think council officers do not feel the need to conduct a proper consultation because they have training, feel that they understand the issues, and believe there is little public interest in whatever they decide. But, in failing to consider the opinions of local people, they can often find themselves like rabbits in the headlights. Huge controversies erupt because they underestimate just how much the public cares about issues that affect them. A good recent example is the fiasco regarding allotment management in Bristol. A draconian set of new rules appeared just before Christmas 2024, together with hefty price hikes for allotmenteers. What seemed like a done deal provoked a serious rebellion – and forced concessions. I argued in *Bristol 24/7* that the whole thing could have been done collaboratively by conducting a proper consultation [13].

Lord Woolf is a judge with a reputation for simple common-sense judgments, one of which defined a proper consultation [14]. He wrote: "To be proper, consultation must be undertaken at a time when proposals are still at a formative stage; it must include sufficient reasons for particular proposals to allow those consulted to give intelligent consideration and an intelligent response; adequate time must be given for this purpose; and the product of consultation must be conscientiously taken into account when the ultimate decision is taken."

These are a pretty simple set of guidelines – not followed in the BCC allotment consultation – which would have saved hard-pressed council officers time and avoided the conflict they found themselves embroiled in.

BTF has found the failure to consult properly endemic within the council. Decisions are taken to fell important individual urban trees with no proper attempt to consult, sometimes by subverting the planning process [15]. One example was the removal of a beautiful willow near Temple Meads railway station, to the shock of passers-by during National Tree Week in 2022 [16]. In many other cities, the tree would have been celebrated.

When such things are done, council officers tend to defend the bad decision to the hilt, however untenable their position becomes. In terms of the larger policy decisions, a failure to consult results in bad outcomes that often have to be reversed later. For example, the 2017 Highways decision to slash the street tree maintenance budget for Bristol by 78 per cent was eventually overturned following BTF intervention and extensive press coverage [17]. It became apparent, through questions at a BTF meeting, that BCC Highways hadn't even consulted the tree officers within the council. It was a decision which would have resulted in huge financial liabilities caused by a failure to manage street trees to ensure that they were safe.

By far the most important consultation has been regarding the new draft Local Plan which will shape planning decisions in Bristol for the next decade. Yet, the draft Local Plan has received little media coverage. In October 2023, BTF wrote to all councillors expressing serious concern with the way that the plan had gone. A major concern was that our previous comments (during two consultation phases) had been ignored, rendering the consultation flawed.

As a result, our concerns remained that protection for green spaces had been reduced, contrary to council policy and despite the Climate and Ecological Emergency declarations [18, 19]. The draft provided fewer environmental protections than the current adopted Local Plan. In addition, there was insufficient information about the individual sites to allow for a proper consultation or independent examination. BTF had contributed detailed comments on two previous occasions and we are left wondering what was the point of contributing to the process. Our letter to all councillors was ignored and Full Council adopted the draft in October 2023.

In trying to get to the bottom of what had gone wrong, we asked for the minutes of the Local Plan Working Group. The refusal of a Freedom of Information request (after internal review) stated rather dramatically that releasing the minutes "would create a chilling effect" [20]. So we have no idea whether the Working Group ever saw, or even discussed the comments that we had spent many hours putting together. There is one last chance to be heard, and we have asked to participate in the Planning

Inspector's Hearings [21]. Bristol Civic Society's comments at earlier stages were also largely ignored, so it has done the same. The Civic Society states that the Local Plan does not even seem to be consistent with national planning policy [22]. It remains to be seen whether the Planning Inspector will re-open the process, or whether the flawed draft will be rubber-stamped to the delight of developers and property speculators.

Without a commitment from BCC to conduct consultations properly in the future, local democracy will remain damaged to the detriment of our city and its citizens.

Trees and planning

The Local Planning Authority plays an important role in determining how Bristol is shaped. In Bristol we no longer seem to have planners who see a value in building developments around existing trees. There are the local and national policies to support the retention of existing trees, but these policies need to be conveyed to developers at an early stage in the application process so that the proposed buildings are designed appropriately.

Once the proposal is brought before the planning committee, it is usually too late to influence the design to secure the retention of trees. The current unwritten policy in Bristol seems to be to flatten everything on the site and pay a fee to BCC for future trees that are unlikely to be planted because there is no room.

Goram Homes, set up by the council to provide much-needed housing, must radically rethink its attitude to existing trees on its sites. The Baltic Wharf Caravan Site, which is a Goram Homes development site, is one example. The developer has chosen to remove 82 established trees rather than incorporate them into the design [23]. This in an area where the tree canopy cover is low and there are very few sites available to plant replacement trees. It is shocking that a council-established development company does not set a good example to other developers; the proposal was given planning approval by a unanimous decision in April 2024, just before the local elections.

An additional problem in Bristol is that the lack of effective planning enforcement with respect to trees. Neighbouring local authorities take substantive action and fine unscrupulous developers that illegally damage trees. BTF has lost count of the number of times we have tried to get action, to no practical effect.

We need a radical re-think, and to hire planners who will implement existing local planning policies to ensure that new developments retain existing trees wherever possible. Other local authorities manage to do it and create far better local environments as a result. A case study by the Trees and Design Action Group of the Angel Building, Islington, London is headlined, 'Effective tree protection unlocks planning consent and letting success at the Angel Building'. Considerable effort was made to protect an existing large-form tree close to a large development and as a result the new building is greatly improved. In Oxford, the new University Physics building was set back to allow the retention of a large and important tree. I have mentioned just two examples from elsewhere, but there are many others [24].

Promises, promises...

When developments are consented, the councillors on Bristol's Development Control Committees are led to believe that replacement trees will actually be planted. But this is often not the case. Instead of actually planting trees, developers give some money to the council which accumulates in a special bank account. This is known as 'Section 106' money, from Section 106 of the 1990 Town and Country Planning Act [25]. At February 2024, the account contained approximately £700,000 of unspent money. For many developments there are no tree planting sites within the one-mile vicinity requirement, so the money just builds up and Bristol's tree canopy cover decreases with each big development. The St Mary le Port and Baltic Wharf developments are two examples of pending tree destruction on a large scale where there are almost no sites for replacements. The solution is simple. If there are no replacement sites, existing trees must be retained. If we want to retain trees in our city centre, we need to make a stand.

Even when BCC is the developer, such as for Bristol Metrobus, tree planting planning conditions have not been honoured. For example, the tree planting promised in 2014 on Avon Crescent still has not happened, despite ongoing requests over ten years. In October 2023, BCC even applied to remove its own the tree planting conditions, but councillors on the committee unanimously agreed the council should abide by the conditions it had agreed in 2014 [26]. There is, of course, little prospect of any planning enforcement taking action.

Highway trees

When I visited Washington DC, I met the tree officer responsible for Washington's amazing street trees. He worked within the Highways Department, giving him a unique perspective and far more influence than if he had worked for the Parks Department. By planting trees from within the same department that plants traffic lights, he understood the processes of digging up sidewalks and he made sure that the Highways Department understood trees. Yet often it seems in Bristol that Highways neither understands nor values trees. Historically, Highways has had extensive powers to remove trees without consultation, though that has now changed. Largescale tree removals resulted from the road realignment around Temple Meads railway station and also the access bridge to what was once going to be Arena Island. We will never know how many of those trees could have been saved because there was no attempt to engage or consult over these proposals with the Bristol Tree Forum. Section 115 of the new 2021 Environment Act which came into force on 30 November 2023 may change all that by introducing a duty to consult [27].

Conclusion

Everybody likes planting trees and no one more than politicians. The publicity photos of politicians planting trees in the run-up to elections often seem a glib response to the complex issues that must be addressed regarding urban trees in Bristol. As a new administration takes over the running of the city, we are at a turning point in Bristol. The new 2021 Environment Act imposes a duty to consult regarding street trees and it remains to be seen how this will be implemented in Bristol. We need to prevent the new Biodiversity Net Gain requirements, which came into force on 12 February 2024, resulting in the hollowing out of biodiversity within the city in favour of planting somewhere else; 'in some foreign field that is forever Bristol' [28]. We hope that the draft local plan will be improved to provide proper protection for existing trees and green spaces. Collectively we need to grasp the nettle and dramatically improve the protection of existing trees. The new councillors need to make sure that there are advocates for trees within key BCC departments such as Highways, Planning and Education. A mechanism needs to be found for ensuring that future consultations are done properly and the council runs its business in an open, transparent and fair fashion. Only by having support from people in a position of power can Bristol's existing tree heritage be retained and new ambitious planting schemes realised, for the benefit of ourselves, our children and our grandchildren. ■

ACKNOWLEDGEMENTS

I would like to thank John Tarlton and Mark Ashdown for commenting on the draft. I'd also like to thank the council officers and councillors who have been prepared to debate urban tree issues with the Bristol Tree Forum, and especially those who have fought to save existing trees.

REFERENCES

1. Peter Floyd. Frank Kelf obituary. Bristol Civic Society, 11 April 2014. Available at: https://www.bristolcivicsociety.org.uk/frank-kelf/ (Accessed 21 May 2024)

2. Cicely Kelf. Frank Kelf Obituary. *The Guardian*, 30 October 2013. Available at: https://www.theguardian.com/politics/2013/oct/30/frank-kelf-obituary (Accessed 21 May 2024)

3. Billy Stockwell. Is Bristol prepared for more intense heatwaves? *The Bristol Cable*, 30 August 2022. Available at: https://thebristolcable.org/2022/08/is-bristol-prepared-for-even-more-intense-heatwaves/ (Accessed 21 May 2024)

4. Ballester et al. Heat-related mortality in Europe during the summer of 2022. *Nature medicine*, 2023;29(7):1857-1866. Available at: https://doi.org/10.1038/s41591-023-02419-z (Accessed 21 May 2024)

5. Alex Marsh. Haringey Tree Protectors protest at ABI conference. *Ham & High*, 28 Feb 2024. Available at: https://www.hamhigh.co.uk/news/24150596.haringey-tree-protectors-protest-abi-conference/ (Accessed 21 May 2024)

6. LTOA. Joint Mitigation Protocol. Available at: https://www.ltoa.org.uk/resources/joint-mitigation-protocol (Accessed 21 May 2024)

7. https://bristoltreeforum.org/category/love-of-trees/ (Accessed 21 May 2024)

8. https://bristoltreeforum.org (Accessed 21 May 2024)

9. Trees of Bristol. Available at: https://bristoltrees.space/Tree/ (Accessed 21 May 2024)

10. Sheffield Street Tree Inquiry. Independent Chair Sir Mark Lowcock KCB. 6 March 2023. Available at: https://www.sheffield.gov.uk/sites/default/files/2023-03/sheffield_street_trees_inquiry_report.pdf (Accessed 21 May 2024)

11. https://www.onetreeperchild.com/ (Accessed 21 May 2024)

12. Papastavrou V. Community engagement in urban tree management decisions: the Bristol case study. *Arboricultural journal*, 2019;41(2):91-104. Available at: https://bristoltreeforum.files.wordpress.com/2021/03/papastavrou-2019-community-engagement-in-tree-management-decisions.pdf (Accessed 21 May 2024)

13. Vassili Papastavrou. Consultations in Bristol seem just to be a box ticking exercise. *Bristol 24/7*, 8 February 2024. Available at: https://www.bristol247.com/opinion/your-say/consultations-bristol-seem-just-box-ticking-exercise/ (Accessed 21 May 2024)

14. R. v North and East Devon HA Ex p. Coughlan [2001] Q.B. 213 (16 July 1999). Available at: https://unece.org/sites/default/files/2021-03/Annex1g_RvNE_Devon.pdf (Accessed 21 May 2024)

15. Vassili Papastavrou. The Council is creating a city which will be unliveable in the climate crisis. *Bristol24/7*, 7 December 2022. Available at: https://www.bristol247.com/opinion/your-say/the-council-is-creating-a-city-which-will-be-unliveable-in-the-climate-crisis/ (Accessed 21 May 2024)

16. Vassili Papastavrou. The council is creating a city which will be unliveable in the climate crisis. *Bristol24/7*, 7 December 2022. Available at: https://www.bristol247.com/opinion/your-say/the-council-is-creating-a-city-which-will-be-unliveable-in-the-climate-crisis/ (Accessed 21 May 2024)

17. McEwan G. (2017). Can local authority tree managers utilise influence of urban tree advocates? Horticulture Weekly. Available at: https://www.hortweek.com/local-authority-tree-managers-utilise-influence-urban-tree-advocates/arboriculture/article/1434385 (Accessed 21 May 2024)

18. Ellie Pipe. Bristol declares climate emergency and pledges to become carbon neutral by 2030. *Bristol24/7*, 14 November 2018. Available at: https://www.bristol247.com/news-and-features/news/bristol-declares-climate-emergency-and-pledges-to-become-carbon-neutral-by-2030/ (Accessed 21 May 2024)

19. BBC News. Bristol declares it faces 'ecological emergency'. 4 February 2020. Available at: https://www.bbc.co.uk/news/uk-england-bristol-51376517 (Accessed 21 May 2024)

20. BTF 2023. Request for copies of the minutes of the Local Plan Working group. Freedom of Information Request. *WhatDoTheyKnow*. Available at: https://www.whatdotheyknow.com/request/request_for_copies_of_the_minute_3 (Accessed 21 May 2024)

21. Bristol Tree Forum representations in relation to the Bristol Local Plan 2023 Publication Version consultation.

Available at: https://bristoltreeforum.org/wp-content/uploads/2024/01/BTF-Representations-on-the-Bristol-Local-Plan-2023-publication-version.pdf (Accessed 21 May 2024)

22. Bristol Civic Society 2024. Local Plan review – final consultation. Available at: https://www.bristolcivicsociety.org.uk/local-plan-review-final-consultation/ (Accessed 21 May 2024)

23. Martin Booth. 166 new flats to be built at Baltic Wharf despite flood risks. *Bristol24/7*, 24 April 2024. Available at: https://www.bristol247.com/news-and-features/news/166-new-flats-built-baltic-wharf-despite-flood-risks/ (Accessed 21 May 2024)

24. Papastavrou V. 2020. New Developments should be built around existing trees. Available at: https://bristoltreeforum.org/btf-2020-newsletter/new-developments-should-be-built-around-existing-trees/ (Accessed 21 May 2024)

25. https://www.legislation.gov.uk/ukpga/1990/8/section/106

26. Alex Seabrook. Community win battle over replacement trees for Harbourside road reopening to cars. *BristolLive*, 19 October 2023. Available at: https://www.bristolpost.co.uk/news/bristol-news/community-win-battle-over-replacement-8841026 (Accessed 21 May 2024)

27. Legislation.gov.uk. The Environment Act 2021 (Commencement No. 7) Regulations 2023. Statutory instruments 2023 No 1170 (C.77) Environmental Protection. 2 November 2023. Available at: https://www.legislation.gov.uk/uksi/2023/1170/made#:~:text=Section%20115%20inserts%20new%20section,consult%20before%20felling%20street%20trees (Accessed 21 May 2024)

28. Mark Ashdown. It seems inevitable Bristol will see a steady inexorable biodiversity decline. *Bristol 24/7*, 12 February 2024. Available at: https://www.bristol247.com/opinion/your-say/it-seems-inevitable-bristol-will-see-a-steady-inexorable-biodiversity-decline/ (Accessed 21 May 2024)

City
Planning

The 26-storey tower at Castle Park viewed from Bristol's historic Old Market Street. Credit: Martin Booth, *Bristol24/7*

Gaol Ferry Steps at Wapping Wharf, where high density was achieved with streets of five and six storeys. Credit: Amelia Banfield, *Bristol24/7*

Planning by numbers

George Ferguson CBE, Mayor of Bristol 2012-2016 and President of the Royal Institute of British Architects 2003-2005, argues that Bristol's housing crisis must not be addressed by a hotch-potch of second-rate towers...

———

BRISTOL'S PLANNING HAS gone horribly wrong over the past few years, but why?

I have spent much of my life learning from cities and communities across the UK, Europe and the world, and have generally returned to Bristol thankful that I live in such a characterful human-scale city. I fear that we are now on a course of trashing much of that character and environment that has made us one of the most attractive places to live in the UK.

I talk of Bristol's character but, as with its population, it has a multitude of characters. It is this very diversity that makes it so interesting. However, the 110 or so villages, out of which the city has grown, are generally made up of walkable streets and spaces, with parks or green open space never far away. It is the curse of all cities that these streets and spaces designed for people have now become throughways and storage for cars, a trend that we have to manage, if not reverse, if we are to regain our freedom to roam and to play.

As Bristol's first elected Mayor for a short four years from 2012 to 2016, I had the tremendous privilege and opportunity of applying some of what I had learnt to the post-war city I first arrived in to study architecture in the 1960s. Some terrible planning mistakes were made in the two or three decades following World War 2 but we were fortunate that the worst of the post-war urban highway and mass housing plans were thwarted and we did not go the way of Birmingham's 'Concrete Collar'.

During the 1960's and 70's Birmingham City Centre underwent rapid change on an unprecedented scale in terms of building and highway construction. Although this resulted in considerable commercial activity and a very high level of vehicular access into the heart of the City it also produced a physical environment that fell short of public aspirations. Part of the legacy of the 60's and 70's growth was an Inner Ring Road drawn tightly around the City Centre. This "concrete collar" created a pedestrian barrier around the Central Core presenting a depressing and unfriendly environment. [1]

My first employment on leaving the University in 1970 was as a planning assistant at Bristol City Council planning office. We were defining Bristol's first Conservation Areas, in a race to save much of the city from post-war plans to demolish and replace with a brave new world of bland office towers, elevated concrete walkways and blocks of flats. It is hard to imagine how crass some of the plans had been. Much of St Paul's would have been flattened to make way for more urban highway, as did happen across Easton. There were plans to demolish whole swathes of Totterdown for a huge spaghetti junction, part of Bristol's very own 'concrete collar', and the Cliftonwood hillside of terrace houses were condemned, ready for replacement with three massive blocks of flats akin to those that were built at Dove Street, Kingsdown. Bristol would never have had its coloured hillside terrace houses which are now famous across the world!

In the post war years and right into the 1970s, property developers made money all over the country; in London, Office Development Permits had to be introduced to slow the rate at which the old city was disappearing before the march of the office blocks. These did not apply in Bristol. Anyone could see the commercial attractions of a city which was to be at the junction of the M4 and M5, and offered a range of recreational and cultural facilities for workers. Offices sprang up like weeds, mainly built 'on spec' for letting. For the most part their design was of the lowest standard acceptable to planners. [2]

The 1970s were a turning point when planners had to start listening to the public who had not previously been consulted. In 1980 Bristol Civic Society published *The Fight for Bristol* subtitled *Planning and the growth of public protest*. It featured Lodge Street on its front cover, a group of derelict listed buildings that my architectural partner, Philip Mann, managed to persuade Bristol Churches Housing Association to take on, saving them from demolition and replacement by a large office block towering over what was the Colston Hall, now Bristol Beacon. This conservation scheme, which we eventually delivered, provided 60 new social low-rent homes, starting the re-population of an abandoned city centre.

Building fast and high is not the solution

I honestly felt that the bigger battle had been won, and in many ways it had. It is therefore unbelievable that we now seem to find ourselves in the equivalent of the post-war 'planning by numbers' which resulted in an appalling period of low-quality big boxes with little or no regard for their historic neighbours or their social or environmental consequences. What has popped up again in Bristol recently is only the beginning of a planning assault on the city by developers who have been encouraged to build high in a short-sighted race for housing numbers while turning a blind eye to the loss of community and quality.

We are all too aware of the housing crisis with a lengthening waiting list and some 1,500 families housed in temporary accommodation. It is vital that we respond to the challenge. However, a short-sighted political reaction to build fast and build high to tick off promised numbers is not the solution. We must find sustainable ways of meeting the demand, in terms of numbers and affordability, and we do not have to look far to find the solutions.

My successor as elected Mayor started his term in 2016 with the sweeping statement that a city with ambition goes for height. John Frenkel, of Bristol Civic Society, wrote at the time:

> Last week Bristol mayor Marvin Rees said: "I want Bristol's skyline to grow. Years of low level buildings and a reluctance to build up in an already congested city is a policy I am keen to change. Tall buildings built in the right way, in the right places and for the right reasons, communicate ambition and energy." Back in the 1960s the same thought occurred to national and local politicians. Building tall was the way to solve the chronic housing crisis. The

Government added a premium to housing grants for tall blocks of flats. The programme left a legacy of poor quality tall buildings in Bristol, often unloved by their occupants, which dominated their neighbours. [3]

There may be a place for some high buildings appropriately sited, but it seems that this damaging mayoral declaration has been taken by all landowners to believe that they can double, or even treble, the height of their previous plans – creating a hotch-potch of second rate towers with little or no consideration for their historic setting, such as the 26-storey tower on Castle Park which is soon to be joined by others with the fatuous notion that Castle Park could be our Central Park New York! [4].

It is a lazy assumption that building high creates high densities. Of course, on any single site a high building houses more people or creates more office space than a lower one, but some of our most densely populated European cities are those made of planned civilised streets with houses and apartments with a host of individual doors onto those streets. That is how communities are made. To achieve this, we need the ambition to revive pro-active public or community master-planning, incorporating compulsory purchase powers where necessary, as is common in many European countries, if we are to create sustainable mixed-use neighbourhoods instead of being led by the nose by the random aspirations of individual private or corporate landowners.

Maybe one of the biggest disappointments in recent years has been the so-called Bedminster Green development, which had everything going for it when it first came to me as a proposal in 2015. I asked that it should start with a proper masterplan and that the Windmill Hill and Malago Community (WHAM) should be a partner in the process. The vision was for a sociable and sustainable medium-rise, high-density neighbourhood of streets and green spaces made up of a mix of terrace houses and flats of up to five or six storeys. Sadly, the council has conceded to developers who are set to create an oppressive monoculture of high buildings, destroying any idea of the exemplary mixed urban community it could have become [5].

A mixed community approach

We have been close to achieving such a mixed community approach via Neighbourhood Planning along Redcliffe Way for some 12 years or so, although nothing has yet happened [6]. While this scheme lacked the ambition of moving, or even removing, Redcliffe Way to give St Mary Redcliffe an appropriate setting, it will hopefully become an exemplar for future development in Bristol [7]. There are other opportunities to create low- to medium-rise, high density, mixed-use developments. But, with a decimated planning department, we need our city's architects and urban designers to take it on themselves to demonstrate what is possible, as we did with some success for the creation of Harbourside in the nineties.

One exemplar scheme that did get built, after I had the privilege of digging the 'first sod' with developer Stuart Hatton, was the Wapping Wharf and Gaol Ferry Steps development behind M-Shed. It followed the principles we had been advocating with our proposed masterplan for Harbourside and demonstrated that high densities can be achieved with streets of five and six storeys – walk up heights – with independent shops and cafes animating the ground level and a mix of 'meanwhile uses' in the shipping containers of 'Cargo'. I have often cited this development as one of the best of its kind anywhere.

Wapping Wharf was the result of a thoughtful masterplan but, encouraged by the call to 'go for height', and endorsement by the mayor, Umberslade replaced their excellent architectural team. After being seduced by some sexy drawings dripping with greenery, the proposed height of the final phases behind M-Shed and Museum Square has nearly doubled, which will destroy the iconic view of the recently listed Princes Wharf cranes that a group of us saved from destruction in the 1970s.

> From the start, the survival and rebirth of these iconic machines has been the work of the city's people. They were saved by the actions of a small group of individuals in 1975. Their restoration has only been possible by dozens of volunteers contributing an estimated 55,000 hours to the work. Their operation and maintenance is similarly achieved by volunteer effort. What we have done with our cranes is unique in the world. There are other preserved cranes but very few that still operate and none that you can visit like ours. [8]

The implication is that a taller development at Wapping Wharf will house more people, but it is a fallacy. The original masterplan with its street layout housed virtually the same number of people as the new plans. The truth is that it will give a select few, willing to pay for the privilege, a view of the city over M-Shed. This is at the huge expense of one of Bristol's most appealing public views as well as acting as a dangerous precedent to build high around the harbour.

This of course leads us to 'Western Harbour' an idea first promoted by John Savage in his book *2050 High in Hope* [9]. It is an idea that has much merit and one that I do support in principle. We have an unnecessarily complicated road junction at Cumberland Basin with some redundant infrastructure, and it has long been realised that it would be possible to remove some of that infrastructure to the south of the basin. The swing bridge, built in the 1960s, has served us well and requires major maintenance. However, it was brilliantly designed and can be fully restored for a fraction of any replacement cost which would run into hundreds of millions and not necessarily do a better job.

The consultation in 2019 was an unmitigated disaster. It was entirely focussed around roads rather than vision. Of ten road options explored by Arup, in a feasibility report commissioned by the mayor, we were only allowed to see three. This was accompanied by putting an arbitrary number of proposed dwellings on the site to fit a political narrative. A petition to publish the full feasibility report gained over 3,800 signatures and triggered a debate at Full Council during which opposition councillors expressed their concerns.

Green Cllr Paula O'Rourke told the meeting: "The words that really leap out of the petition are 'confusion', 'concern', 'fear' and 'harm'. There must be some accountability about the fear and scepticism that the proposals have caused because this petition would never have got to this stage if there had been inclusion from the beginning. People fear that something is being done to them and they are struggling to have their voices heard. There is genuine confusion. The petitioners are here today because they're afraid the mayor is going to rob the area of their heritage and rob them of their amenity. Instead of using it as an opportunity to improve the city, there is concern that he will in fact overdevelop a very historic site, and these fears are justified because way too early we've been told there will be over 2,000 homes built in Western Harbour" [10].

Five years later, master planners have been appointed – a London based practice with an excellent reputation [11]. However, their brief includes the expectation of 2,000 dwellings which is putting the cart before the horse, driving planning into a numbers game. The site, straddling the river Avon and Cumberland Basin, is a very special one lying, as it does, in view of the Avon Gorge, Georgian Clifton and Brunel's great bridge and the adjoining listed Bonded Warehouses. The opportunity to do something special is an exciting one, but that 'special' depends on its relationship with its neighbours and the rich landscape and industrial archaeology in the immediate area. That requires design to dictate the numbers, not numbers determining design. I hope that, under a new administration, the arbitrary stipulation on numbers will be removed in favour of an appropriate scale and mix of uses that is essential to good place making.

Planning for a sociable and sustainable city

So how do we achieve the numbers that are required to deal with the current housing emergency within an artificially tight Bristol boundary without wrecking what we have? Of course we should make the most of what we have within clear planning guidelines, but we need to redefine what we mean by Bristol. Bristol's somewhat artificial municipal boundary contains 42 square miles, but the urban area has expanded beyond that boundary by some 20 more square miles of suburban development. We are part of the Bristol and Bath city region, currently known as the West of England, which including North Somerset covers some 600 square miles.

The bulk of Bristol's urban expansion has been low-density housing estates and a mess of commercial and retail development spreading into South Gloucestershire. I have advocated a properly planned expansion to the north of Bristol [12], contained by the M4 to the north and M5 to the west, that revamps and builds on that largely unplanned development that could create homes and jobs for up to another 100,000 people, although we should not stipulate a number but be driven by design and the desire to build beautifully and maximise green space. This is a wonderful opportunity for a metro mayor now freed of the rivalry with his or her Bristol city counterpart.

One of the saddest episodes during Bristol's mayoral experiment was the apparent decision by my successor to talk down and undo as much as possible of what we had achieved in the first term, but I suppose that is the stuff of party politics! Cancelling the Arena Island project adjacent to Temple Meads station, for which we had a fixed price and planning permission, displayed a serious misunderstanding about the way cities tick. Pushing such facilities to the suburbs flies in the face of both economic and environmental good practice – a huge lost opportunity. Jon Usher, while in post as Sustrans Head of Partnerships for England South, argued:

> "It's my firm belief that an arena located next to Temple Meads would serve more of the people of Bristol, than one stuck out on the edge of the city. Even though there's been an offer of cash from YTL, the Malaysian developers of Filton Airfield, an arena on the very fringe of the city isn't good for anyone who actually wants to get there. Public transport in Bristol, and in most regional cities for that matter, works on the commercial principle of taking people from where they live to where they want to go. That in Bristol's case is in and out of the city centre... A Temple Meads location also means people are in the city. They'll spend money on food and drink in the city. They'll stay in the city. Bristol will benefit from an arena on Arena Island. People in the past have criticised Sustrans for being beige. Well, this is black and white. An arena in Filton would be bad for transport, and bad for the people of Bristol [13]."

The Bristol Arena decision, combined with an equally destructive re-location of Bristol's famous Zoo to an M5 motorway junction, risks shifting Bristol's leisure centre of gravity to the north of the city for which there needs to be a huge improvement in transport infrastructure. Urban expansion to the north must come with a radical improvement in the public transport service. I hope that a strengthened metro mayor will be able to invest in further park-and-ride facilities and dedicated bus routes into and across a city that should, in my opinion, be completely covered by an Ultra Low Emission Zone (ULEZ).

We have now moved to a less autocratic government for Bristol, which is a disappointment for some but a great relief to others. It is so easy to characterise a committee system as indecisive, as former cabinet member Paul Smith acknowledged:

> "the deceit is that mayors somehow 'gets things done' while committees flounder in indecision – all too reminiscent of the claim that dictators like Mussolini 'make the trains run on time'. The

committee system in Bristol built almost 50,000 council homes. Under the committee system, the 'corporation' set up and ran the electric and gas infrastructure, trams, buses, schools, a polytechnic (now UWE Bristol), health services and Bristol's plethora of parks. The committee system got things done. Alternatively, some people argue that decision making in the committee system is better because decisions are made in public. This does not stop them making poor decisions. Pushing a road through the middle of Queen Square was made by a committee (so was the decision to remove it)" [14].

The committee system is, as with all things, dependent on the application of a large dose of goodwill and the burying of axes in an adversarial party system. However, I do believe that individual councillors with restored authority will do all they can to make it work. The new system is also dependent on a more cohesive West of England Combined Authority which will hopefully bring North Somerset back into the fold [15]. Strategic planning, transport and housing provision should now all rest under the wing of the metro mayor and cabinet of four council leaders, which becomes more likely without an opposing Bristol mayor [16].

In spite of the damage that has been done in the distant and recent past, Bristol remains my favourite city and I am hopeful that a collective of Bristol councillors with strong environmental and social ambitions will do all they can to avoid being pushed into damaging planning decisions driven solely by numbers, but take all factors into consideration to ensure we do meet our environmental goals and that we make a city that is sociable and sustainable for generations to come. ■

REFERENCES

1.   Select Committee on Environment, Transport and Regional Affairs. *Memorandum by Birmingham City Council* (WTC 16). UK Parliament publications. January 2001. Available at: https://publications.parliament.uk/pa/cm200001/cmselect/cmenvtra/167/167ap17.htm (Accessed 6 June 2024)
2.   Gordon Priest, Pamela Cobb (eds). *The Fight For Bristol: Planning and the growth of public protest.* Bristol Civic Society and The Redcliffe Press. Bristol, 1980.
3.   John Frenkel. New Tall buildings should not harm the character of an area. *Bristol24/7*, 10 October 2016. Available at: https://www.bristol247.com/opinion/your-say/new-tall-buildings-should-not-harm-the-character-of-an-area/ (Accessed 6 June 2024)
4.   Martin Booth, Amanda Cameron. St Mary Le Port Development Plans Split Opinion. *Bristol24/7*, 21 December 2021. Available at: https://www.bristol247.com/news-and-features/news/st-mary-le-port-development-plans-split-opinion/ (Accessed 6 June 2024)
5.   Tristan Cork. Bedminster Green flats will be 'slums of the future' claims councillor. *Bristol Live*, 4 April 2024. Available at: https://www.bristolpost.co.uk/news/bristol-news/bedminster-green-flats-slums-future-9204274 (Accessed 6

June 2024)

6. Redcliffe Neighbourhood Development Forum. *Redcliffe Neigbourhood Development Plan*, November 2016. Available at: https://www.redcliffeforum.org/wp-content/uploads/2016/11/Redcliffe-online-version.compressed.pdf (Accessed 6 June 2024)

7. LDA Design. A Bristol Street Re-imagined. 18 May 2020. Available at: https://www.lda-design.co.uk/kindling/news/a-bristol-street-reimagined/ (Accessed 6 June 2024)

8. M Shed's cargo cranes. Bristol's Free Museums and Historic Houses. Available at: https://www.bristolmuseums.org.uk/stories/m-sheds-cargo-cranes/ (Accessed 6 June 2024)

9. John Savage. *2050 High in Hope*. The Initiative, Business West, 2011.

10. Adam Postans. Controversial Western Harbour plans branded "insane" as campaigners trigger council debate with 3,800 name petition. *Bristol Live*, 15 November 2019. Available at: https://www.bristol247.com/news-and-features/news/controversial-western-harbour-plans-branded-insane/ (Accessed 6 June 2024)

11. Martin Booth. Western Harbour masterplanners 'to map out future of one of UK's most extraordinary place'. *Bristol24/7*, 20 March 2024. Available at: https://www.bristol247.com/news-and-features/news/western-harbour-masterplanners-map-out-future-one-uk-most-extraordinary-places/ (Accessed 6 June 2024)

12. George Ferguson. We need to start planning now for a new town in North Bristol. *Bristol24/7*, 11 October 2023. Available at: https://www.bristol247.com/opinion/your-say/need-start-planning-now-new-town-north-bristol/ (Accessed 6 June 2024)

13. John Usher. An arena in Filton is bad for transport and bad for Bristol. *Bristol24/7*, 1 February 2018. Available at: https://www.bristol247.com/opinion/your-say/arena-filton-bad-transport/ (Accessed 6 June 2024)

14. Paul Smith. Mayor vs Committee: Which System Delivers? *Bristol Ideas*, Referendum 2022, 17 January 2022. Available at: https://www.bristolideas.co.uk/read/referendum-paul-smith/ (Accessed 6 June 2024)

15. Matt Griffith. Business community urges regional leaders to bring N Somerset into WECA fold. Business West, 30 October 2020. Available at: https://www.businesswest.co.uk/blog/business-community-urges-regional-leaders-bring-n-somerset-weca-fold (Accessed 6 June 2024)

16. Henry Woodsford. North Somerset will not join WECA after Bristol mayor 'veto'. *North Somerset Times*, 16 December 2020. Available at: https://www.northsomersettimes.co.uk/news/20405020.north-somerset-will-not-join-weca-bristol-mayor-veto/ (Accessed 6 June 2024)

The vacant site near Bristol Temple Meads railway station, was the planned location for Bristol's long-awaited arena. Credit: *Bristol24/7*

The sign affixed to a fence near the Brabazon Hangars points to YTL's promised arena that is, as yet, unbuilt. Credit: Martin Booth, *Bristol24/7*

The Bristol Arena project: A chronicle of ambition

Joanna Booth, citizen journalist writing about Bristol and local politics, recalls the events leading to the cancellation of Bristol's central arena for an alternative on the outskirts of the city...

———

IN 2003, THE South West Regional Development Agency (SWRDA) and Bristol City Council (BCC) entered into a partnership to develop a site near Temple Meads railway station in Bristol. The Bath Road diesel depot was bought by the developmental agency as a potential site for a 10,000-seat indoor arena.

SWRDA was to contribute £9m for land acquisition and infrastructure in addition to £4m from the council. The latter already owned some adjacent land, which it would make available for vehicles and pedestrians. The plans were now in motion with the hope of delivering the arena by 2008 which, according to Diane Bunyan, Labour leader of the council, would "enhance Bristol's reputation as a leading UK and European City" and "form a significant part of Bristol's City of Culture bid" [1].

But by 2007 concerns were raised after a 'public funding gap' was identified [2]. SWRDA indicated that the arena was dependent on "the public and private partners coming up with the right funding package" and there were no guarantees that the public sector would cover costs if the funding gap was too great. Helen Holland, then Labour leader of Bristol City Council said: "We are keen on the Arena, but it is a complex project."

Although SWRDA had pledged a further £14m towards decontamination, its Deputy Chief Executive Colin Molton admitted there was no guarantee an arena would be built. By the end of 2007, the costs were acknowledged as being too high and the arena was scrapped. The partners had pledged £46m towards the scheme, £16m from BCC and £30m from SWRDA, but an additional £40m "would simply not be a good use of public money" [3].

Plans to regenerate Temple Quarter continue

In 2010, the collation government formally announced the abolition of RDAs, including SWRDA. Instead, Local Enterprise Partnerships (LEPs) were to be established – essentially slimmed down versions of the RDAs that had been criticised as wasteful quangos. Bristol was to be part of the new West of England LEP, to be chaired by Colin Skellett, the long-standing chairman of (YTL-owned) Wessex Water [4].

The area around Temple Meads was still in sight for regeneration and the coalition government's policies on new enterprise zones started to make it look attractive for investment again. Temple Quarter Enterprise Zone was announced in 2011. Colin Skellett welcomed "a number of advantages to businesses by reducing both the amount of planning red tape and the cost of their rates" as well as "benefits for the area as a whole since we are able to retain the business rates that are generated which can be used to improve the other five areas we have identified" [5].

There was also the promise of ultrafast broadband across a proposed Digital Enterprise Zone, comprising the Temple Quarter Enterprise Zone, Harbourside and the University of Bristol [6]. New ideas about how to use the land and available capital started forming, particularly when the university saw an opportunity to expand. On 27 April 2012 "more than 200 businesses from across the South West, including representatives from the University of Bristol, gathered in a temporary circus tent which has been erected in the heart of the new Temple Quarter Enterprise Zone to hear an update on the exciting redevelopment project" [7]. This focus on technology, aligned with higher education, would persist throughout the years.

The first elected mayor of Bristol

In 2012, Bristol's governance saw big changes. George Ferguson, standing as an independent candidate, was elected mayor of Bristol – beating the Labour candidate, and favourite to win, Marvin Rees [8]. David Sweeting, an academic studying the transition to the mayoral system, said: "The general mood is one of optimism because George has a good track record of doing things for the benefit of Bristol, from being involved with the Tobacco Factory to the harbourside redevelopment. He's very well-connected within influential Bristol networks and I'm sure he'll use this influence for the good of the city" [9].

Along with the introduction of a mayor's designated bicycle parking bay, in front of the renamed City Hall, Ferguson wanted to revive the plans for an arena. He made it clear that the project in Temple Quarter was a key objective of his administration: "Bristol is left off the concert map because we are the only city without a proper arena. It shouldn't be a box in a car park, like so many arenas tend to be. It must be outward-looking and animate the space around it, and be really embedded in the city" [10].

By 2013, the arena had been costed, but funding was still to be found. When the Regional Growth Fund turned down a bid for £40m, Labour councillor Helen Holland said: "During his campaign for Mayor, George Ferguson prioritised an arena for Bristol, stating that he would knock on the doors that previous leaders had failed to open. It seems that those doors have slammed shut again, and Bristol is the loser. The arena is a big ambition for the city, not just to match the entertainment and conference venues of our competitors, but as a catalyst for job creation, for regeneration, and for stimulating the local economy" [11].

But the local paper started spreading a different message. In 2011, BAE Systems Ltd had announced its decision to close Filton Airfield on the edge of the city in South Gloucestershire [12]. A review of options for the site mentioned that "a number of respondents suggested a concert/exhibition arena" [13]. YTL had a new neighbourhood in mind for Filton, and its Chief Executive was in charge of the LEP.

In August 2013, a letter was published in *Bristol Post* about Filton being be a better site for an arena [14]. This was followed up by another supporting letter about the Brabazon hangars (in which Brabazon and Concorde aircraft had been constructed) which were on the edge of the Filton site and just inside the Bristol boundary. A couple more letters were sent that year from Downend locals, offering titbits of an alternative idea. The most relevant aspect of this might be the prominence provided to them by *Bristol Post*.

Also in 2013, L&G created Legal and General Capital. As part of this, the company became "committed to a homebuilding programme as one part of [their] direct investment programme" investing funds from their "shareholder and policyholder capital to achieve a long-term financial return, sometimes for 30, 40 or 50 years" [15]. L&G were stepping into a role previously provided by banks and governments because there was profit to be made.

The momentum was beginning to build for a change of plan. While Ferguson was in power, however, there would be no policy move from an arena at Temple Quarter. Other doors were to open and in 2014, the LEP offered £53m of grant funding for the Temple Island arena. Bristol City Council announced that the arena could be completed by 2017 [16]. But a confluence of events was occurring.

In 2015, the former Filton Airfield site was acquired by Malaysian developer YTL Group with plans to transform the site into a new mixed-use development. Colin Skellett, Chair of YTL UK, said he was "delighted to have acquired this significant site, which is a strategically important development for South Gloucestershire and the South West region" [17]. South Gloucestershire Council had already announced a £110m funding package for the Cribbs Patchway New Neighbourhood (CPNN) [18].

At the same time, L&G were keeping contact with Bristol City Council about their investment vehicle, which would "act as a conduit for property investors to get involved in regen schemes across the country with much of the risk removed" [19]. This meant that the risk of spending a lot of money in regeneration projects was reduced. In fact, there was profit to be made. L&G had access to a lot of money and they wanted to invest somewhere.

Conversations had begun with council officers in 2014, bypassing the elected mayor, Ferguson. In 2015, the conversations became more concrete. Barra Mac Ruairi, the Strategic Director for Place at Bristol City Council, was invited to Downing Street to meet up with L&G. In 2016, L&G's head of corporate affairs became head of the Number 10 policy unit. This was an environment where investment in regional development seemed very promising.

The second elected mayor of Bristol

The biggest shift however may have come from a left-wing backbencher who, in September 2015, was elected Labour leader; this was Jeremy Corbyn. The future seemed to offer more hope for many voters who got swept up on a Corbyn wave. The inexperienced Marvin Rees was elected as Labour Mayor of Bristol in 2016 [20]. Rees was now in charge of a billion-pound budget and had a deciding vote for all cabinet decisions.

One the first things Rees did was to invite the spirit of God into the city at Hope Chapel, his church. Before the 2016 election, Rees had been meeting regularly with the churches and was known to be a believer. He was very much a Christian mayor. Rees had spent some time in Washington volunteering for Sojourners, a Christian charity, and Tearfund. He'd also become acquainted with Bill Clinton's faith advisor, Tony Campolo, and attended Eastern University, a Christian university in Pennsylvania [21]. The US influence, with Christianity a strong strand, runs through Rees's speeches and actions.

One of the next things he did was to put up a poster in his office of an extract from a speech by the 26th president of the USA, Teddy Roosevelt: The Man in the Arena.

"It is not the critic who counts; not the man who points out how the strong man stumbles, or where the doer of deeds could have done them better. The credit belongs to the man who is actually in the arena."

As Rees began his first term, Ferguson's cycle bay was quickly erased [22]; getting rid of the arena, which was in progress, was to take a bit longer.

Under the first mayor, a design competition had been undertaken and won, contractors had been appointed, city maps had been created, and Brocks Bridge was named and ready to provide improved road access to Bristol's 'Arena Island', with an £11m investment from Homes England [23].

Meanwhile, the University of Bristol were seeing investment in technology as even more attractive. There was talk of 5G and smart cities. A £16m investment for a 5G hub came in 2017 [24]. In March 2017, the council's Strategic Director of Place, Mac Ruairi, oversaw the sale of the Council's freehold interest in "land comprising all of the Cattle Market Road site and the part of Arena Island not required for the Arena development" to the University of Bristol [25]. The university's plans for expansion included the creation of a new Temple Quarter campus including a digital innovation hub, a new business school and a student residential village [26].

Two months later, Mac Ruairi left the Council to take up the post of Chief Operating Officer for YTL where he, together with another ex-council boss, Robert Orrett, began working on plans to convert the Brabazon Hangar into an alternative site for Bristol's arena. A year later, amidst concerns about back room deals and revolving doors, Mac Ruairi left YTL to become Chief Property Officer at the University of Bristol [27].

To fill the gap of the missing Executive Director of Growth and Regeneration, the Council hired SWRDA's ex-Deputy Chief Executive, Colin Molton in September 2017. By November 2017, alarms started going off about the arena plans as Rees commissioned KPMG to produce the £100,000 report on whether there could be a better use for Temple Island. When the value assessment was published, it argued that "the University of Bristol's purchase of the remainder of the Temple Island site and the Post Office Sorting Depot site has weakened the likely catalytic impacts of the Arena and, therefore, the strategic case of the project" [28].

YTL had initially approached George Ferguson in 2015 about their privately funded arena but he had not been interested. In December 2017, YTL paid for Marvin Rees to fly to Malaysia with hospitality at the Ritz Carlton in Kuala Lumpur [29]. At unminuted meetings, Rees met with YTL officers. We don't know what was said or agreed but a BCC spokesperson later confirmed: "The mayor received hospitality from YTL during a stop-off in Malaysia last December. This was to attend discussions about infrastructure and investment opportunities in Bristol" [30].

One further aspect of YTL may have served as a link between the new mayor and the Malaysian multinational company's chief, Dato Hong Yeoh – their Christian beliefs. In an interview with *Bristol Post* in 2019, then-editor Mike Norton asked Yeoh about how his company's faith and family shape YTL's business decision-making [31]. He replied: "'Our ethos is very simple. We are a Christian family and the concept is about stewardship. Because the family are all Christians, we have a unity of purpose from one generation to another."

Dato Hong commented on the criticism Rees received for meeting YTL in Malaysia at the company's expense: "To be fair to Marvin, if you were him and you had the ambition to build an arena and you didn't want to subsidise it and someone wants to build an arena in his own place with his own proper money, you'd be biting his hands off! The only question is whether he's real or not. The fact that he is coming to Malaysia to check that out I think means that he's doing the due diligence he should do. For himself and for the Bristol community."

Within days of Rees' visit to Kuala Lumpur, BCC's interim Executive Director of Growth and Regeneration, Colin Molton, met with L&G. We know that he talked to them about housing and office buildings on the Arena Island site because the communications were disclosed through a Freedom of Information (FOI) request. In January 2018 an email from

L&G asks: "Is there anything put to paper around yours/Marvin's vision for the site? I seem to recall you mentioned offices and housing in our meeting" [32].

Paving the way for the YTL arena

Within weeks, a consultant who had previously worked for YTL's Cribbs Patchway New Neighbourhood, Nigel Greenhalgh, was appointed on Molton's recommendation to prepare a report for cabinet on the Bristol arena. A Freedom of Information request uncovered numerous, partially-redacted documents in which an arena on the Filton site was being favoured over the Temple Quarter site [33]. Minutes of a meeting to discuss transport plans for an arena at Filton show a BCC spokesperson, believed to be Nigel Greenhalgh, saying he had been appointed to "prepare a statement of support for the Brabazon Arena project proposed by YTL".

BristolLive reported that the FOI documents showed: "A senior [BCC] strategy boss helped YTL draw up their Filton Arena proposal; a council officer reassured the Malaysian firm they would 'assist them' on their proposal as much as they could within the law; Council chiefs from both Bristol and South Gloucestershire held a private meeting with YTL and Network Rail in March to create a transport plan for a Filton Arena, which ended with plans to draft a letter from both councils in support of the Filton project, and; a meeting was held in City Hall to discuss the marketing and PR strategy for the Filton Arena in May" [34].

The biggest planning issue was the sequential test. This is the principle that seeks to identify, allocate or develop certain types or locations of land before others. For example, brownfield housing sites before greenfield sites, or town centre retail sites before out-of-centre sites. In the case of the arena, if there was a more suitable location for an arena close to the town centre, the Filton arena would fail the test. Meeting the sequential test for the Filton arena was a priority for Molton and Greenhalgh. *BristolLive* reported: "To 'beat' the sequential planning test rules Mr Rees is expected to give the city centre site over to housing, a conference centre, shops and offices as a way to eliminate the land from the decision" [34].

At the Extraordinary Full Council meeting on 3 September 2018, where the arena project was discussed, 200 comments were sent in objecting to the move from central Bristol to Filton. Only 11 public forum comments were supportive of the move [35].

Liberal Democrat Councillor Anthony Negus moved the motion: "This

Council believes that the best site for Bristol's Arena, for the benefit of Bristol as a whole, is Temple Island in the centre of Bristol and that the decision taker should be guided by the vote at this meeting." Councillor Rachel Combley (Green) seconded the motion, which was carried with 50 members voting in favour (including Marvin Rees), none against, and two abstentions.

Rees said: "I have always said the city centre would be the best location. So let me say it again tonight and make it clear, I support this motion... I support the motion because of its simplicity but it shows that opposition councillors have consistently failed to understand the decision we have to make. Just because the best place for the arena is Temple Island, it doesn't follow that the best use of Temple Island is an arena" [36].

Greenhalgh's report went to Cabinet the next day, 4 September. It recommended cancelling the proposed arena on Temple Island and "to take all steps necessary and incidental to the cessation of that project" [37]. At the same time, it recommended that the Council "continues to work with partners to develop an alternative mixed-use scheme for the Temple Island site". The mayor and cabinet rubber-stamped the decision to proceed with the alternative scheme. The L&G work could progress.

The public were outraged. Councillors, MPs, architects, planners, and transport planners were also critical of the decision. Greenhalgh's role to make the Filton arena viable was predetermined from the start. L&G had to have a cabinet decision in place for use of the Temple Quarter site in order for YTL's arena in Filton to be given planning permission.

After experiencing defeat at the hands of Ferguson in 2012, Rees had succeeded in cancelling his predecessor's arena project, saying: "The reality is without an arena the only legacy from the previous administration is 20mph and RPZs" [38].

A key reason Rees gave for cancelling the central arena is that there would be no cost to the taxpayer for the YTL arena in Filton. However, this claim does not reflect reality [39]. The £53m grant money for the LEP was now redirected. £32m would go towards preparing Temple Island (no longer Arena Island) for L&G [40]. Meanwhile the transport plan for the proposed Filton arena required major infrastructure improvements including improved train links between Temple Meads and existing Filton stations, a new train station serving YTL's development plans, and completion of Metrobus Phase 2. Other improvements to the road network, as well as surrounding walking and cycling routes, would also be required. Almost all of this infrastructure would fall on the public purse.

Rees' decision to change the arena's location was also predicted to be the death knell to Bristol's central shopping area. Building the arena at Filton would compound the effect of the city centre's competitor, the Mall at Cribbs Causeway in South Gloucestershire. The threat was seen in the strengthening of "the retail and food and beverage offerings surrounding the Filton site". BCC had previously challenged a proposed expansion of Cribbs Causeway on the basis that it would cause irreparable damage to Bristol's City Centre shopping district, noting "with 39% and 33% of the average spend of a day visitor in Bristol consisting of shopping and food and drink respectively, these two spending areas, collectively make up more than two thirds of the total average expenditure for a day visitor in Bristol" [41].

In Filton, YTL are now the beneficiaries of millions of pounds in public investment, which benefit their expanding housing development. Meanwhile work on the arena, which initially had an opening date of 2024, has been delayed year after year [42].

The man in the arena

In 2022, the people of Bristol voted to abolish the role of elected mayor. Some say the arena saga contributed to this decision. Also in 2022, Bristol's 'man in the arena' moved out of the city to South Gloucestershire, although his term of office continued until local elections in 2024. Despite ongoing delays and uncertainty, in his final major speech before leaving office, Rees said: "With our partner, YTL, we are delivering the fourth biggest arena in the UK and the most sustainable in Europe" [43].

Roosevelt had given what some would say was his most famous speech, in 1910, a year after he left office. He spoke with hindsight. He spoke of the man "who spends himself in a worthy cause" [44]. It was also quoted by US President Richard Nixon in his resignation speech after he was caught spying on opponents: "Sometimes I have succeeded and sometimes I have failed, but always I have taken heart from what Theodore Roosevelt once said about the man in the arena".

Teddy Roosevelt fought against business interests so as to protect the public from deregulation. The fight for a private arena was against the public will, and was engineered alongside business interests with direct involvement of the mayor's office. Time will tell if the last elected mayor of Bristol spent himself well. We already know the arena haunts his legacy. ■

REFERENCES

1. City's 10,000-seater stadium plan. *BBC News*, 12 March 2003. Available at: BBC NEWS | England | City's 10,000-seater stadium plan (Accessed 26 May 2024)

2. Cash fears over city arena scheme. *BBC News*, 6 June 2007. Available at: BBC NEWS | England | Bristol | Cash fears over city arena scheme (Accessed 26 May 2024)

3. Bristol's arena plan is abandoned. *BBC News*, 13 December 2007. Available at: BBC NEWS | England | Bristol | Bristol's arena plan is abandoned (Accessed 26 May 2024)

4. West of England council partnership to be closed. *BBC News*, 27 June 2011. Available at: https://www.bbc.co.uk/news/uk-england-bristol-13906153 (Accessed 26 May 2024)

5. Land near Temple Meads named as Bristol enterprise zone. *BBC News*, 7 June 2011. Available at: https://www.bbc.co.uk/news/uk-england-bristol-13681651 (Accessed 26 May 2024)

6. Ultrafast Broadband coming to the Zone. Bristol Temple Quarter blog, 3 October 2012. Available at: https://www.bristoltemplequarter.com/ultrafast-broadband-coming-to-the-zone/ (Accessed 27 May 2024)

7. New enterprise zone set to transform the centre of Bristol. University of Bristol Press release, 27 April 2012. Available at: https://bristol.ac.uk/news/2012/8441.html (Accessed 27 May 2024)

8. Marvin Rees Loses Bristol Mayor Race. *The Voice*, 16 November 2012. Available at: https://www.voice-online.co.uk/news/uk-news/2012/11/16/marvin-rees-loses-bristol-mayor-race/ (Accessed 27 May 2024)

9. Bristol mayor now 'needs to deliver what the voters want'. University of Bristol Press release, 16 November 2012. Available at: https://www.bristol.ac.uk/news/2012/8947.html (Accessed 29 May 2024)

10. Oliver Wainwright. Bristol's architect mayor wants the city to be a 'laboratory for change'. *The Guardian*, 21 January 2013. Available at: https://www.theguardian.com/artanddesign/architecture-design-blog/2013/jan/21/bristol-architect-mayor-george-ferguson (Accessed 27 May 2024)

11. Bristol arena funding bid turned down. *BBC News*, 19 July 2013. Available at: https://www.bbc.co.uk/news/uk-england-bristol-23357655 (Accessed 27 May 2024)

12. BAE Systems issues report justifying Filton Airfield closure. *South Gloucestershire Post*, 19 October 2011. Available at: https://www.southglospost.co.uk/2011/10/19/bae-systems-issues-report-justifying-filton-airfield-closure/ (Accessed 29 May 2024)

13. South Gloucestershire Council. Review of the BAE Systems Aviation Options Report for Filton Airfield, December 2011.

14. B.E.J. Blestowe Downend. Brabazon hangar should become an arena; Your say... Filton airfield. *The Bristol Post*, 28 August 2013.

15. L&G Annual Report 2015. Available at: https://group.legalandgeneral.com/files/ar/2015fastread/index.html (Accessed 28 May 2024)

16. Bristol Arena: £53m funding provision approved. *BBC News*, 6 February 2014. Available at: https://www.bbc.co.uk/news/uk-england-bristol-26075213 (Accessed 27 May 2024)

17. YTL acquires the former Filton Airfield. YTL Group, 11 April 2015. Available at: https://www.ytldevelopments.co.uk (Accessed 28 May 2024)

18. Pamela Parkes. Multi-Million Pound Plan For Cribbs Patchway. *Bristol24/7*, 3 February 2015. Available at: https://www.bristol247.com/news-and-features/news/multi-million-pound-plan-for-cribbs-patchway/ (Accessed 29 May 2024)

19. FOI. 2015 Meeting with Legal and General. *WhatDoTheyKnow*, 13 January 2020. Available at: https://www.whatdotheyknow.com/request/2015_meeting_with_legal_and_gene#incoming-1563885 (Accessed 29 May 2024)

20. Louis Emanuel. Corbyn in Bristol to congratulate new mayor. *Bristol24/7*, 7 May 2016. Available at: https://www.bristol247.com/news-and-features/mayor-election-2016/corbyn-in-bristol-to-congratulate-new-mayor/ (Accessed 28 May 2024)

21. Who is Mayor Marvin? *Bristol 24/7*, 5 May, 2016. Available at: https://www.bristol247.com/news-and-features/mayor-election-2016/who-is-mayor-marvin/ (Accessed 28 May 2024)

22. Now you see it, now you don't. *Bristol 24/7*, 19 September 2016. Available at: https://www.bristol247.com/news-and-features/news/now-you-see-it-now-you-dont/ (Accessed 28 May 2024)

23. Brock's Bridge. Bristol Temple Quartet. Available at: https://www.bristoltemplequarter.com/key-projects/infrastructure-brocks-bridge/ (Accessed 28 May 2024)

24. £16m investment will create new 5G Hub partnership linking three universities' test beds. University of Bristol press release, 7 July 2017. Available at: https://www.bristol.ac.uk/news/2017/july/5g-funding.html (Accessed 29 May 2024)

25. Bristol City Council. Decision details. University of Bristol – Second Campus at Temple Meads East, 7 March 2017. Available at: https://democracy.bristol.gov.uk/ieDecisionDetails.aspx?Id=197 (Accessed 28 May 2024)

26. Michael Yong. Bristol University to take over old sorting office by Temple Meads for new £300m campus. *BristolLive*, 29 November 2016. Available at: https://www.bristolpost.co.uk/news/bristol-news/bristol-university-take-over-old-603 (Accessed 28 May 2024)

27. Tristan Cork. Now former Bristol council chief leaves new Arena job for the University of Bristol. *BristolLive*, 14 June

2018. Available at: https://www.bristolpost.co.uk/news/bristol-news/now-former-bristol-council-chief-1677138 (Accessed 28 May 2024

28. Bristol Arena Value for Money Assessment: Summary conclusions. KPMG report for Bristol City Council. June 2018. Available at: https://democracy.bristol.gov.uk/documents/s24714/Appendix%20II%20FINAL%20Bristol%20 Arena%20Value%20for%20Money%20Assessment%20summary_vSTC%20QA.pdf (Accessed 28 May 2024)

29. Marvin Rees China/Mayalsia trip. *WhatDoTheyKnow*, 1 March 2018. Available at: https://www.whatdotheyknow. com/request/marvin_rees_chinamayalsia_trip (Accessed 28 May 2024)

30. Martin Booth. YTL have paid for flights, a hotel and meals for Rees in last seven months. *Bristol 24/7*, 8 August 2018. Available at: https://www.bristol247.com/news-and-features/news/ytl-pay-flight-hotel-meals-bristol-mayor-marvin-rees/ (Accessed 29 May 2024)

31. Mike Norton. Meet the man behind YTL Arena plans and why he's willing to invest millions into Bristol. *BristolLive*, 19 November 2019. Available at: EXCLUSIVE: Meet the man behind YTL Arena plans and why he's willing to invest millions into Bristol – Bristol Live (bristolpost.co.uk) (Accessed 28 May 2024)

32. Legal and General (L&G) meetings and emails (01/12/2017-31/01/2018). *WhatDoTheyKnow*, 21 January 2020. Available at: https://www.whatdotheyknow.com/request/legal_and_general_lg_meetings_an (Accessed 28 May 2024)

33. Bristol arena project – meetings and emails with YLT Corporation. *WhatDoTheyKnow*, 24 May 2018. Available at: https://www.whatdotheyknow.com/request/bristol_arena_project_meetings_a#incoming-1163971(Accessed 28 May 2024)

34. Esme Ashcroft. Private talks of a Bristol Arena at Filton started six months before the council claims. *BristolLive*, 13 August 2018. Available at: https://www.bristolpost.co.uk/news/bristol-news/private-talks-bristol-arena-filton-1890201 (Accessed 29 May 2024)

35. Bristol City Council Minutes of the Extraordinary Full Council, 3 September 2018. Available at: https://democracy. bristol.gov.uk/ieListDocuments.aspx?CId=142&MId=3330 (Accessed 28 May 2024)

36. Esme Ashcroft. Bristol Mayor votes to keep arena in city centre – but still looks set to scrap the project. *BristolLive*, 4 September 2018. Available at: https://www.bristolpost.co.uk/news/bristol-news/bristol-mayor-keep-arena-scrap-1967119 (Accessed 28 May 2024)

37. Bristol City Council. Decision details. Arena update. Available at: https://democracy.bristol.gov.uk/ieDecisionDetails. aspx?Id=361 (Accessed 29 May 2024)

38. Esmee Ashcroft. 'People elected me for my opinion': Marvin Rees remains defiant on ability to make arena decision. *BristolLive*, 16 August 2018. Available at: https://www.bristolpost.co.uk/news/bristol-news/people-elected-opinion-marvin-rees-1905500 (Accessed 29 May 2024)

39. Joanna Booth. Millions in cost to the taxpayer for the Brabazon arena. 3 May 2021. Available at: https://joannab. substack.com/p/millions-in-cost-to-the-taxpayer-for-the-brabazon-arena-e3985aa084a3 (Accessed 29 May 2023)

40. Bristol Temple Island redevelopment deal completed. *BBC News*, 31 August 2022. Available at: https://www.bbc. co.uk/news/uk-england-bristol-62737138 (Accessed 29 May 2024)

41. Bristol City Council. Report of the OSM board to cabinet re the arena VFM study outcomes. Cabinet Supplementary Information, 3 July 2018. Available at: https://democracy.bristol.gov.uk/ieListDocuments.aspx?CId=135&MId=3092 (Accessed 29 May 2024)

42. Bristol Arena will not open until 2026, says developer. *BBC News*, 16 January 2023. Available at: https://www.bbc. co.uk/news/uk-england-bristol-64292524 (Accessed 29 May 2024)

43. Estel Farell Roig. Bristol mayor Marvin Rees' speech at the Bristol Beacon in full. *BristolLive*, 14 March 2024. Available at: https://www.bristolpost.co.uk/news/bristol-news/bristol-mayor-marvin-rees-speech-9164218 (Accessed 29 May 2024)

44. Erin McCarthy. Roosevelt's "The Man in the Arena". *Mental Floss*, Mar 9, 2023. Available at: https://www.mentalfloss. com/article/63389/roosevelts-man-arena (Accessed 29 May 2024)

Disused and decaying buildings are currently on the site of a proposed out-of-scale development at St Mary le Port. Credit: Martin Booth, *Bristol24/7*

The evocative entrance to ruins of St Mary le Port. Credit: Suzanne Audrey

St Mary le Port: Something rotten at the historic heart of the city

Joe Banks, freelance writer who has written for *VICE* and *The Bristol Cable*, reveals a troubling lack of probity around large developments in Bristol and a need to restore public confidence in Bristol's planning system...

WHY WOULD BRISTOL do this to itself? That was the question baffling me in early 2022 when I first saw the recently approved plans for three large office blocks at the historic heart of the city. The jarring quality of these buildings, their bulky eight- and nine-storey commercial dimensions so out of scale with what remains of the Old City, left me with the sense that something peculiar had happened. They had a bullying presence, claustrophobically close to the 15th century tower of St Mary le Port and crowding out the famous grouping of church spires at the city's ancient core. With their bland, monolithic design they could have been dropped in from anywhere. At the time I had only a hazy awareness of planning and local governance issues in the city, but the proposed development at St Mary le Port became a portal through which some of the forces shaping Bristol came into much sharper focus.

I came to understand the political attempt to control planning by the mayoral administration, the wider penetration of local government by the development industry, the revolving door between the public and private sectors, and the increasing role of global institutional investors in Bristol. I saw the way that this is being facilitated by a tightly enmeshed professional network of consultants, developers, and corporate architects. Perhaps most shocking of all for the redevelopment of such a sensitive part of this great historic city was the apparent disdain for democratic accountability and due process.

Special qualities

From its medieval beginnings, Bristol's dynamic commercial character as a place of trade and industry mean that it has never stood still in terms of its built environment, but it has retained some very special qualities. Despite the destruction of the Second World War and a lot of infamously bad post-war development that followed, the centre of Bristol still throws up moments of startling beauty. Its rich architectural inheritance covers every period from the Norman Romanesque to the modern day. Its special character also lies in its undulating topography and the openness of its largely midrise skyline, the watery expanses of the floating harbour and the Avon New Cut, and the glimpses of fields and wooded hillsides beyond the city's edge. This makes it a uniquely stimulating place to be, with a human scale sympathetic to mental health and wellbeing, and in marked contrast to the oppressive urban character typical of so many other British city centres.

The site for the proposed St Mary le Port development is beside the crossroads of High Street, Wine Street, Broad Street and Corn Street, that formed the original layout at the centre of the late Saxon settlement. This is where Bristol began, on the high ground beside a crossing point of the River Avon. To the east is Castle Park, once a tightly-packed warren of half-timbered medieval buildings and the city's busy shopping and entertainment district before it was devastated by German bombing in 1940. Directly across High Street to the west is the dense concentration of Victorian and Georgian listed buildings that survived in the Old City, with its streets and alleyways of Bath stone.

The three derelict buildings currently standing on the St Mary le Port site are the Norwich Union Building, Bank House and Bank of England House. Built in the 1960s and 1970s, they are in a shabby condition and were never much loved. They wrap around the 15th century church tower and low-standing fragments of wall which are all that survived from the bombing.

At the time of writing there is still some doubt about whether the recently proposed office block scheme, with retail and food outlets at ground floor, will actually get built. Following the approval given by a planning committee in December 2022, Bristol Civic Society – who, along with Historic England, had strongly objected to the scheme on the grounds that it would dominate the Old City – made a request to the Secretary of State for the application to be called-in and assessed by the planning inspectorate [1]. When that request was rejected in September 2022, planning permission was granted. But nothing has happened on site since. The developers are still making positive noises in the local press [2], but they and the investors may well be deliberating on whether to push the button for construction in uncertain times or settle with the rising value of their assets. Either way, the story of this development's journey through the planning process offers an illuminating insight into the city's planning and development regime through this period.

Ambition and energy

Marvin Rees had said in his first State of the City address in 2016 that he wanted Bristol's skyline to grow and that tall buildings communicated "ambition and energy" [3]. This was a radical departure from his predecessor George Ferguson, the architect enamoured with mid-rise European cities who had come to prominence in the 1970s as part of the campaign to resist the crass development that was happening in the city at the time, including a boom in speculative high-rise office buildings.

Rees' announcement signalled an intent to take an interventionist role in planning issues, also reflected in the fact that he gave himself the Cabinet portfolio for planning. It was an approach that would come to strain the legally mandated separation of a local authority's executive from its planning function. But the first step was not in itself an unreasonable one: to begin a review of the local development plan. These are the policies and site allocations that, along with the National Planning Policy Framework, all new planning applications are assessed against, and need to be updated from time to time. Brought in to oversee this process was newly-elected Labour councillor Nicola Beech, who joined Rees' Cabinet in July 2017 with the portfolio for Spatial Planning and City Design. Significantly, Beech had come directly from the lobbying and PR firm JBP, specifically working for developers in the planning process. The year she joined the council, she was working to get a controversial 24-storey tower built on Cardiff's waterfront [4].

The review of Bristol's local plan started with a 'call-out' to developers in 2017, asking them to make representations about sites in the city they were interested in developing. The US-based global asset manager

Federated Hermes expressed interest in the St Mary le Port site. Together with the BT Pension Scheme as investor and MEPC as developer, they have built large-scale commercial developments across the UK in the last decade, including offices and business parks. In September 2018 they bought the leasehold for two of the buildings at St Mary le Port: Bank of England House and Bank House. One wonders what the discussions with Bristol City Council, who continue to own the freehold, had been up to this point. Large office block developments had been concentrated in recent times outside the historic centre at Temple Quay. And there was never going to be a possibility of this developer of exclusively commercial real estate providing any much-needed residential use. But in February 2020 the final building was purchased and later in the year a joint statement was released by the developers and Councillor Beech announcing plans to redevelop the site [5].

Friends of Castle Park?

Council minutes show that, during the same month as the first two leaseholds were bought up in 2018, a council Area Committee meeting had taken place, attended by Nicola Beech, where it was noted that: "Castle Park does not have a support/friends group, so there is no one lobbying on its behalf. It would be helpful for members and officers to set one up." [6]

A 'Friends of Castle Park' Facebook group appeared the following week. I first became aware of Friends of Castle Park two years later, through seeing references in the local media to their support for the St Mary le Port scheme [7]. Despite the fact that it had remained simply a Facebook group, with no formal structure, no voting and no meetings of members, this 'community group' was given prominence as a key stakeholder. No doubt conscious of the grassroots campaigns to oppose previous proposals, the developer featured the group's support prominently in their online public consultation presentations. Friends of Castle Park were mentioned three times in the developer's short statement read out at the planning committee meeting, and the founder of the Facebook group also provided a statement to the planning committee, claiming the ratio of members supporting the proposals was 10 to 1. This figure was later questioned as it had been arrived at by counting emojis on the Facebook page [8,9]. Nevertheless, two Labour councillors directly referenced the group's support during the meeting when they declared their reasons for voting to approve the application.

Telling a different story

Having seen several Freedom of Information requests about 'interference' in the planning process for St Mary le Port and other sites across the city [10,11,12], I put in my own request for the formal pre-application correspondence between the council and the developers [13]. This revealed that all the way through this five-month process, the council's planning managers and specialist urban design officers were telling the developers that the height, scale and massing of the scheme did not comply with policy and was unacceptable. The final pre-application response stating this position came from the Head of Development Management, Gary Collins, who a few months later would, contrariwise, be encouraging councillors on the planning committee to vote through an unchanged proposal.

The officer report was written by Collins and planning manager Peter Westbury. Westbury presented the case to councillors for approving the scheme alongside Collins at the meeting in December 2021. He had been an officer in Bristol City Council's planning department since 2008 but became Team Manager for Major Applications in October 2016, five months after Marvin Rees came into office. Westbury was also the Chair of Trustees at Hope Chapel, the same church in Hotwells that Rees was a member of during his mayoralty [14,15].

Contrary to accepted practice, the view of the City Design team was excluded from the officer's report. These were the council's internal heritage and place-making specialists that had, along with planning officers, strongly opposed the height and scale of the scheme. In my view, the exclusion of a conservation officer's opinion from the councillors assessing a development at the historic core of the city – that was recognised to cause harm to listed heritage assets – would have made the report vulnerable at a judicial review. Mrs Justice Lang's judgement, delivered earlier that same year in *Kinsey, R (On the Application Of) v London Borough Of Lewisham*, quashed planning permission for a series of residential blocks in London because of exactly the same omission from the case officer [16].

Having left out the council's own internal specialists, the officer's report leaned heavily on feedback from a Design West review panel that had been positive about the scheme. The developer's planning statement also emphasised Design West's support for the height of the proposed buildings.

With the encouragement of the council, the services of Design West, a design and placemaking consultancy based on the harbourside, are engaged during the pre-application process by developers of major schemes in Bristol. Their 'independent' feedback from development experts is meant to drive up design quality during the pre-application process. But a closer look at the make-up of the review panel raises serious questions about its ability or desire to provide the kind of rigorous, independent assessment that is claimed.

The architects for St Mary le Port, Feilden Clegg Bradley Studios (FCBS), had designed several of the mayoral administration's most heavily-backed schemes. This included the University of Bristol's 'Enterprise Campus' in the emerging 'Temple Quarter', the masterplan for YTL's residential development at Filton airfield, and the high-rise 'Boatyard' scheme on the river beneath Totterdown [17,18,19].

One member of the five-person review panel from Design West was a director of a landscape architecture firm that was working at the time with FCBS on the 'Boatyard' project. Another was a director of Arup's Bristol office and had recently been arranging a deal for Arup to become a 'Strategic Partner' to Bristol City Council, providing consultancy services for infrastructure projects. This was a policy managed by Stephen Peacock, then the council's Executive Director of Growth and Regeneration. Furthermore, the chair of the review panel, who wrote the feedback letters to the developers, was also the chair of Bristol Beacon's 'Strategic Advisory Group', a small board overseeing the venue's refurbishment project, which was spiralling massively over budget and requiring vast amounts of extra funding from the council [20].

The incestuousness of these networks, shot through with potential conflicts of interest, can also be seen in the fact that the director of the Bristol-based communications consultancy working for the developer on St Mary le Port, Marengo, was a former colleague of councillor Beech's from JBP. The 'public consultation' Marengo ran for St Mary le Port lasted less than three weeks in April 2021, with the planning application being submitted to the council's planning department the following month. Meeting notes released through an FOI request show that the May submission was planned in advance of the consultation and was always going to be too short a timeframe to make any significant changes to the scheme's design based on feedback from the public [21].

Off the record

Internal email correspondence then shows various off-the-record meetings being arranged after the application had been submitted. In July, after Historic England had formally objected to the proposal, Marengo contacted Beech to ask if she'll "have a coffee" with the developer's commercial director, which she agrees to [22]. Referring to a less-than-positive article in the *Bristol Post* that had been published a few days previously – 'New offices planned for Bristol park likened to 'giant slabs' as opinion divided ahead of council decision' [23] – Marengo also asked Beech if the developers might meet the mayor. The answer came back from the Mayor's Office that it "doesn't need to be Marvin right now". Instead, a meeting with Kevin Slocombe – Head of the Mayor's Office – and Stephen Peacock, was arranged. I was told by the council that no minutes or notes for these meetings exists.

Stephen Peacock, then Executive Director of Growth and Regeneration, carried out a review of the planning system shortly after coming into Bristol City Council in late 2019. Out of this emerged regular 'driving development' meetings, which he chaired and were attended by Kevin Slocombe and the mayor's closest advisors [24]. Without any scrutiny from the public or elected councillors, these meetings focused on ways to progress particular developments designated as 'mayoral priorities', one of which was St Mary le Port. Inevitably this weight of expectation would be felt by both planning officers and Labour councillors on planning committees, despite the fact that both sets of decision-makers are meant to operate on a non-party political basis and exercise their independent judgement based on the Local Plan and the National Planning Policy Framework.

There was clearly disquiet at this time among some opposition councillors about this approach. In September 2021, the most senior planning officer, Zoe Wilcox, contacted Peacock and Slocombe to say that the chair of one of the planning committees had brought an agenda item to their regular meeting: 'Politicisation of the planning process'. Wilcox went on to say, "Obviously in days gone by I'd have had Cllr Beech/the Cabinet Member join me and give some cover. Should I invite someone from the Mayor's Office or will that just look odd?"

At this point Nicola Beech no longer had the Spatial Planning brief (although that had not stopped her being a key point of contact for the St Mary le Port developers). Slocombe's response was that the officer should not engage with the issue but refer the councillor to Full Council if they wanted to raise it.

The correspondence between the planning department, the Mayor's Office and Stephen Peacock during this period gives the unavoidable impression of close working relationships that placed considerable pressure on the Head of the Service, Gary Collins. This is captured particularly vividly in a brief exchange that occurred following the planning committee meeting for St Mary le Port in December 2021 [25]. Minutes after permission was granted, Collins – who, remember, had expressed a fundamental objection to the proposed scheme over months of pre-application meetings and formal correspondence with the developers – emailed Peacock, Slocombe and Wilcox:

> "Hi All, You may know already but DC Cttee resolved to grant PP! Vote was 5/3 with one abstention."
> Peacock replied: "Fantastic! Head down so missed it. Thanks to you and the team. Great work."

Stephen Peacock was made Chief Executive of Bristol City Council the following year. Towards the end of 2022, he and the mayoral administration brought an item to Cabinet that would break up City Design as a distinct entity and create a new Chief Planner role with overarching management powers for the planning system. A former colleague of Peacock's from the South West Regional Development Agency, Simone Wilding, took up the new position in May 2023. This reform – heavily criticised at the time by figures such as Celia Davis of the Town and Country Planning Association, who submitted a statement to that Cabinet meeting – appeared to be another move to centralise control and further remove potential checks on developers in the planning process.

The new Chief Planner was also tasked with reducing the huge backlog of planning applications that had built up. But, unable to retain experienced staff or adequately replace them, progress has been slow, resulting in the government putting the department into 'special measures' in March 2024 [26]. A further consequence of the continuing dysfunction has been the almost complete disappearance of planning enforcement across the city, with nearly all resources focused on reducing the backlog [27].

Reflection

The St Mary le Port story highlights a troubling lack of probity around large developments in Bristol and the need to restore integrity, transparency and public confidence in Bristol's planning system. But it is also about the bad outcomes the current model has been producing.

'Getting stuff done' was the mantra of Marvin Rees' tenure as mayor, and the scale of development taking place across the city was pitched as an ambitious response to the pressure of a growing population, the need for economic development, and a chronic housing crisis. But the largely private developer-led model has not been providing the affordable housing required to make a dent in the housing crisis (indeed it cannot, because that would require the industry, dominated by big players, to supply enough housing to drive down their own prices), while the urgency and intensity of the problem has been used to make lower standards of building design acceptable to planning committees. Meanwhile, the ongoing expansion of the universities, driven by a fragile dependency on ever-larger numbers of overseas students, is currently the largest contributory factor to both population growth and new development across the city centre's scarce brownfield sites. Bland student accommodation blocks sprout with increasing frequency, at ever larger heights, but never quick enough to meet demand.

Cities have to evolve and change but Bristol is in danger of throwing away something precious that, once lost, cannot be recovered, and for reasons that don't stack up. I believe the city has taken an important step in the right direction by abolishing the mayoral system, whose concentration of top-down power was vulnerable to pressure from vested interests. But the same external pressures remain. Councillors recently elected to the council with its new committee system need to make it a priority that the planning and urban design functions are fit for purpose. They have many other serious issues pressing on a chronically underfunded local authority but the profound consequences for the city if this isn't tackled should not be underestimated.

I would encourage those councillors to reflect on the words of the Portuguese former politician and writer Bruno Maçães, who was a guest at Marvin Rees' annual State of the City address in 2019 [28]. A perceptive and well-travelled outside observer, Maçães had recently been visiting new cities being built in China. During the panel discussion that followed the mayoral address, the Chair, Andrew Kelly, asked the guest how 'traditional cities' like Bristol could compete with these futuristic new metropolises. Maçães responded:

> *"It's a tough world out there. And Bristol has to compete. What I worry about – and I want to make this point also to the Mayor – this need to compete, this need to be as productive, as efficient, as modern, as future-oriented as you possibly can, has the danger that cities start to be thought of almost as smart gadgets that have to be up to the latest standard. They all start to resemble each other. I see that in China a lot. They lose their past and their identity because that's the only way to survive and to be successful. And I wonder what we can do about that.*
>
> *Sometimes I think public authorities, local authorities, think that it's up to the people to preserve the identity of Bristol and up to the authorities to make it competitive. But I would say that people alone cannot do that. And we need cities as a whole, and we need local authorities to also be concerned – among all the other goals that the Mayor listed, and they're all very important – about preserving the identity, the uniqueness, the special character of a city like Bristol and not leave it to chance, because if it's left to chance, it might not survive."*

If Bristol isn't to throw away its precious inheritance and become like any other generic British, North American or even new Chinese city, it has to find a better balance in managing inward investment. This means negotiating positively but firmly with developers, being truly ambitious for design and placemaking excellence, and resisting the idea that blandness is the inevitable price of progress. The historic centre should not be treated as an asset for global finance capital to extract maximum returns from. This is a threat to the soul of the city *and* its future economic success, potentially creating an 'anywhere' place that won't foster a sense of belonging or encourage people to visit.

The government's introduction of Design Codes needs to be embraced seriously, with these being shaped through public consultation and having the express and unashamed purpose of creating beautiful places, with popular appeal, that can stand the test of time [29]. Design Codes have the aim of establishing clear design expectations at the outset of the planning process. This should have a benefit for developers that are willing to comply with these rules, through speeding up (and therefore lowering the cost) of their journeys through the planning system. There needs to be genuine engagement from the council with the Office of Place, the recently established arms-length government department tasked with helping local planning authorities implement these reforms.

These are some of the practical ways we can try to safeguard the special character of Bristol for future generations. If we drift on as we are, it will be gone pretty quickly. It will take real energy and ambition, as well as adequate resourcing from central government. And it will require ongoing scrutiny of local government, which remains deeply vulnerable to cronyism, short-term thinking and the predations of the private sector with its legions of consultants and lobbying firms. A clear-eyed and critical view on how the city council, the planning system and the broader development ecosystem are functioning needs to be allied to positive, imaginative visions of the city that offer a constructive way forward. Having learnt from its wartime losses and its postwar mistakes, drawing on its historic genius for radical innovation, Bristol should lead the fightback against the forces that have made so much of Britain's built environment a soulless mess. ∎

REFERENCES

1. BBC News (2022). Bristol: Public inquiry sought over plans for historical area. Available at: https://www.bbc.co.uk/news/uk-england-bristol-60203879 (Accessed: 25 April 2024).

2. Bristol Live (2024). Bristol's biggest eyesore buildings won't be demolished until later this year. Available at: https://www.bristolpost.co.uk/news/bristol-news/bristols-biggest-eyesore-buildings-wont-9083979 (Accessed: 25 April 2024).

3. Bristol Ideas (2016). Marvin Rees: State of the City 2016: A City for All (Bristol Festival of Ideas). Available at: https://www.youtube.com/watch?v=h5RlaH7ZYtw&ab_channel=BristolIdeas (Accessed: 25 April 2024).

4. Gorkana (2016). Associated British Ports appoints JBP for Cardiff Bay development. Available at: https://www.gorkana.com/2016/09/associated-british-ports-appoints-jbp-for-cardiff-bay-development/ (Accessed: 25 April 2024).

5. Bristol Live (2020). What's happening with eyesore buildings at Castle Park as new owner named. Available at: https://www.bristolpost.co.uk/news/bristol-news/whats-happening-eyesore-buildings-castle-4614867 (Accessed: 25 April 2024).

6. Bristol City Council (2018). Minutes of the Area Committee 4, 13 September 2018. Available at: https://democracy.bristol.gov.uk/documents/s31723/Minutes%20Public%20Pack%2013092018%20Area%20Committee%204.pdf. (Accessed: 25 April 2024).

7. Bristol 24/7 (2022). The Old City has been abandoned, neglected and unloved for many years. Available at: https://www.bristol247.com/opinion/your-say/the-old-city-has-been-abandoned-neglected-and-unloved-for-many-years/ (Accessed: 25 April 2024).

8. Edwards, M (2022). Community Support for Castle Park development was overstated, claim members of local group. The Bristol Cable. Available at: Castle Park development support overstated: local group members (thebristolcable.org) (Accessed 09 May 2024)

9. Banks, J (2024). St Mary le Port: A Bristol planning case study. Available at: https://joebanks.substack.com/p/st-mary-le-port-a-bristol-planning (Accessed: 25 April 2024).

10. WhatDoTheyKnow (2022). St Mary le port interference. Available at: https://www.whatdotheyknow.com/request/st_mary_le_port_interference?nocache=incoming-1977045 (Accessed: 25 April 2024).

11. WhatDoTheyKnow (2022). I want to know what Kevin Slocombe is saying to the planning department. Available at: https://www.whatdotheyknow.com/request/i_want_to_know_what_kevin_slocom#incoming-1987336 (Accessed:

25 April 2024).

12. *WhatDoTheyKnow* (2022). Council cabinet interference with the planning process. Available at: https://www.whatdotheyknow.com/request/council_cabinet_interference_wit#incomin (Accessed: 25 April 2024).

13. *WhatDoTheyKnow* (2022). Pre-application documents for St Mary le Port. Available at: https://www.whatdotheyknow.com/request/pre_application_documents_for_st#outgoing-1455566 (Accessed 25 April 2024).

14. Premier Christianity (2021). 'I used to be quite literal about my faith. It's much messier now' – Marvin Rees, Mayor of Bristol. Available at: https://www.premierchristianity.com/interviews/i-used-to-be-quite-literal-about-my-faith-its-much-messier-now-marvin-rees-mayor-of-bristol/5282.article (Accessed: 25 April 2024).

15. Charity Commission (2024). Hope Chapel. Available at: https://register-of-charities.charitycommission.gov.uk/charity-search/-/charity-details/4044473/full-print (Accessed 25 April 2024).

16. Local Government Lawyer (2021). High Court judge quashes grant of planning permission for 110-unit scheme. Available at: https://www.localgovernmentlawyer.co.uk/planning/401-planning-news/47140-high-court-judge-quashes-grant-of-planning-permission-for-110-unit-scheme (Accessed 25 April 2024).

17. Feilden Clegg Bradley Studios. An inspiring campus embedded in the culture and fabric of Bristol. Available at: https://fcbstudios.com/projects/university-of-bristol-temple-quarter-enterprise-campus/ (Accessed 25 April 2024).

18. Architects Journal (2019). Green light for 'thoughtful' 278-home FCBS Bristol scheme. Available at: https://www.architectsjournal.co.uk/news/green-light-for-thoughtful-278-home-fcbs-bristol-scheme (Accessed 25 April 2024).

19. Construction Enquirer (2019). Green light for 17-floor Bristol housing scheme. Available at: https://www.constructionenquirer.com/2019/07/09/green-light-for-17-floor-bristol-housing-scheme/ (Accessed 25 April 2024).

20. BBC News. (17 January 2023). Bristol concert venue revamp costs soar again to £132m. Available at: https://www.bbc.co.uk/news/uk-england-bristol-64302085 (Accessed: 25 April 2024).

21. *WhatDoTheyKnow* (2022). St Mary le port interference. Available at: https://www.whatdotheyknow.com/request/st_mary_le_port_interference?nocache=incoming-1977045 (Accessed: 25 April 2024).

22. Ibid.

23. Bristol Live (2021). New offices planned for Bristol park likened to 'giant slabs' as opinion divided ahead of council decision. Available at: https://www.bristolpost.co.uk/news/bristol-news/new-offices-planned-bristol-park-5686385 (Accessed 25 April 2024).

24. *WhatDoTheyKnow* (2022). Driving Development Meetings. Available at: https://www.whatdotheyknow.com/request/driving_development_meetings. (Accessed 25 April 2024).

25. *WhatDoTheyKnow* (2022). St Mary le port interference. Available at: https://www.whatdotheyknow.com/request/st_mary_le_port_interference?nocache=incoming-1977045. (Accessed: 25 April 2024).

26. Bristol Live (2024). Bristol's failing planning department taken over by Government. Available at: https://www.bristolpost.co.uk/news/bristol-news/bristols-failing-planning-department-taken-9145539. (Accessed: 25 April 2024).

27. *Bristol Live* (2024). Planning enforcement in Bristol has almost no staff to investigate cases. Available at: https://www.bristolpost.co.uk/news/bristol-news/planning-enforcement-bristol-almost-no-9234425. (Accessed: 25 April 2024).

28. Bristol Ideas (2019). Delivering for Bristol: The Mayor's Annual State of the City Address and Debate. Available at: https://www.youtube.com/watch?v=zvmwTo8TDkE&ab_channel=BristolIdeas. (Accessed 25 April 2024).

29. GOV.UK (2023). Creating a design code. Available at: https://www.gov.uk/guidance/creating-a-design-code. (Accessed 25 April 2024).

Note: Joe Banks' full-length investigation into the St Mary le Port development can be found at www.joebanks.substack.com

A beautiful day in Bristol Zoo Gardens. Credit: Tom Jones

Protestors object to the Zoo's plans to sell their historic site for housing.
Credit: Mia Vines Booth, Bristol24/7

Sell out at Bristol Zoo Gardens

Tom Jones describes building a campaign to save Bristol Zoo at its Clifton site, while Alistair Sawday and Iain Boyd set out an alternative vision for Bristol's historic gardens...

———

Save Bristol Zoo Gardens

PICTURE THE SCENE. It is 2062 and I, Tom Jones, am walking past Bristol Zoo's iconic entrance with my grandchildren. They turnaround and ask me: *"What's behind those walls Grandad and why does it say, 'Zoo' when there aren't any animals in there?"* I answer: *"Once upon a time there was a Zoo here, Bristol Zoo. It was 186 years old and everyone in Bristol loved it very much. But the people who were in charge chose to move the Zoo to another home outside of the city without asking anyone what they thought. The site was closed for 10 years and when it did finally reopen, the gardens were supposed to be for everyone, but after a few years the residents changed the rules. Now they're private and I haven't been in there for over 30 years. They were the most beautiful gardens I have ever seen. How terribly sad that the people running the Zoo and the city back then didn't have the vision or imagination to find another way to keep the Zoo in Bristol and open for everyone."*

Now. Rewind to 5pm, Thursday 12 May 2022. I find myself in one of my favourite places in the whole world, Bristol Zoo. We are in the midst of a mini-heatwave and today has been one of those astonishing English summer's days, hazy but clear blue skies, a crisp yet simultaneously soft light, and rarely-felt heat has been beating down on the Zoo's many visitors throughout the day. But it is quiet now, 30 minutes before closing, most people have left for the day and I am standing in dappled shade, created by an array of extraordinarily majestic trees. Everywhere I look

I see trees and flowers, gardens astonishingly mature, verdant and lush. And wildlife. Exotic wildlife. I'm in the middle of Bristol. I'm also in Eden. I don't know how many times I have stood here and yet it never ceases to move me.

I have my 4-year-old son on my shoulders and we are watching meerkats scurrying around right in front of us while, in the near distance, we can see golden-headed lion tamarin monkeys swinging through the trees. As I stand here in these sacred surroundings, I cannot believe that in just over two months' time these gardens are to be closed to the public for *at least* five years, sold to a private developer and turned into a housing development. If the Zoo's current proposal gets planning permission and goes ahead, where I'm standing right now will become someone's multi-million-pound private home and garden, as will the iconic herbaceous border just behind me which will be bulldozed. Until then, this unique slice of paradise, 186 years of historic fabric, woven into the heart of the city, will be a building site. And afterwards, it will never be the same again.

Earlier today, my son and I left our home and travelled to the Zoo by bike. Fifteen minutes later, we were making eye contact with an Asiatic lion just metres in front of us. We then walked a short way along the famous top terrace and watched red pandas peacefully munching on bamboo. Shortly afterwards we were spending time with South American fur seals moving through invitingly crystal-clear salt water. I look up and see the graceful architecture of Clifton College watching over. A phenomenal juxtaposition of natural and urban, of people and wildlife; Bristol Zoological Gardens are unique. They are a jewel in the crown of this city *we all love*. They are 186 years of the natural world, history and collective memories contained within a 12-acre site in the heart of a city. Once they are sold off to a private developer to be turned into housing, they are gone forever and not coming back.

Someone had to do something

It was these experiences, both real and imagined, which led me to where I am now. Bristol Zoo is closed to the public but it still has not been sold. Behind the closed doors it is still a Zoo housing a family of gorillas. On the other side of the boarded-up gates remains a stunningly beautiful botanical garden. But we the people of Bristol, are no longer allowed inside, however much we might dream of walking on the hallowed ground once more.

When I heard the fateful news that Bristol Zoo was to close on 27 November 2020, my first thought was, *"It's not going to happen, someone will step in and do something, because it literally, cannot happen. Bristol Zoo cannot close."* But almost two years later, and after much soul-searching, I finally realised that no one else *was* going to do anything. So in that moment, I decided that I would at least try to do something. I didn't know what, I just knew I had to do something.

Since then, a lot has happened. In the following months, I undertook hundreds of hours of research into the Zoo's annual reports, accounts and strategic plans to understand their sudden change in direction. It was very much a labour of love as I am a working musician and parent, not an investigative reporter, so a lot of the work was done in the early hours. I started making notes on all the research I was doing and I wrote a blog which I posted online. I also started the petition 'Save Bristol Zoological Gardens from Becoming a Private Housing Estate' [1] whilst my wife was in labour with our second child. It's safe to say she was not happy but I did stop well before the baby came!

Up until that point, I had casually spoken to many staff members at Bristol Zoo whilst visiting regularly, and I had continually picked up on the fact that something just wasn't right about the impending closure. But I knew that I needed access, inside information, if I was going to get anywhere. After trying and failing with a few different staff members, the breakthrough came just a couple of weeks before the Zoo closed in late August 2022 when I received a message on Facebook from someone who had seen my blog and petition online. At that stage, I didn't know for sure if they worked for the Zoo, but I had my suspicions. They simply said that like me, they cared very much about the site and wanted to talk.

We agreed to meet a few days later on the bench opposite the lions at 3.30pm. As I sat down at 3.25pm, I felt like I was in a movie, looking out for someone but not quite knowing who. As they approached and I caught their eye, I realised they were a senior staff member from what they were wearing. We only talked for 10 minutes as they said they were taking a serious risk by talking to me at all. They told me that having read what I'd written, I was way ahead of the game and that many people within Bristol Zoological Society were deeply unhappy with what had been going on but couldn't speak out publicly because of fear of retribution or because many staff had signed quasi non-disclosure agreements, precluding them from talking about the Zoo's closure. They said that although they couldn't speak out themselves, they wanted to help me get the truth out there because I had a voice. We agreed to meet properly at the Alma Tavern the following week, just days before the Zoo closed.

After that first meeting at the Alma, where another staff member joined us, we met up regularly and developed a close working relationship which subsequently became a friendship. The information I was able to elicit, as well as the questions I could finally ask and have answered, led to my writing a report investigating the reasons behind the decision to close Bristol Zoo [2].

I was initially motivated by a very strong feeling that closing the world's fifth oldest Zoo, and selling it off to become a housing development, was morally bankrupt. But from my continuing research, and as I began to find out what had been going in within the Society, I was also driven on by a dawning perception that a great injustice had been perpetrated. The past two years have been an extraordinary journey of discovery. I have spent several thousand hours working on this, along the way talking to over 40 Bristol Zoological Society employees, both past and present, current and former Bristol Zoological Society trustees, as well as an array of internationally renowned Zoological and Conservation experts.

I started the petition, which has over 11,600 signatures, and co-founded the 'Save Bristol Zoo Gardens' (SBZG) campaign with Alastair Sawday and Iain Boyd [3]. Amongst other things, it helped generate over 500 objections to the Zoo's planning application, and staged two public meetings to raise awareness of our campaign [4]. We organised and led a protest march in objection to the Zoo's plans to sell their historic site for housing [5]. I have crowdfunded over £27,000 (with a target of £50,000) to help me continue with my work on an alternative plan for Bristol Zoological Society to adopt [6].

A monumental error

All of this inspired a disgruntled Bristol Zoological Society shareholder to transfer one of their shares to me to help me further in my quest to save the Zoo. From this new enlightened position, I believe it is beyond reasonable doubt that Bristol Zoological Society's current strategy to sell Bristol Zoo Gardens and invest everything they have, including the proceeds from their prize asset, into the renamed 'Bristol Zoo Project' in South Gloucestershire is a monumental error which far from ensuring the long term survival of Bristol Zoological Society, exposes the Society to existential risk.

I am shortly to publish a second report which interrogates the original decision to close Bristol Zoo, as well as all the projections upon which Bristol Zoological Society are predicting their future success. The report finds almost all the projections to be questionable. It also finds that Bristol Zoological Society's decision in 2020 to sell Bristol Zoo Gardens in Clifton, and invest all the capital raised in their visitor attraction in South Gloucestershire, was based on limited information. This calls into question whether the original decision to close and sell Bristol Zoo Gardens should be revisited by Bristol Zoological Society's shareholders and trustees.

Until 2020, Bristol Zoological Society's strategy was to retain and invest in both of its sites. What changed, so suddenly and so dramatically? The Society says Covid forced it to radically rethink its strategy. But for a Zoo which had been open for almost 200 years, survived two World Wars and welcomed 90 million visitors, was being closed for a few months enough to provoke such a radical rethink as to sell their core asset and Bristol's crown jewels? Would we accept Clifton Suspension Bridge being permanently closed and sold down the river during a global pandemic? If the answer to these questions is no, then what is the motivation for selling Bristol Zoo Gardens?

Why does Bristol Zoological Society say its housing development plan for Bristol Zoo Gardens is to give the public continued access to the gardens, when in reality the Society knows it can offer no long-term guarantee of that public access? As a conservation charity, how does the Society feel about felling 156 of its own trees at Bristol Zoo Gardens and bulldozing the herbaceous border enjoyed by generations? Do the purported gains of building at Cribbs Causeway, infrastructure that already exists in Clifton, outweigh the irreplaceable loss of the world's fifth oldest Zoo site?

Where do we draw the line?

What makes towns and cities what they are, and what do we want them to be in the future? Is pretty much anything up for grabs to become housing? When I wrote to the mayor about the closure of Bristol Zoo in the summer of 2022, Marvin Rees replied: "The fact that we can use the existing buildings for conversion to unique and much needed homes is exactly the right outcome for the site."

Bristol Zoo themselves frequently talk about how proud they are to be building "much-needed homes for Clifton and Bristol" [7]. But is it the right outcome for the site? If more homes are so necessary in Clifton and Bristol, why not start building on the Downs as well? Our parks? Ashton Court? These spaces are great assets to *all* of our mental health, they help us find perspective in the busyness of modern life. Bristol Museum, M Shed, Cabot Tower, Central Library, Bristol Old Vic?

Where do we draw the line if we continue on this road of travel and value housing developments above all else? When do you start undoing what makes a place what it is? Surely we can all agree that some places are just too important and valuable – in a strictly *uneconomic* sense – to be turned into housing? Do we want housing developers, whose primary motivation is profit, to get their hands on these spaces that belong to all of us?

When asked about whether cinema-going had a place in the 21st century, Steven Spielberg said: *"A great story can get you on your iPhone, but I prefer a super-size screen because, what you get with that experience leaving home to go out to the movies is, you get basically to be with civilisation, to sit with strangers, who probably in real life don't agree with anything that you agree with. But it doesn't matter because you may agree on one thing and that's what's coming off the screen, what's coming out of that soundtrack, the themes. There may be common ground found in movie theatres between people and ideologies that are so far apart in everyday life, but all come together to share one single experience. You can't get that at home on a television screen, you can in a movie theatre."* [8]

I think you can extrapolate that argument to Bristol Zoo. Visitors at Bristol Zoo represented a diverse cross-section of society. It gave people across Bristol a reason to visit Clifton. At zoos, just like Steven Spielberg says about cinemas, strangers with different ideologies, backgrounds and experiences, people you may not agree with anything else about in life, can share and be united by the same experience of making eye contact with a roaring lion, a munching gorilla, a playful seal or a cheeky meerkat. In that moment, you have common ground and frequently look at each other and smile. You can't get that at home on a television screen watching a David Attenborough documentary, no matter how good it is.

Bristol Zoo's move to the Wild Place site in South Gloucestershire means access will be mostly limited to people with cars. Closing Bristol Zoo is erecting barriers for many people who live in the city – young and old – many of whom will need to make a difficult and off-putting drive *out* of the city.

Sir David Attenborough once said: "No one will protect what they don't care about, and no one will care about what they have never experienced". Taking the Zoo out of the heart of Bristol may mean that fewer people from Bristol will have the chance to experience amazing, exotic and endangered wildlife and consequently may not want to protect it.

On 26 April 2023, six out of nine members of Bristol City Council's Development Control A Committee took the historic decision to grant provisional planning permission for Bristol Zoological Gardens to be turned into a housing development [9]. Given the well documented backlog of applications in Bristol City Council's planning department, how was an application as complex and detailed as Bristol Zoological Society's proposals for Bristol Zoo Gardens able to gain planning permission with such apparent ease and relative speed?

As of now, that planning permission is vulnerable to a Judicial Review but, should it stand, how will history judge that decision for Bristol?

Sometimes in life you see something, and you just know instinctively, you feel deep down, that it's not right. You just know. Going to Bristol Zoo in its final few weeks before it closed was like that. One of my son's friends recently said to me: "*I miss the Zoo.*" So do I. And I want it back. Bristol Zoo has not been sold and until the keys have changed hands and the money has been transferred, that is still possible. If the Zoo's trustees can summon up the courage to take back control, we can have our Zoo back.

A safe, natural retreat for the next century

Bristol's beloved and ancient Zoo has closed, most of the animals and staff gone, and the beautiful 12-acre site is threatened by development. Tom Jones continues his campaign for the Clifton site to be reopened as a more modern zoo. Meanwhile we, Allastair Sawday and Iain Boyd, together with other members of Save Bristol Gardens Alliance, have set out to find an alternative vision for this magnificent and precious site, one which will do justice to the original dreams of the founders rather than to the property market.

Developers v Bristol?

Bristolians have long battled against developers, against the invasion of our beautiful city by crass profiteering, mediocre vision and craven bureaucracy. These battles are immediate, compelling, exhausting, and usually won by those with deep pockets.

The battles have mostly been fought in the last 50 years, triggered by the destruction of so much during the last war, the dominance of the motor car and a new enthusiasm for modernist ideas in architecture. The main influence in planning was road engineering. Indeed, the City Engineer ran the planning department! So it is hardly surprising that historic buildings all over the city were crushed to make way for ribbons of asphalt. So powerful were the road builders that they even planned, in the 1970s, to force a major highway through the city, along and over the docks and through Clifton. The City Council cheered them on until a small group of objectors challenged the plans and won, after a titanic struggle against the odds [10]. Imagine the harbour part-filled, a dual-carriageway striding along it and through some of our loveliest places. Bristol came close to losing much of its soul.

Most of us are unaware how touch-and-go it has been. For example, a multi-storey car-park was intended for the Avon Gorge below the hotel, but was fought off by a local group in the early 1970s. This can be seen as the starting point for Bristol's conservation movement, which went on to save the ferries, the harbourside cranes, churches, Georgian houses a'plenty and more. Once we have lost handsome buildings and public places, they very rarely return – in any form. New developments that nourish the community are as rare as hen's teeth.

A simple truth about development is that it is frequently a matter of private companies seizing an opportunity and dressing it up in jargon: 'planning gain', 'public realm improvements', and nods towards 'community engagement'. There is often a sense of urgency generated by the developers, whereas the community is often happy to wait – for years if need be. The best development practice involves city (or neighbourhood) plans, real consultation, and then competition.

There is another angle to the sale-and-development pattern to be repeated with Bristol Zoo Gardens. Andrew Marr wrote a powerful piece last year called 'The Idiot Rich are taking over our cities' [11]. Nobody is suggesting that it is they who will buy into the Zoo's proposed housing, but many will certainly be rich. They will reap the rewards of almost two centuries of care of the site by generations of Bristolians.

The 1960s (and later) invasion of the supermarkets is perhaps the clearest example of the deep pockets of the victors in development battles.

Rarely were they wanted, frequently they were opposed. People were only too aware of the threat to the familiar high street, to the people they knew, and to modest ways of living to which they had become attached. But the supermarkets persuaded local authorities to give way. Fast forward to 2024 and governments are now panicking about the loss of the high street, carbon emissions, and waste: crises that are strongly driven by supermarkets. It didn't have to be like this, and now that generation of planners has gone and we are left to pick up the pieces.

It would be a fine thing for cities to look into their futures, to see what the real threats to their citizens are, and then to avoid them. Climate change is the biggest by far, and Bristol is one city that has been pushed hard to acknowledge this. There are green policies, but we all know that none of them go far enough. Saving our green spaces is a 'no brainer'.

Part of the problem is that politicians and planners are by their nature interventionists. They want to bring about visible change. Even though they know that maintenance and care of existing fabric is better than demolition, their preferred starting point is the blank sheet of paper: cleared and empty sites within the city. Developers love it, and then construct their profitable, bland, tall buildings. Or, as proposed for the Zoo Gardens, their unattractive blocks of 'luxury'.

Jane Jacobs saw cities not as discreet plots and building sites but as joined-up ecosystems evolving over time, naturally giving rise to a mix of styles and uses with planning based on communities and local needs. In her seminal book, *The Death and Life of Great American Cities*, she wrote: "Cities need old buildings so badly it is probably impossible for vigorous streets and districts to grow without them. By old buildings I mean not museum-piece old buildings, not old buildings in an excellent and expensive state of rehabilitation – although these make fine ingredients – but also a good lot of plain, ordinary, low-value old buildings, including some rundown old buildings" [12].

The French team, Anne Lacaton and Jean-Philippe Vassal, who received the coveted Pritzker Architecture Prize in 2021, were forthright in expressing their philosophy: "Demolition is a waste of energy, of materials, of history. It's an easy option, short term. Moreover, it has a negative social impact. For us it is an act of violence ... Never demolish, never remove or replace, always add, transform and reuse" [13]. This is what we are arguing for at the Zoo Gardens, plus some serious forward-thinking.

How special are the gardens?

Keenly aware of the constant threats to Bristol's grace, scale and unity, the Save Bristol Gardens Alliance unites several groups that see the threatened loss of the Gardens as another blow to Bristol. It certainly would be. But being 'much-loved' is perhaps not quite enough. There needs to be some added reason for battling so painfully against the odds, to save an empty 12 acres of space in the city. It is, quite simply, that these are the finest urban walled gardens in the UK of such size. They are 'heritage' gardens, a place of inestimable emotional value to Bristolians of all ages and many generations. Alongside this sits the constant awareness of climate change.

The gardens were designed by Richard Forrest, a respected landscape gardener and designer who designed several other plans for zoological gardens, of which Bristol may be the last survivor [14]. What remains is a green sanctuary, free of cars and rich with horticulture. Trees have been brought to the gardens from all parts of the world over more than 185 years and there is a famous herbaceous border. Bristolians have long scattered family ashes there. The zoo has welcomed more than 90 million visitors since opening in 1836 [15]. It was part of the very fabric of people's lives, an oasis of beauty and peace, a family outing. In other words, part of Bristol's heritage.

Visit Bristol described Bristol Zoo Gardens as: "... home to beautifully colourful and scented gardens that are every bit as impressive as the animals and contain one of Bristol's most important collections of plants. There are unusual trees, shrubs and plants from around the world. Visit a buzzing nectar garden, butterfly forest, Lemur Garden and the 'Smarty Plants' area, or wander along long avenues flanked by brightly coloured seasonal borders and relax on the lush green lawns" [16].

The British Zoos website stated: "A ticket to Bristol Zoo Gardens opens a door into a plant collection boasting unusual and rare trees and shrubs, such as the monkey puzzle, Kashmir cypress, oblong woodsia and flax lily, as well as two national collections of Caryopteris and Hedychium. Bristol Zoo Gardens has also set up a three-year national garden performance trial for Hedychium and contains Tree Register 'Champion trees' in the Trithrinax campestris (by the entrance to Zona Brazil) and Crataegus laciniata (opposite the herbaceous border)" [17].

Bristol Tree Forum, which has battled to have the trees protected by Tree Preservation Orders, reminded us that of 381 on-site trees, 162 will be removed [18]. In objecting to the recent planning application, Bristol Tree

Forum said: "The loss of the integrity of this historic garden asset, from a botanical garden with a serious scientific purpose to pleasure gardens – managed for the benefit of those who live there – will be significant. We also understand that barely 25% of the gardens will be made accessible to the public, as opposed to the 100% they can now enjoy. Cars will also be able to access the site for the first time ever. Not only will this destroy the current amenity of the site, but it will also introduce a new source of pollution into the gardens that never existed before (save for service vehicles) and will damage the unique habitat and ecology of the site."

A new vision

A bold vision is needed if the Gardens are now to be saved. The Zoo Trustees nearly have the required formal planning permission to sell it on as a housing development. Although charitable trustees may feel bound to sell to the highest bidder, to extract maximum financial value to help fund their project in South Gloucestershire, this is a moot point. It can be argued – on ethical grounds alone – that the sale should be consistent with their charitable aims and objectives, and that they should seek a better outcome for the Gardens rather than one that destroys nature and community value.

Following on from the long-fought campaign to block the Zoo's planning application, the campaign group turned its mind to positive alternatives and asked the question: what would YOU do with 12 acres of walled garden in the heart of a major conservation area in Bristol?

We have drawn up a set of ideas for the Gardens that offer nature as a central theme: how to celebrate it, encourage its protection, generate ideas for its reinforcement – use the Gardens as a teaching place and conservation tool. For, if we don't save nature, surely she cannot save us. In the long term it will be nature that emerges, scathed but unbeaten, from the climate catastrophe. But she can support us if given the support.

The Zoo Gardens are not an easy project to take on. Even in the Zoo's own scheme there is an obligation to conserve listed assets and some green space [19], which are off-putting complications for any developer. The site is full of interesting and rare trees, an expanse of water and is surrounded by high walls of traditional rubble masonry. It is beautiful, but a headache for any owner or builder who generally prefers a quiet profitable life of low maintenance and high margins.

So the place comes with challenges, but as the architect Frank Lloyd

Wright observed: "Limitations seem to have always been the best friends of architecture." He meant being forced to accommodate externalities, such as nature or history or geology or (worst of all!) people, would in the long term produce more thoughtful and creative solutions. Look at his masterpiece Fallingwater in Pennsylvania with its projections over-sailing the river and imagine what problems they had to address.

But many of these issues disappear once you dispense with a developer's mindset. Historic walls, lovely trees and listed buildings within the boundaries become key to the place's character and attraction not irritations to be dealt with for pesky legal reasons, diminished and hemmed in. But the biggest mindset changes relate to the twin factors of time and profitability. Developers in most cases fund their projects through debt. The longer a project takes, the more interest they pay and the less profitable it becomes.

On the Zoo site we are applying a number of principles which circumvent these pressures. The first will be to acquire the site purely through philanthropy so that the Trust that owns the site is not carrying a huge burden of debt for which it has to constantly generate income to service.

The second principle is the overarching ethos of 'Nature First'. In a 12-acre garden there is room for a multitude of activities and interests and, as long as they benefit nature in some way, there is a home for them at the Zoo Gardens site. We have already identified over 120 local nature-focussed organisations and businesses who could benefit from existing in close proximity.

The Gardens would be a uniquely safe, green, urban sanctuary and offer a range of leisure and work activities, even office and research facilities, an auditorium and spaces for events and exhibitions. There would be physical and mental health benefits through play, contemplation and exploration. Two thirds of the space could be freely accessible to the public, and there would be no cars. It will be a suitable venue for non-government organisations, enterprises and businesses as well as research dedicated to sustainability and climate resilience. It can provide a central facility where complementary disciplines can meet. It will be a crucible for research and the translation of ideas into practical solutions. Start-ups around nature-based solutions and renewables will be encouraged.

The third issue is time. We have seen how time is the enemy of the developer and how they are forced by their business model to work as quickly as possible, sell, and move on to the next project. And we, the unlucky ones, are then surrounded by their grim contribution. We love places like old city centres and the Zoo Gardens for precisely the reasons that Jane Jacobs outlined, for their slow and natural development over time during which places acquire layers of interest and history. We have time – time to take it on, get it back on its feet again and let the Gardens site grow organically under the 'Nature First' banner.

But is it an economic impracticality? We think not. Free of developers, we wouldn't need to 'max out the opportunity'. A modest amount of commercially rented space – for nature related organisations, business and academic research – can provide the turnover to maintain the majority of the 12 acres for trees, greenery, water, and safe enjoyment. Much of the floor space is already available in existing buildings to which we would apply the principles of adaptive reuse. In our vision, the amount of built space needed is less than half the proposed housing in the current housing development scheme.

Success for a 'place' is about people and giving them reasons to come. Arguably the Gardens are unlikely to serve the whole of a far-reaching and expanding city like Bristol, and both transport and parking will have to be addressed. But again we are trying to establish something for the next hundred years and we cannot know how things will change. For certain no-one came by car to the Zoo in its first century of life and yet it was a huge attraction.

There is also a serious social function as cities increasingly think about climate resilience. One purpose for the site is as a refuge from future heat waves. The value and need for urban green spaces is only increasing, and this is an area that councils and city planners are actively pursuing.

As any Bristolian knows, almost every school-child in the city once had an opportunity to visit the Zoo. But thinking has rightly moved on when it comes to caging and displaying animals, and the Nature First principles open up doors to new worlds of learning. The Natural History Museum in London has embarked on a mission to use its few acres of outdoor space in exactly this way. We foresee every new generation of Bristol children continuing to visit and enjoy the Gardens as part of their growing up.

Imagine a place with some new building, but not housing, and with at least two-thirds kept as green space. There would be no roads. Imagine somewhere that embodies the best aspects of sustainable building in a site that demonstrates overall biodiversity and environmental net gains;

somewhere that provides space for everything from children's play to artists, from work-space for academics and start-ups, to labs for research into our biggest challenges.

All over the world visionaries have created astonishing spaces. The Eden Project was a dream brought to life in old china clay pits. The SS Great Britain was hauled back from the Falklands as a rusted wreck. Can we not imagine a renewed Gardens on the old Zoo site? Imagine a place of which all of Bristol can be proud in a hundred years. ■

REFERENCES

1. Save Bristol Zoological Gardens From Becoming A Private Housing Estate. *Change.org*. Available at: https://www.change.org/p/save-bristol-zoological-gardens-from-becoming-a-private-housing-estate (Accessed 7 June 2024)
2. Tom Jones. Bristol Zoological Gardens: The Most Beautiful Zoo In The World. Available at: https://savebristolzoogardens.org/the-report (Accessed 7 June 2024)
3. Save Bristol Zoo Gardens. Available at: https://savebristolzoogardens.org (Accessed 7 June 2024)
4. Mark Taylor. 'It's not too late' – packed public meeting held as support to save Bristol Zoo grows. *Bristol World*, 23 February 2023. Available at: https://www.bristolworld.com/news/its-not-too-late-packed-public-meeting-held-to-save-bristol-zoo-4037939 (Accessed 7 June 2024)
5. Steven Morris. 'It's an act of greed': hundreds protest over Bristol zoo closure. *The Guardian*, 12 Mar 2023. Available at: https://www.theguardian.com/uk-news/2023/mar/12/its-an-act-of-greed-hundreds-protest-over-bristol-zoo-closure (Accessed 7 June 2024)
6. Help Tom Jones Save Our Zoo Gardens. *Gofundme*. Available at: https://www.gofundme.com/f/help-tom-jones-save-bristol-zoo-gardens (Accessed 7 June 2024)
7. Tristan Cork. The seven options for Bristol Zoo as decision day looms. *BristolLive*, 16 April 2023. Available at: https://www.bristolpost.co.uk/news/bristol-news/seven-options-bristol-zoo-decision-8353180 (Accessed 7 June 2024)
8. Steven Spielberg. Desert Island Discs. BBC Radio 4. 23 December 2022
9. Alex Seabrook. What next for Bristol Zoo site after plans to build 200 homes given the green light. *BristolLive*, 27 April 2023. Available at: https://www.bristolpost.co.uk/news/bristol-news/what-next-bristol-zoo-site-8392069 (Accessed 7 June 2024)
10. Gordon Priest, Pamela Cobb (1980). "Urban renewal". The Fight for Bristol. Bristol Civic Society and The Redcliffe Press.
11. Andrew Marr. The idiot rich are taking over our cities – and our culture. *The New Statesman*, 8 February 2023. Available at: https://www.newstatesman.com/culture/2023/02/idiot-rich-taking-over-cities-culture (Accessed 6 June 2024)
12. Jane Jacobs. The Death and Life of Great American Cities. 1961. Random House, New York City.
13. Oliver Wainwright. 'Demolition is an act of violence': the architects reworking buildings instead of tearing them down. *The Guardian*, 16 August 2022. Available at: https://www.theguardian.com/artanddesign/2022/aug/16/demolition-is-an-act-of-violence-the-architects-reworking-buildings-instead-of-tearing-them-down (Accessed 6 June 2024)
14. Bristol Zoological Garden – Bristol – Parks & Gardens. Available at: https://www.parksandgardens.org/places/bristol-zoological-garden-1 (Accessed 6 June 2024)
15. Bristol Zoo to celebrate 186-year history. *BBC News*, 15 February 2022. Available at: https://www.bbc.co.uk/news/uk-england-bristol-60377243 (Accessed 6 June 2024)
16. VisitWest. Press sheet. Bristol gardens. Available at: https://www.visitwest.co.uk/dbimgs/Bristol%20gardens_press%20sheet.pdf (Accessed 6 June 2024)
17. www.britishzoos.co.uk (Accessed 6 June 2023)
18. Bristol Tree Forum. Bristol Zoo Application Comments Summary 22/02737/F Appendix 1 – Contributor Comments. Available at: https://democracy.bristol.gov.uk/documents/s83106/2%20-%20Part%202%20-%20Appendix%201%20-%2022.02737.F%20Zoo%20Comments%20-%20Consultees.pdf (Accessed 6 June 2024)
19. Bristol Zoo Gardens site brought to the market with plans for residential development. Abigail Turner. *BusinessLive*, 6 October 2023. Available at: https://www.business-live.co.uk/economic-development/bristol-zoo-gardens-site-brought-27854526 (Accessed 6 June 2024)

A Celebrating Sanctuary event at the Cumberland Piazza during Bristol Refugee Festival. Credit: Anna Haydock-Wilson

Flooding at Cumberland Basin. Credit: Rob Browne

Rebranded or re-imagined?

Anna Haydock-Wilson, artist and community engagement practitioner specialising in place-making in urban environments, considers the response of a community to rebranding...

———

CITIES EVOLVE, PEOPLE come and go, but fundamental to a sense of place are the ways in which citizens relate to their neighbourhoods. The social histories people create together, combined with forces of nature, enrich our day-to-day lives. This chapter aims to represent a specific community, Hotwells in Bristol, describe local feelings about council-led development plans for the Cumberland Basin, and reveal community-led ideas and dreams for a sustainable future for humans and nature.

> *We are the Guardians of the Gateway where hillside tumbles down from horizon to river bed*
> *Where Avon New Cut and River Waters meet, where waters come and go*
> *Spring tide, low tide, ebb & flow, ebb & flow*
> *Where history is herstory, where our story is your story is their story, it is all one story.* [1]

> *Hotwells probably wasn't developed before Georgian times because the river smelt so badly. It actually smelt badly until about the 1970s but in those days it was Bristol's open sewer and everything went into it, so I don't think people would have rushed to have a house alongside the river. You've got to consider the history before putting new things in.* [2]

Hotwells and Cliftonwood Community Association (H&CCA) was formed in 1974 to represent the interests of locals and to manage The Hope Centre, a converted 18th century chapel, as an inclusive community arts centre. The area is defined by an old parish boundary and includes Spike Island west of the SS Great Britain [3].

In the late 1960s, the area experienced the destruction of three streets of Victorian housing, with most residents moved to Knowle West and Hartcliffe.

The traffic was busy because they all used the little bridge by the Nova Scotia. Hotwell Road was quite a busy little shopping area back then. It was a very working class area. The minister of housing came down and bash, the wrecking ball. [4]

The demolition was followed by the construction of a complex system of roads together with leisure space designed by the English landscape architect Dame Sylvia Crowe.

Crowe had recommended a piazza scheme for the northern, Hotwells side of the Basin which would be 'frequented and enjoyed by the people' with a playground, pond and fountain, flower stalls, open-air art exhibitions and a cafe, while the southern side was to be planted with trees and shrubs. Most of Crowe's report was implemented, however over the next forty years, the area became rundown with the café closing and the pond grassed over. [5]

As dock activity decreased, new housing developments added to the diverse demographic mix; Baltic Wharf was built in the late 1970s, Rownham Mead in 1980, and Pooles Wharf Court in 1998. Stories abound of the Hope Centre in its hey-day; Hotwells Panto and the primary school still perform their annual shows on its stage, but this hub of creativity and connectivity was taken back by the church in 2000 and now serves a Christian community.

Secular community activists, who had given so much of their time to the Hope Centre building, turned their attention to other local spaces and ventures. They delivered a regular community newsletter, organised events, and in 2008 H&CCA set up the West Bristol Arts Trail attracting thousands of visitors, and is still going strong. A Community Traffic Strategy was developed, the Cumberland Piazza revived, community gardens created, and the Hotwells Panto returns year on year with its hilarious mix of politics and slapstick.

Council houses were and continue to be sold off. House prices rise. Hotwells Primary is still the only school in the area. The doctor's surgery sadly closed in 2017 and there are lots of empty shops on Hotwell Road. The tidal Avon continues to ebb and flow twice a day. Some things have changed; others stay the same.

It's not Western Harbour

While H&CCA members were busy trying to improve open public spaces, road safety and address the climate crisis, the elected mayor of Bristol, Marvin Rees, announced in his 2017 annual address to the city that he had plans to develop the Cumberland Basin area and rebrand us 'Western Harbour'.

In August 2019, Bristol City Council asked for people's views on some changed road configurations. A number of open public engagement sessions were held by the Council and there was the opportunity to complete an on-line survey. But, while an important feasibility report had outlined 10 road options, only three were presented to the public for consideration. A petition to 'Publish the full feasibility report on the Cumberland Basin road options' gained city-wide support [6].

The three chosen options all list considerable weaknesses including: environmental harm to the river and riverbank, community severance (areas being 'cut off' from each other by busy roads), harm to historic assets, harm to iconic views of the Clifton Suspension Bridge, changing the cycle route from a rural to a heavily-trafficked area, increased heavy traffic alongside the Nova Scotia and Pump House pubs, and increased air pollution. Local residents and businesses are also fearful about the future of their homes and premises. [7]

Strategic community response to Western Harbour

In February 2018, Dennis Gornall (then Chair of H&CCA) and local councillor Mark Wright met with Alison Bromilow from Bristol's Neighbourhood Planning Network to discuss creating a Cumberland Basin Stakeholder Group (CBSG); the idea being that CBSG should act as both a vehicle for dialogue with Bristol City Council and to protect the interests of local people as the plans developed.

The make-up of the group altered slightly over time but has included four local residents, two local businesses, eight local and community interest groups (H&CCA, CHIS, Underfall Yard, BS3 Planning Group, Hotwells and District Allotments Association, Friends of Avonquay House, Avon Gorge activities, and Action Greater Bedminster), local councillors (from Clifton, Hotwells and Harbourside, Southville, and Bedminster), Bristol Civic Society, and Bristol Neighbourhood Planning Network.

In October 2019, Western Harbour Advisory Group (WHAG) was established 'to help create objectives for the proposed future redevelopment of Western Harbour and shape its direction' [8]. Membership was by invitation only from the Mayor who was keen to see the area transformed, and argued:

> We need something that's transformative. We can't tinker around with the city. We need to get stuff done. Those [road options] that have been brought forward are those that give us the opportunity to have a really transformative development... I heard the statement earlier on, that this is central to our city's identity. Not mine, okay. My experience of Bristol as a kid did not come down to Clifton or Hotwells. We didn't come to this part of Bristol. [9]

Dennis Gornall, as Chair of the CBSG, was the only local resident on the Western Harbour Advisory Group. (After he stepped down in 2022, local representation was effectively excluded.) Membership of WHAG was criticised by local councillors who were not permitted to join the group. Southville councillor, Stephen Clarke, said:

> It seems to be a growing trend that when major decisions in the city have to be made, the mayor pulls together unscrutinised, unelected groups full of the usual suspects to discuss them and provide 'advice'. The people that seem to be left out of these ad-hoc groups are local people and their elected representatives; this cannot be justified and the mayor should reconsider the makeup of this advisory group. [10]

In January 2020, the Mayor attended a packed public meeting in Hotwells at which he stated:

> I've not said much about this publicly, but I have been quite dismayed on

occasion about the level of confusion, conflict and conspiracy that's been floating around about it. Where we are on the timeline of this is we are in what I call the pre-process period. In a normal process you go through a regeneration process, we're not even in the first stage. Some of it may have been ham-fisted in some sense, and I don't think it's been a perfect process, but I can tell you where we are in the process is the trigger has not even been pulled. [11]

Later that month, CBSG wrote to the Mayor: firstly, to encourage him to take a step back and, rather than focus on the three road options presented in August 2019, to take note of the future planned engagement, to be carried out in 2021, regarding the whole Western Harbour idea [12]; secondly, to express concern about the Mayor's portrayal of a public meeting held in Hotwells, during an online webinar with the University of Pennsylvania [13], which did not match residents' experience of it.

I was deeply shocked by Mr Rees's representation of how the meeting went. He presented it as the usual NIMBYS stopping the building of decent affordable houses. It was nothing of the kind.

Requests for information went unanswered. As a result, people began to assume that the Mayor's vision of Western Harbour was a 'done deal' and large-scale development was inevitable. The existing community felt invisible, threatened and ignored by the proposed developments, some even selling up and moving away.

Harbour Hopes – the council consults the city

Because of the widespread discontent with the initial 'consultation', a new approach was tried. In September 2021, the new 'Harbour Hopes' engagement programme explored people's aspirations for the future transformation of the area [14]. The engagement tender was awarded to Turner Works, with Place Bureau and Burgess and Beech, delivering a 6-month programme of community engagement. Much of the city-wide engagement was facilitated by Play:Disrupt, a Bristol-based community engagement organisation, who employed me as a local facilitator as part of their team.

Residents felt that the views of other communities in the city were prioritised over those of Hotwells, Spike Island and Ashton residents who live adjacent to the designated areas and would be most affected. The architects and their team seemed to sometimes share that frustration, and much of the feedback from other communities across the city was along the lines of 'Where is this?' or 'I would go there more often if the bus service was better'.

The Harbour Hopes Community Engagement Report [15] and the draft Vision for Western Harbour [16] were published in March 2022 asserting:

> *Western Harbour will be a distinctive gateway to Bristol, support a thriving community, build on its tradition of innovation, and embrace freedom and nature.*

Many locals were frustrated by the vagueness of the vision, seeming to want certainty about what was going to happen. Others were more positive as the engagement report valued the local heritage and environment, and reflected many local concerns. The main issues raised by H&CCA and those whose views were sought remained the lack of ongoing communication between Bristol City Council and the community, and the lack of local representation in decision-making.

Community expertise

As a community engagement practitioner with 30 years' experience of working with multiple neighbourhoods in London and Bristol, I have a strong belief that local people are experts in their own environments. It's often assumed that people living in areas under threat of redevelopment are opposed to any kind of change, but that is not my experience. Mainly they want to be involved and share their ideas, although it is true that the noise, dust, disruption and chaos caused by multiple road and housing developments are understandably unpopular.

I moved to Hotwells 20 years ago and began working as a Community Development Administrator for H&CCA in 2006. Since then I've had various roles within the organisation and delivered many creative events and placemaking projects involving thousands of locals and visitors, including West Bristol Arts Trail, Art Under the Flyover and the Peaceful Portway. I am currently working with the Bristol Climate and Nature Partnership who are supporting us to create a Community Climate Action Plan.

Bristol City Council owns most of the land around Cumberland

Basin and maybe they have the right to decide how assets are used and developed. On the other hand, some feel that local authorities should serve the needs of their residents in terms of the best use and value of realising those assets. Preparing this land for high density housing development will be incredibly expensive. Locals see the need for housing, but at what cost and for whom?

Over the years, I have heard from people who live and work in our area about what they see for the future and how traffic, bridges, homes (ideally more affordable, sustainable and social housing), leisure space and flood mitigation could be achieved. Exploring residents' relationships with our urban environment, I worked closely with the late great Ray Smith to develop Cumberland Piazza Projects and Art under the Flyover [17], running events, surveys and consultations with 2,500 households via our tri-annual printed newsletter, Art under the Flyover blog, and online. Our mission was to enliven an underused open public space.

In 2010 artists began to help us all reimagine the Cumberland Piazza as a community space, prioritising children and young people as Sylvia Crowe had done when she designed the play park and the fountain in the 1960s. We planted trees and shrubs, built planters, a skate spot, a pocket park, painted pillars and many murals. Poets mused on pre-history:

> Bang! Crash! Whoosh! Swoosh...
> Ah! The earth shook, heaving, surging, the sky was alight, crimson, vermillion.
> Ah! Those were the days, 300 million human years ago, so exciting, explosive, effervescent!
> We are the highway spirits, the bold concrete spirits. We find the spirit of the engineer.
> Crush the houses, where will the people go? We are being transformed, transferred.
> We need some softening, call in the natural spirits, water, fountains, trees and children. [18]

In 2018 we celebrated the Women of Hotwells and Cliftonwood for the centenary of women's suffrage – Angela Carter, Mary Wollstonecraft and her daughter Mary Shelley, Dinah Black and Ellen Craft freed slaves, Eliza Walker Dunbar, a local physician who treated the poor, and Dame Sylvia Crowe.

A committed gardening group now meets once a month to come up with new ideas for community use of the piazza, litter pick and increase biodiversity in the space. We have recently connected with Avon Wildlife Trust who are supporting our mission to continue to green this former park space. If the roads are knocked down, we will lose the work we have been doing but will continue to push for wildlife corridors and community green space.

Roads and bridges – traffic, Plimsoll, and BOB

Hotwells is not without major traffic issues. A Hotwells Community Traffic Strategy was instigated by Richard Walker in 2008 following successful work on home zones and traffic calming in New Cross, London in the early noughties. H&CCA consulted the whole neighbourhood and a design was drawn up and integrated into the Council's local plan. Along with 'hotspots' of danger, such as the 'run-for-your-life' crossing point outside the Pump House car park, the overall strategy hinged around the reduction of road widths and traffic speeds to increase safety, particularly along Hotwell Road. Sadly, not much has changed since then, apart from an increase in empty shops.

The need for repairs to the Plimsoll Bridge is becoming quite urgent. When the bridge swings or an accident occurs the ramifications are felt by Bristol commuters more than they are by locals. Recent Bristol City Council development plans seem to have been based on finding alternative solutions to repairing the Plimsoll Bridge which, the response to a Freedom of Information request suggests, has a £40 million+ price tag [19]. Citing this expense, Mayor Rees preferred new road options, including an infamous 4-lane highway requiring the demolition of homes on Ashton Avenue and threatening the much-loved Riverside Garden Centre. By tearing down Dame Sylvia Crowe's roads, it was argued that extensive Council land would be released for housing development. But the roads had been designed this way to allow the movement of cars above, and people and boats below, with the intention of minimal impact on the community and additional space for parks. Proposed alternative layouts make little sense:

> The layout of roads is efficient and works, don't change it.
> The Plimsoll bridge needs fixing, fix the bridge.
> Regarding the need for housing, why not begin with converting the

Bonded warehouses into flats, as they have successfully done with similar buildings in Liverpool. [20]

Meanwhile, Brunel's other Bridge (BOB) group has been active around the Cumberland Basin since 2006 with a mission to reinstate the former swivel bridge below the Plimsoll Bridge and highlight the importance of the unique dock heritage assets around the Cumberland Basin [21]. BOB were one of the players in sharing Historic England's review of the listed building and scheduled monument designations in and around Cumberland Basin and Underfall Yard in February 2023, at the request of Bristol City Council. Several assets within the designated development area were listed, including the Electricity Substation on Avon Crescent [22].

Water, water everywhere

March 2024 saw the highest tides in nearly ten years and it is these Spring tides that remind us of the immense quantity of water that comes through the Cumberland Basin area. We are home to a fantastic piece of Victorian engineering that helps protect Bristol from flooding. The lock gates at the entrance to the Cumberland Basin and the floating harbour are designed to let maximum amounts of water out of the harbour at the lowest tide and therefore increase the amount of water we can store at the highest tides. So should we be worried about tidal flooding?

With sea level rises and storm surges there is a very real danger that homes could be flooded in Hotwells and right across the city centre [23]. Local opinion is also wary of Council plans to increase the hard surfacing at Cumberland Basin cited in its latest Flood Risk Strategy [24]. Our day-to-day vistas of such a massive volume of water mean we view attempts to further funnel it as dangerous. Water is good at finding its way through barriers, and needs space. Nationally and internationally the talk is of blue/green solutions. Adding more concrete and building at density in the area will further increase pressure on this incredible, fragile environment.

Many locals have discussed potential solutions, especially following the 2014 Spring tides when water covered Avon Crescent in January, February and March. HighWaterLine Bristol took place in 2014, initiating conversations throughout the city about flood risk [25]. Suggested solutions include strengthening the existing defences and permanently lowering the floating harbour, to give space for more water in times of need, such as spring tides and storm surges. This could be a low cost, low carbon solution which would require longer ropes for boats and a survey of safe water levels in the harbour. The lock gates may need additional updating. Looking at the tidal Avon, together with the Council and with other communities at risk, would be a great starting point.

Another option is to look at water storage downstream; is there anywhere along the Avon Gorge that could offer spaces for more blue/green solutions which would avoid water over tipping on to the Portway? Interventions such as an expensive barrage in the gorge have been flagged over the years, perhaps mainly by engineers, but there is general agreement that these are not beneficial to our unique environment. Urban waterways offer potential for incredible biodiversity corridors, which we will increasingly need more of, as our climate changes.

Re-imagining

Over the years, through conversations and creative engagement, our communities of Hotwells, Cliftonwood and Spike Island have been imagining how the area can be shaped for a sustainable future. During Covid lockdowns the traffic decreased to the levels of the 1970s when the roads were newly built. It highlighted how urban planning that assumes ever-increasing road traffic is not how we should be thinking. People wondered about using half the road surfaces for cars and the rest for active travel, cycle super highways, planted walkways suspended above the Cumberland Basin which would be full of boats again. Brunel's other Bridge would swivel again to increase pedestrian and cycle access. The water would be clean enough for swimmers, both human and animal.

Sibussiso Tshabalala, Director of Cognitive Paths, and myself have recently been working with MA Architecture students from UWE on one of their Live Projects for Hands on Bristol. This partnership with H&CCA allowed us to re-engage with residents and Hotwells Primary School to find out what the key priorities are for our neighbourhood. The Re-imagining Hotwells Report lays out child-friendly visions for Hotwell Road, the Cumberland Piazza, traffic calming ideas and enhancing small pockets of green spaces [26]. Through detailed consultation and data analysis, as well as some superb ideas from 10 and 11 year-olds, they've helped us visualise how this area could function better for people and planet in the future.

Not forgetting that the Council have the final say, a masterplanner was commissioned in March 2024 by Bristol City Council to create their version of the area for the future [27]. A partnership exploring potential development could yet happen, as key local stakeholders have been selected as part of the new Western Harbour Advisory Group. Perhaps the change of administration at Bristol City Council, from an elected mayor to a new committee system, will bring recognition of what an incredible opportunity for enhancing this unique environment through sensitive development could bring.

Locals have dreamt of hanging gardens festooned from the flyovers with plants absorbing motor vehicle emissions and blossoms buzzing with pollinators. Birds could find homes in the fruit orchards in Ashton Meadows, trees which produce fruit to be enjoyed by all. Buses and ferries would be frequent and cheap from all parts of the city, giving everyone access to the harbour and a new community arts centre. It would finally be recognised that it is possible to convert the bonded warehouses into flats and maisonettes and the problem of low ceilings is not insurmountable, as previously thought. Experiments with prefabricated new builds for people on low incomes using sustainable materials could be raised high enough to allow the river space to rise and fall on its twice daily journey. Ebbing and flowing. ■

ACKNOWLEDGEMENTS

With thanks to Hotwells & Cliftonwood Community Association, Bob and Carol Walton, Sue Stops, Ray Smith, Rich Walker and Dennis Gornall.

REFERENCES

1. Extract from Voices of the Pillars by Bob Walton and poetry group, 2011. Available at: https://vimeo.com/78917488
2. Sue Stops, local historian, 2021. Interview for Hotwells & Hartcliffe Podcast. Available at: https://drive.google.com/file/d/1FktBYlxz8KS0sG8Lwe1gcxDRXtYMKt3L/view (Accessed 4 June 2024)
3. https://www.hotwellscliftonwood.org.uk/about (Accessed 4 June 2024)
4. Ian, former resident of 1 Brunswick Square, destroyed to build the roads in 1960s. Interview by Elizabeth Purnell, 2011. Ian's Story. Available at: https://vimeo.com/76878454
5. Visit Gardens blog. Sylvia Crowe at Cumberland Basin, Bristol. 27 January 2020. Available at: https://www.visitgardens.co.uk/sylvia-crowe-at-cumberland-basin-bristol/ (Accessed 4 June 2024)
6. Adam Postans. Controversial Western Harbour plans branded 'insane'. Bristol24/7, 17 November 2019. Available at: https://www.bristol247.com/news-and-features/news/controversial-western-harbour-plans-branded-insane/ (Accessed 4 June 2024)
7. Publish full feasibility report on Cumberland Basin road options. 38Degrees. Available at: https://you.38degrees.org.uk/petitions/publish-full-feasibility-report-on-cumberland-basin-road-options (Accessed 4 June 2024)
8. Bristol City Council. Western Harbour Advisory Group terms of reference, October 2019. Available at: https://www.bristol.gov.uk/files/documents/3208-western-harbour-advisory-group-terms-of-reference/file (Accessed 4 June 2024)
9. Martin Booth. Rees: 'The bridge, the gorge and balloons are not central to my city's identity'. Bristol24/7, 7 November 2019. Available at: https://www.bristol247.com/news-and-features/news/rees-the-bridge-the-gorge-and-balloons-are-not-central-to-my-citys-identity/ (Accessed 4 June 2024)
10. Martin Booth. Makeup of Western Harbour Advisory Group criticised for being too close to mayor. Bristol24/7, 4 November 2019. Available at: https://www.bristol247.com/news-and-features/news/makeup-of-western-harbour-

advisory-group-criticised-for-being-too-close-to-mayor/ (Accessed 4 June 2024)

11. Tristan Cork. Feisty residents of Hotwells tell Mayor to think again on Western Harbour project. *BristolLive*, 23 January 2020. Available at: https://www.bristolpost.co.uk/news/bristol-news/feisty-residents-hotwells-tell-mayor-3768602 (Accessed 4 June 2024)

12. Letter to Marvin Rees, December 2020. Available at: https://d3n8a8pro7vhmx.cloudfront.net/hcca/pages/185/attachments/original/1608144933/Letter_to_Marvin_Dec_2020.pdf?1608144933 (Accessed 4 June 2024)

13. Perry World House. Bristol and Beyond: A Mayor on the World Stage with Marvin Rees, Mayor of Bristol, United Kingdom. 25 November 2020. Available at: https://www.youtube.com/watch?app=desktop&v=ShJn4fXHLiw&feature=youtu.be from about 33 minutes. (Accessed 4 June 2024)

14. https://harbourhopes.co.uk/ (Accessed 4 June 2024)

15. Turner Works. Harbour Hopes Community Engagement Report. Available at: https://harbourhopes.co.uk/report.pdf (Accessed 4 June 2024)

16. Harbour Hopes. A Vision for Western Harbour. 2022. Available at: https://harbourhopes.co.uk/index.php?contentid=82#gallery1-1 (Accessed 4 June 2024)

17. Art under the Flyover: Instigating change through arts at the Cumberland Piazza, Hotwells. Available at: https://artundertheflyover.com (Accessed 4 June 2024)

18. Extract from Voices of the Pillars 2011 by Bob Walton and poetry group.

19. WhatDoTheyKnow. Costs of repairs to Plimsoll Bridge, 4 October 2019. Available at: https://www.whatdotheyknow.com/request/costs_of_repairs_to_plimsoll_bri#incoming-1461855 (Accessed 4 June 2024)

20. Rupert Martin, local resident 2024.

21. https://www.brunelsotherbridge.org.uk (Accessed 4 June 2024)

22. Heritage assets in Bristol Western Harbour. Underfall Yard Electricity Substation. Available at: https://bwhha.wordpress.com/Underfall-Yard-Electricity-Substation/ (Accessed 4 June 2024)

23. Get the data. Hotwells flood map. Available at: https://www.getthedata.com/flood-map/hotwells (Accessed 4 June 2024)

24. Bristol City Council. Bristol Local Flood Risk Management Strategy, May 2023. Available at: https://www.bristol.gov.uk/files/documents/790-local-flood-risk-management-strategy/file (Accessed 4 June 2024)

25. HighWaterLine. Available at: https://annahaydockwilson.com/highwaterline/ (Accessed 4 June 2024)

26. Re-imagining Hotwells. Available at: https://www.hotwellscliftonwood.org.uk/reimagining_hotwells (Accessed 4 June 2024)

27. Martin Booth. Western Harbour masterplanners 'to map out future of one of UK's most extraordinary places'. *Bristol24/7*, 20 March 2024. Available at: https://www.bristol247.com/news-and-features/news/western-harbour-masterplanners-map-out-future-one-uk-most-extraordinary-places/ (Accessed 4 June 2024)

Campaigners celebrate when a hyperdense proposal for the Broadwalk Shopping Centre is refused by the planning committee. Credit: Tim Kent

Protestors outside Bristol's City Hall following the shocking reversal of the planning decision. Credit: Helen Evans-Morris

Broadwalk betrayal

Laura Chapman, a leading campaigner with the Broadwalk Redevelopment Community Group, reveals troubling behaviour by a planning committee chair and the elected mayor's office...

———

THE BIG DAY. I met my co-campaigner Helen in the sandwich aisle of Tesco, opposite College Green on 31 May 2023. "I really don't want to do this. Why are we doing this to ourselves? We know it's a done deal..." "I know, but we just need to see this through, a couple of hours more stress is worth it to know that we did absolutely everything we could. We've come so far; let's just get it over with..."

Our shoes felt like lead as we dragged ourselves over the road to City Hall. We had spent the previous 18 months putting every drop of blood, sweat and tears into dissecting the material considerations and forming compelling, policy-informed arguments against the Broadwalk planning application. I don't think either of us knew quite how or why we'd found ourselves at the helm of the fight against the development.

Until Broadwalk, my activism had been focused on global justice issues like human rights and climate change. I'd seen it as my duty to participate in local elections – all elections – but I'd never really engaged with the 'boring' pedestrian issues of local politics. But Broadwalk was on my doorstep, and it seemed just so ridiculous. From the outset, the developers had obscured important details (including the height and number of flats they proposed to build) and attempted to either greenwash their scheme, guilt-trip us into believing it would solve Bristol's housing crisis, or dazzle us with the superficial lure of bringing a few cafes and restaurants to Knowle. It didn't take much digging to expose that there was scant affordable housing and very little benefit for the community, definitely not enough to compensate for their intention to plonk 12-storey tower blocks at the heart of our 2-storey neighbourhood, on the edge of our much-loved park. For me, the proposals quickly turned from being a planning issue, to a social justice issue. Why did these developers and their agents have the right to turn up in our neighbourhood, permanently change it against local wishes, and walk away with the profit?

Helen and I couldn't have done more, and we couldn't have played more closely by the rules; and yet by the day of the Development Control A (DCA) Committee meeting we felt we didn't have a shred of hope. Despite our diligence, our local councillors, Gary Hopkins and Chris Davis – ironically branding themselves as the Knowle Community Party [1] – seemed dazzled by the large sums of money being discussed, and willing to use their public platform to undermine the growing numbers of their constituents who opposed the 12-storey plans [2].

As we walked closer to the council chamber, and bumped into the many Knowle residents who had come out to join us at the DCA meeting, we painted on our positive faces and "We can do this!" attitude. We knew that packing out the public gallery was our best chance of winning the David and Goliath battle, so we had to make people believe that there was a chance our collective action could cause the scheme to be rejected.

I had been in this position before, when the first hyper-dense Broadwalk scheme was debated in March 2019. I could still vividly remember the injustice and disbelief I felt as Cllr Eddy (Conservative) implied it was the best offer we could get for Knowle. We felt the developers had treated us like fools, and our elected representatives didn't do much better, ignoring the many ways that the 420-unit scheme flouted the Council's own recently-introduced Urban Living supplementary planning document with guidance for 'successful places' at higher densities [3].

This time around the developers were asking for permission to build 850 units. Eddy had been promoted to Chair of DCA, so I knew what to expect from him; our 'Knowle Deserves Better' campaign strapline deliberately pre-empted his likely argument in favour of the scheme. Sure enough, Eddy gave a long monologue about how Broadwalk was on the verge of dereliction and was set for the same fate as St Catherine's Place in Bedminster, which had just been named as the saddest shopping centre in England by *The Sun* newspaper [4].

But, as the debate at the DCA meeting progressed, something felt different this time; the dying embers of our hope were fanned by questions from committee members about the proposed degree of hyperdensity, the prevalence of single-aspect dwellings, and discomfort about approving such a huge scheme in outline only, without the all-important details about how the many problems of such high-density living would be mitigated. The level of debate was noticeably more thoughtful than in 2019, and the scrutiny far higher. Helen and I exchanged glances, not quite smiling yet, but starting to feel it maybe wasn't a hopeless outing.

Then Cllr Plowden (Green) said words that I'll always remember: "On the information we have at the moment I am finding it very difficult, and I am yet to be convinced. I will be voting against this." The public gallery broke into applause. Then Cllr Varney (Liberal Democrat) spoke: "To describe the scheme as a new village is an insult to villages across the land, so on that note I will not be supporting this." More applause from the gallery. The other Green councillors – Fi Hance and Tom Hathway – quickly declared that they would also be voting against.

Everyone in the public gallery was doing the maths, and even Helen and I were unsure if the vote had to be unanimous, or a majority. Despite all of our preparation, we hadn't even considered this detail, as it seemed like an impossible outcome. But here we were. Four out of nine DCA committee members had rapidly declared they couldn't support the application. Cllr Chris Jackson (Labour) was up next. At that point our knowledge of the Labour mayor's tall building agenda [5] was fairly superficial, so we had no idea how significant it would be for Cllr Jackson to refuse it. But he did! Helen and I nearly jumped out of our seats; the public gallery took their cue from us, and the room erupted.

Cllrs Geater (Conservative), Hulme (Labour) and Hussain (Labour) followed suit, rejecting it as an unsupportable application. The applause and cheers got louder with each rejection. It was intoxicating. We couldn't believe what was happening, it felt like a dream. When the formal vote happened, even Cllr Eddy voted to reject the scheme. A unanimous rejection. Our friends and neighbours ran down from the public gallery, and we hugged and cried and laughed with relief. A stalwart of Bristol's planning scene told me she had never seen anything like it. David had defeated Goliath!

Over the next few days there were press interviews [6] and conversations to discuss what would happen next; how could we engage the community and work with the developers to develop a mutually agreeable new scheme? But what I remember most was the hopeful messages from other neighbourhood planning groups across the city, asking for advice about how they could defend themselves against equally oppressive schemes in their community. The Broadwalk decision had renewed hope for campaigners across the city. Our victory had shown that if you are able to understand planning policy, and use it to expose the weaknesses in an application, your collective voices might actually be heard.

The U-turn

After our amazing triumph on 31 May we started making plans for a community celebration, but a few days beforehand we received the notification letters for the 5 July DCA meeting, which indicated that Broadwalk was being 'reconsidered' at the meeting. We had heard it was usually a rubber-stamping exercise, but this sounded more substantial and we were worried. I emailed the Planning Manager at Bristol City Council (BCC) to confirm the scope of the 5 July meeting, and whether there was any chance of the committee changing their mind. He replied: "The role of the Committee on 5 July is to confirm the wording of the reasons for refusing this application. The original report will be appended. Whilst technically the Committee could decide to reverse their decision on the 31 May, I think that this is unlikely." [7]

I reflected on this; did we need to be paranoid and turn up on 5 July in our full strength, or should we trust the DCA councillors – and the planning process – to stay consistent and leave them to do their jobs in peace? As another councillor had said, if they had felt strongly enough to unanimously vote against it, why would any of them – especially a majority – change their mind?

I was on holiday when my phone started buzzing relentlessly, just after 6pm. People were reporting that the Broadwalk developers had turned up to DCA *en masse* and were making statements that ignored the fact that their scheme had been refused. Then horror that Cllr Eddy declared his opinion that the scheme had not been formally refused on 31 May. And a few minutes later – unbelievably – the news that the Broadwalk proposal had been approved.

I didn't understand how it could be true. I rewound the DCA live stream in the vain hope that the people messaging me had misunderstood. But no, it was true. Four members of DCA (Cllr Eddy and the Labour trio) had U-turned. A fifth member, Cllr Geater (Conservative), abstained and opened the door for Cllr Eddy to use his Chair's casting vote. The Green and Liberal Democrat members – who had held firm – were bewildered at the *coup* they just witnessed [8].

I immediately packed my things and returned to Bristol. I was home by midnight, and my inbox was full. It took hours to reply to everyone. I set up interviews, scheduled meetings with outraged councillors who offered to help, and called an emergency meeting of our Knowle Neighbourhood Planning Group. The four days before I returned to work were frenetic. We rallied the community into action, triggering 40 statements to Full Council's public forum in less than 24 hours. Hundreds emailed the four councillors who had U-turned, asking them to justify their decision. Others focussed on submitting freedom of information (FOI) requests, attempting to uncover who within City Hall had been discussing Broadwalk between 31 May and 5 July.

The fight back

I cannot overstate how seriously we debated the pros and cons of fighting the U-turn, particularly via the courts. We looked into every angle to scrutinise whether it was responsible to take it to the next level. If we successfully fought it, would the re-run of the planning approval process mean it would just be approved again? If it wasn't approved again, would our community resilience put off other developers from being interested in the site? We even talked to a few local property developers to get their views on whether they would touch it with a barge-pole, and if they thought that a smaller, more sustainable scheme was actually possible at Broadwalk. We also kept our ears wide open, listening to the Knowle community, to make sure that we weren't going against popular opinion. That's why the launch of our Crowdfunder was deliberately positioned as an exercise to assess the appetite of the community for legal action [9].

Every conversation gave Helen and I more confidence that our case was strong and people wanted us to fight the injustice of 5 July. As soon as the U-turn happened, the Broadwalk debate stopped being about the merits of knocking down an old shopping precinct, it became about city-wide democracy being under threat. Even people who supported the scheme approached me to say they were disgusted at the way it had been pushed through on 5 July. Broadwalk become symbolic of the insidious power of property developers within Bristol, and the potential for abuse of executive power at BCC.

By the time we attended Full Council on 11 July, to protest about the U-turn, our Crowdfunder had raised £4,000. This was enough to get an initial opinion from specialist lawyers, who listened in astonishment as we explained what had happened and showed them the initial evidence we had been able to gather. But long-term costs were always a barrier; we realised that we had no chance of securing legal aid for a planning case, and were facing the reality that we'd have to secure £35,000+ if we wanted to take this all the way.

One of the most intimidating decisions we faced was whether to instruct a lawyer or to go direct to a barrister. The latter felt like the most efficient route, but all the barristers we approached would only communicate via their clerks, so we got no sense of who they were or how they felt about our case. It was all horribly formal until we met Simon Bell, a direct access barrister who was happy to chat with us. He shaved his costs down to the bare minimum to ensure our budget could stretch far enough, and set to work on identifying 10 grounds on which we could legitimately request a judicial review.

But this legal action was only one strand of our strategy. We didn't really want to take BCC to court. As well as an unsuccessful call-in request to the Secretary of State [10], we used every lever of soft power at our disposal in an attempt to reach an out-of-court resolution, and to encourage the local planning authority to call-in the application for another layer of scrutiny.

Firstly, we scrutinised the paperwork and spotted that the minutes of the 31 May 2023 DCA meeting didn't quite reflect the truth of what was resolved: the scheme had been refused, but the minutes now indicated the decision was deferred. Was this an innocent mistake, or could BCC be attempting to rewrite history? Even though ensuring the accuracy of minutes should have been a simple matter-of-fact, it took almost two months to agree on the final wording, and culminated in an hour-long debate at the DCA meeting of 20 September, where BCC's legal advisor went to extraordinary lengths to argue that the incorrect minutes should not be amended [11]. The debate concluded with our proposed wording being adopted after Cllr Varney directly quoted it from a banner held aloft by our supporters in the public gallery.

Once the minutes reflected reality, letters from our barrister drew BCC's attention to the constitutional irregularities caused by the inconsistencies between the corrected minutes of the 31 May and the minutes of the 5 July. The record now clearly showed that the scheme was refused on 31 May. How then did DCA have the legal authority to re-vote on the same scheme on 5 July, even though their original resolution still stood and had not been rescinded?

We presented this argument to anyone who would listen to us, and it resulted in our local Labour MP – Karin Smyth – writing to BCC's then Chief Executive Officer (CEO), Stephen Peacock, to express her concern at the way the application had been handled, and to request that it should be called-in for further scrutiny and reconsideration. Cllr Tim Kent and members of the Liberal Democrats also wrote to BCC officers and expressed their concern that the contradictory minutes left BCC vulnerable to legal challenge. But the concerns of these elected representatives were ignored.

Gathering the evidence

While this was happening, other members of our community were facing an uphill struggle to obtain FOI disclosures they had requested. BCC repeatedly rejected requests on the grounds that they were too time-consuming, or that they were being done for 'vexatious' purposes. But – via our new allies on X (formally Twitter) – we picked up tips on how to circumnavigate these evasive tactics.

When we finally received our first dossier of FOI disclosures, it was explosive! The full timeline is available for the public to read [12], but in summary:

- Within days of Broadwalk being rejected on 31 May, planning consultants acting on behalf of the Broadwalk developers reached out to Kevin Slocombe, Head of the Mayor's Office, to discuss "what went wrong at DCA". Mr Slocombe clearly felt the matter was urgent and important as he arranged a same-day meeting and stated that DCA "seemed to implode a bit".

- The developers consulted legal counsel and forwarded their barrister's recommendations to the planning officer and Cllr Eddy, laying out the legal justification for reconsidering the 31 May determination and making a thinly-veiled threat of their intention to take legal action and seek compensation if the scheme was not approved.

- Cllr Eddy asked DCA members to abstain from the Broadwalk debate on 5 July, deferring all debating rights to the DCA 'lead' members from each political group. This was agreed on the understanding that the Broadwalk debate would be brief and confined to approving the wording of the reasons for refusal.

- Cllr Eddy agreed to off-record meetings with the developers, while pre-

and post-meeting 'jokey' emails show an informal, pally relationship between them [13].

- Kevin Slocombe and Cllr Eddy met off-record a week before the 5 July meeting, followed by a meeting between Kevin Slocombe and the Labour members of DCA.
- More off-record meetings between Kevin Slocombe and the developers. BCC's CEO Stephen Peacock also appears to have met with the developers.
- An email chain between BCC's CEO, the Executive Director for Growth and Regeneration, Cllr Eddy and the newly appointed Planning Chief, with the executive team members seeking reassurance that newspaper reports predicting Broadwalk would be rejected were not true.
- Cllr Eddy met with BCC's top legal representative (Tim O'Gara) to ask him if it would be lawful for the Broadwalk decision to be overturned on 5 July.
- Email correspondence between Cllr Eddy and the developers, including several statements anticipating and pre-empting the likely outcome of the 5 July meeting, and making value judgements on "more appropriate" outcomes being reached at the meeting.

It was more evidence than we had ever hoped for. Before receiving the three dossiers that we eventually extracted from BCC, we thought we had little chance of arguing Cllr Eddy's pre-determination on 5 July. But the FOI dossiers provided us with an abundance of evidence. The FOI documents also showed a significant level of interest from senior figures within the BCC executive team, and a cosy relationship between the Broadwalk team and Mayor Marvin Rees's right-hand-man, Kevin Slocombe, giving us a glimpse of the manoeuvres which we believe ultimately led to the U-turn on 5 July. It will be for a judge to decide if that is a fair conclusion to draw from the evidence we've gathered.

We organised a public protest on 13 September 2023 to highlight the strength of feeling over what was now widely recognised as the 'Broadwalk scandal' [14]. Over 100 people joined us outside City Hall – in the rain – to make it clear that they were not happy with the circumstances of the U-turn. Ironically, while we were protesting outside, Marvin Rees was making a somewhat uncomfortable speech to Full Council in which he praised Cllr Eddy "on the way you've chaired planning committee."

A week later, during the 20 September DCA meeting (when the 31

May minutes were formally corrected), one DCA member asked if the Broadwalk decision could still be changed. BCC's own lawyer said that the decision was amendable until the moment the planning notice was issued. We decided it was worth a shot! We wrote to DCA members, laying out the inconsistencies between the 31 May and 5 July minutes which left BCC vulnerable to legal action. We also shared the wording of the relevant committee procedure rules for revoking a decision, and encouraged them to use their right to call-in the decision for reconsideration. There was no guarantee that this 'untangling' of the Broadwalk decision would result in the scheme being rejected on its third hearing, but we took a calculated risk that it might.

What followed on 13 December was one of the most bizarre and confusing scenes ever witnessed in the council chamber [15]. Democratic Services had advised Cllr Hathway that the time limit for challenging the decision had passed, but he could override this time limit by invoking rule 12.1, which suspends normal standing orders. Cllr Eddy tried to block Cllr Hathway's attempt, but a concerted effort from the Green and Liberal Democratic members of DCA enabled Cllr Hathway to press on and ask for a vote on his request to call-in the Broadwalk decision for further scrutiny. Instead, it was resolved that the DCA 'leads' (the head of each political group within DCA) would meet and discuss the possibility of a Broadwalk recall in January 2024. For us, this was the closest we had got to the decision being overturned.

Ten days later, however, BCC pulled the rug out from under our – and some DCA members' – feet by issuing the planning decision notice at 6pm on 23 December, the last working day before the Christmas break. It was the most cynical timing possible. It immediately started the 6-week countdown for requesting a judicial review, and the holiday period meant two working weeks would effectively be lost.

Fortunately, we were ready. I had to pull our evidence together into a witness statement which substantiated the grounds for requesting a judicial review. Our barrister asked me to "keep it succinct" and Helen was a ruthless editor, but we had so much to say that it was still 33 pages long – and the evidence dossier was a further 517 pages! I hadn't anticipated the level of detail required, and can safely say that it was one of the most exhausting and stressful things I've ever written. But we submitted our court papers on time and robustly argued the case for five grounds that warranted a judicial review of the Broadwalk decision.

On 23 May 2024, we received news that the High Court had given us permission to go ahead with the Broadwalk judicial review [16]. Judge Jarman agreed that all of the five grounds we had identified were legitimately concerning and should be explored by the High Court.

Changing landscape

At the time of writing, we don't know what will be the outcome of the judicial review. We have always said, we would love to settle this out of court and prevent taxpayer's money being spent on defending a development that simply isn't good enough for Knowle. What we do know is that the Broadwalk betrayal triggered a change in Knowle's political landscape. At the local elections in May 2024, the incumbent councillors – who had strongly supported the Broadwalk scheme and heavily criticised our campaign – lost their seats.

But there were wider implications. What happened with Broadwalk on 5 July 2023 sent shockwaves around the city. A petition about loss of confidence in Bristol's planning system gained over 3,500 signatures from residents across Bristol and triggered a debate at the December 2023 Full Council meeting [17]. Nevertheless, other hyperdense planning applications were rushed through DCA for approval before the mayoral administration was finally removed and Labour lost control of the Council [18]. Consequently, more judicial review requests have been submitted to the High Court.

Whatever happens with our judicial review, I already feel better knowing that we now have local councillors who are committed to scrutinising the next set of plans for Broadwalk properly. I hope the city's new DC committee members focus on how a city can be successfully densified with gentler height, more intelligent architecture, and the support of local communities. Developers will still try to influence the planning process but I feel hopeful that we've made it a little bit harder for them to run roughshod over the people of Knowle. ■

ACKNOWLEDGEMENTS

With thanks to: Helen Evans-Morris, for sharing my passion about Broadwalk, none of this would have been possible on my own. And her husband Clive for his endless patience! Our awesome Barrister Simon Bell, for caring about communities not profits. Councillors Ed Plowden, Andrew Varney, Graham Morris, Tim Kent, Lisa Stone, Jos Clark, Tom

Hathway, Fi Hance, Paula O'Rourke, Jon Geater, Sarah Classick, Tony Dyer and Ani Stafford Townsend for their support and advice. Zac Barker and Anna Fry, who felt more like Knowle's councillors than our elected representatives did. Every single member of Broadwalk Redevelopment Community Group, who have donated generously, attended meetings at City Hall, made FOI requests, transcribed videos, and put thousands of leaflets through doors. Tristan Cork, Mark Taylor, Alex Seabrook, Adam Postans, Joe Banks and Charlie Watts for documenting the whole saga. Suzanne Audrey, Sian Ellis-Thomas, Lesley Powell, Danica Priest, Dan Ackroyd and Joanna Booth for calling out corruption and fighting for a fairer Bristol. Knowle Neighbourhood Planning Group and Bristol Civic Society. Andrew Hill and Katie Reid for teaching us so much about Judicial Reviews. My incredibly understanding boss Kate James. And my wonderful parents, for raising me to be the sort of person who won't let Knowle residents be treated like second-class citizens!

REFERENCES

1. Bristol Lib Dems: Councillors deny 'fraudulent' actions over cheque. *BBC News*, 21 January 2022. Available at: https://www.bbc.co.uk/news/uk-england-bristol-60073202 (Accessed 5 June 2024)

2. Tristan Cork. Fury as campaigners told refusing 'Redcatch Quarter' plans will 'damage community'. *BristolLive*, 17 January 2023. Available at: https://www.bristolpost.co.uk/news/bristol-news/broadwalk-shopping-centres-future-hangs-8062555 (Accessed 5 June 2024)

3. Bristol City Council. Urban Living SPD: Making successful places at higher densities. Adopted November 2018. Available at: https://www.bristol.gov.uk/files/documents/2675-urban-living-spd-making-successful-places-at-higher-densities/file (Accessed 5 June 2024)

4. Clara Bullock and Pete Simson. Bedminster shopping centre dubbed the 'UK's saddest'. *BBC News*, 18 April 2023. Available at: https://www.bbc.co.uk/news/uk-england-bristol-65273524 (Accessed 3 June 2024)

5. Ellie Pipe. Sky high ambitions for Bristol. *Bristol 24/7*, 8 October 2018. Available at: https://www.bristol247.com/news-and-features/news/sky-high-ambitions-for-bristol/ (Accessed 5 June 2024)

6. Adam Postans. Broadwalk shopping centre redevelopment plans refused. *Bristol24/7*, 1 June 2023. Available at: https://www.bristol247.com/news-and-features/news/broadwalk-shopping-centre-redevelopment-plans-refused/ (Accessed 5 June 2024)

7. Joe Banks. Councillor emails reveal behind-the-scenes effort to reverse Broadwalk planning decision. Substack. Available at: https://joe-banks.com/2023/09/18/councillor-emails-reveal-behind-the-scenes-effort-to-reverse-broadwalk-planning-decision/ (Accessed 5 June 2024)

8. Alex Seabrook. South Bristol shopping centre will be knocked down after planning councillors' shock U-turn. *The Bristol Cable*, 6 July 2023. Available at: https://thebristolcable.org/2023/07/south-bristol-broadwalk-shopping-centre-will-be-knocked-down-planning-councillors-shock-u-turn/ (Accessed 5 June 2024)

9. Save Knowle from the Broadwalk tower-blocks. Gofundme. Available at: https://www.gofundme.com/f/save-knowle-from-the-broadwalk-towerblocks (Accessed 5 June 2024)

10. Charlie Watts. Developers 'delighted' at government's refusal to review shopping centre plans. *Bristol24/7*, 19 September 2023. Available at: https://www.bristol247.com/news-and-features/news/developers-delighted-at-governments-refusal-to-review-shopping-centre-plans/ (Accessed 5 June 2024)

11. Alex Seabrook. Row over errors in how Broadwalk development decision was recorded. *BristolLive*, 21 September 2023. Available at: https://www.bristolpost.co.uk/news/bristol-news/row-over-errors-how-broadwalk-8769069 (Accessed 5 June 2024)

12. Broadwalk U-turn. Timeline of Communications & Events. Available at: www.tinyurl.com/BroadwalkTimeline (Accessed 5 June 2024)

13. Tristan Cork. Broadwalk controversy escalates after release of jokey emails before 'stitch-up' planning U-turn. *BristolLive*, 6 September 2023. Available at: https://www.bristolpost.co.uk/news/bristol-news/broadwalk-

controversy-escalates-after-release-8729937 (Accessed 5 June 2024)

14. Adam Postans. Bristol shopping centre 'scandal' protest outside City Hall as Mayor backs planning decision. *BristolLive*, 13 September 2023. Available at: https://www.bristolpost.co.uk/news/bristol-news/bristol-shopping-centre-scandal-protest-8749462 (Accessed 5 June 2024)

15. Alex Seabrook. Greens try to overturn Broadwalk decision during 'confusing' planning committee row. *BristolLive*, 18 December 2023. Available at: https://www.bristolpost.co.uk/news/bristol-news/greens-try-overturn-broadwalk-decision-8982147 (Accessed 5 June 2024)

16. Tristan Cork. Judge says Broadwalk plan saga can go to Judicial Review. *BristolLive*, 24 May 2024. Available at: https://www.bristolpost.co.uk/news/bristol-news/judge-says-broadwalk-plan-saga-9305410 (Accessed 5 June 2024)

17. Suzanne Audrey. 'We need to restore trust in Bristol's planning system'. *Bristol24/7*, 14 December 2023. Available at: https://www.bristol247.com/opinion/your-say/we-need-to-restore-trust-bristol-planning-system/ (Accessed 5 June 2024)

18. Matty Edwards. The elected mayor system has been removed, and leadership of the city has changed from Labour to the Green party. *The Bristol Cable*. 3 May 2024. Available at: https://thebristolcable.org/2024/05/breaking-greens-surge-secures-historic-victory-at-bristol-council-elections/ (Accessed 5 June 2024)

In Conclusion

Bristol City Council, Full Council meeting at City Hall. Credit: Rob Browne

Representatives of all political parties, and members of It's Our City Bristol, begin their campaign to replace the elected mayor with a new committee system. Credit: It's Our City Bristol

Scrutiny, democracy and the demise of Bristol's elected mayor

Suzanne Audrey, freelance writer and community activist, describes mounting problems with scrutiny and local democracy in Bristol that contributed to the demise of the mayoral system...

———

THE SYSTEM OF local governance is an important context for many of the stories in this book. In 2012, a referendum had been held in Bristol about future governance of the city. The majority of those who voted opted for change – to a directly elected city mayor. This, it was argued, would provide a strong, accountable leader. But, as the years progressed, the voices of residents and their elected councillors were increasingly sidelined. Ten years later, councillors exercised their limited powers and voted to hold another referendum asking the people of Bristol to decide if they wanted to continue with an elected mayor, or change to a system of committees reflecting the political balance in the council chamber. In 2022, Bristol voted to abolish its elected mayor. This chapter contains four opinion pieces, written between January 2020 and March 2022, that document increasing concerns about the mayoral system.

January 2020: The New Year has not started well as far as scrutiny is concerned

Something is wrong with scrutiny at Bristol City Council.

Guidance issued in May 2019 by the Ministry of Housing, Communities and Local Government described scrutiny within local government as "fundamentally important" to the successful functioning of local democracy and delivery of public services [1]. Effective scrutiny, the guidance asserts, is even more important in local authorities with a directly elected mayor, where particular attention should be given to: rights of access to documents by the press, public and councillors; transparent and fully recorded decision-making processes, especially avoiding decisions by 'unofficial' committees or working groups, and; powers to question and review, including the legal requirement for the mayor, members of the executive and officers to attend overview and scrutiny committee sessions when asked to do so.

Bristol's constitution does contain the building blocks for effective scrutiny. There are currently four scrutiny commissions – Growth and Regeneration (G&R), Resources, Communities, and People – plus an Overview and Scrutiny Management Board (OSMB) responsible for overseeing council business and managing the Scrutiny Work Programme.

Responsibilities of the various scrutiny commissions include: analysing policy documents; scrutinising decisions; reviewing the council's performance against policy objectives and targets; producing reports and recommendations; questioning the Mayor, cabinet members or senior officers, and; exercising the right to call-in, for reconsideration, decisions made but not yet implemented by the executive.

Citizens can, and arguably should, contribute to the scrutiny process. Bristol's constitution states citizens have the right to: attend meetings of the full council, executive and its committees (except where confidential or exempt information is likely to be disclosed); find out which key decisions will be taken and when; see reports, background papers and records of decisions made (except confidential or exempt information), and; inspect the council's accounts.

As well as accessing information, citizens have the right to ask questions, submit statements and present petitions. So far, so good. But, in practice, is effective scrutiny being supported or undermined? In August 2018, Marvin Rees was accused of holding the scrutiny process in contempt when members of OSMB said they were not given enough time to read 842 pages of papers for their meeting [2]. Adding insult to injury, the Mayor cancelled his attendance at the relevant OSMB meeting to prepare for a full council meeting later that day.

Relationships continue to be strained. In November 2019 the Chair of OSMB complained about the process surrounding scrutiny of Bristol's clean air proposals [3]. Delays in publishing papers meant members had only three days to examine more than 1,000 pages of reports. The delay also undermined public engagement, despite considerable interest in the topic.

Further concerns were raised about exempt papers which should be discussed and agreed in advance. The chair, who had received a telephone call on publication day informing him there were exempt papers despite his not having had time to assess them, argued "the established process is an important check and balance to prevent abuse of the exempt status and members would like assurances that this breach will not be repeated".

Lack of commitment to scrutiny may be infectious. In October 2019 the chair of G&R Scrutiny Commission questioned whether scrutiny was being marginalised after six members and an invited cabinet member failed to attend a meeting. A month later, members of the People Scrutiny Commission agreed to submit a formal complaint after senior education officials and an invited cabinet member were absent, leaving junior officials struggling to respond to questions. In response the mayor has criticised "efforts to throw mud and create fake debates" [4]. But is it a fake debate?

The new year has not started well as far as scrutiny is concerned. The agenda for January's meeting of the G&R Scrutiny Commission includes the Temple Island Regeneration Approach – a topic of interest since the cancellation of Bristol's city-centre arena – but, again, the relevant report has not been published in time to meet the council's own deadlines [5]. Under the circumstances it seems important to repeat the functions of scrutiny for local democracy: rights of access to documents by the press, public and councillors; transparent and fully recorded decision-making processes, and; the powers to question and review.

April 2021: Why is Bristol electing 70 councillors in May?

On Thursday 6 May 2021, elections will take place for 70 councillors representing 34 wards in Bristol. Some people may be asking "Why?"

The local government association (LGA) describes the role of councillor as a unique and privileged position with the potential to make a real difference in people's lives [6]. LGA guidance for new councillors explains that residents will expect them to: respond to queries and investigate concerns; communicate council decisions; know their patch and be aware of any problems; work with representatives of local organisations, interest groups and businesses; represent the views of residents at council meetings, and; lead local campaigns. Beyond representing ward interests, the responsibilities of councillors include developing and reviewing council policy, holding the executive/cabinet to account, and a range of regulatory, quasi-judicial and statutory duties.

But, after resigning as a Labour councillor and cabinet member for housing in 2020, Paul Smith indicated "there is a real problem at the moment" and suggested, "we need to look at how those backbench councillors and opposition councillors can have more of a say" [7]. What is the point in having 70 elected councillors, he asked, if almost all decisions are made by an elected Mayor and a small number of councillors in the cabinet?

Despondency about the role of backbench and opposition councillors was evident in a recent speech at full council by Labour backbencher, Mike Davies: "There has been such a disparity between my hopes before I got elected and the reality of being a councillor under the mayoral system – it's been a demoralising experience, and I know that's true not just for me but for many others" [8]. He argued "so much enthusiasm, talent and expertise has gone wasted" and suggested many good councillors are stepping down because "our role is hollow, and our communities are let down".

When asked about the role of councillors, Mayor Rees suggested the mayoral model requires a new set of skills and culture from them and highlighted the importance of city partners, commissions and 'thematic boards' in setting city priorities. But these boards and commissions have been described by others as operating like an unelected alternative council.

When I contacted councillors to ask about their role under an elected mayor, two Labour councillors responded favourably: one indicating, "I sought election in order to help my ward, and I've been able to do just that"; another stating, "I see myself as a representative of my ward community and have been able to work effectively within the current channels."

But other councillors of all parties expressed concerns. A Green councillor referred to the history of local government committee models being dropped for leader and cabinet systems in the 1990s, when many councillors felt side-lined, followed by the more recent switch to an elected mayor and cabinet, with many more feeling disempowered. For some, this sense of disempowerment is made worse by the current mayor's preference for working with selected 'city leaders' to the exclusion of elected councillors: "It's galling when we're then told to stop shouting from the side-lines and 'get involved' – we would all desperately love to get involved if there was any way of doing so" (Green). Others described the current system as "undemocratic, unaccountable, non-transparent and unable to deliver real value-for-money" (Conservative), and as "making a mockery of participatory democracy" (Liberal Democrat).

Almost half of Bristol's city councillors will not be standing for re-election in May, and some have placed the blame with a mayoral model that undermines their ability to fulfil the functions for which they were elected: "I hoped to contribute my skills and experience to the council, but little use was made of them; instead, I found myself a victim of what I describe as a culture of bullying and the suppression of dissent" (Labour).

But other councillors are standing again. One experienced Liberal Democrat councillor argued: "We can sometimes make positive progress despite it being twice as hard as it used to be." And a Green councillor argued: "There's loads to debate about how to run the city better, to achieve a fairer, sustainable, thriving city – I'd like to have that discussion so everyone can work out the pros and cons of different, more democratic ways to achieve positive change."

On Thursday 6 May 2021, the people of Bristol will elect 70 local councillors. Those of us who elect them should be mindful of the challenges they face as they endeavour to represent their wards and the interests of the wider city.

December 2021: It is clear that Bristol's profile is not dependent on its electoral system

On 7 December 2021, at a full council meeting of Bristol City Council, a large majority of councillors voted in favour of a referendum giving the people of Bristol the opportunity to decide if they would prefer the city to be governed through an elected mayor and cabinet system, or by committees of elected councillors reflecting the political balance in the council chamber.

Strong views are likely to be expressed about the pros and cons of the two systems before the referendum in May 2022. For the moment, the discussion seems to be focussed on three issues: whether an elected mayor raises the profile of the city; which system is better for 'getting stuff done', and; what are the implications for local democracy?

Raising the profile of the city

I doubt I am the only Bristolian who feels irritated when people imply that, until ten years ago, the city was a backwater that no one knew or cared about. Bristol's 'high profile' achievements and organisations, pre-dating an elected mayor, include: BBC's Natural History Unit, described as the best known and most loved producer of natural history content in the world and based in Bristol since its formation in 1957; Bristol International Balloon Fiesta, founded 1979; Oscar-winning Aardman Animations, founded 1972; Banksy, a product of the Bristol underground scene in the 1990s which inspired collaborations between artists and musicians; Massive Attack, whose *Unfinished Sympathy* is considered by many to be a masterpiece. Others may choose different examples, but it is clear that Bristol's profile is not dependent on its electoral system.

'Getting stuff done'

Those who champion the elected mayoral system suggest that a 'strong leader' is able to achieve more than other local governance systems. But, for example, in the decade before we had an elected mayor: the Children's Hospital opened 2001; Redland Green School was built 2006; Bristol was declared the UK's first Cycling City 2008; Cabot Circus opened 2008; The Bottle Yard Studios opened 2009; Bristol was declared a City of Sanctuary 2010; M Shed opened in 2011.

It is possible to compile a similar list for the years Bristol has had an elected mayor: patients moved into the new Brunel building at Southmead Hospital in 2014; Bristol was crowned the European Green Capital 2015; Bristol was designated UNESCO City of Film 2017; Bristol was selected as one of Channel 4's new creative hubs, opening 2020. But it is difficult to argue, for example, that Channel 4 favoured Bristol because it had an elected mayor. Leeds, not Bristol, was chosen for Channel 4's national HQ, and Glasgow as a second creative hub, but neither city has an elected mayor.

An important question is whether the 'stuff' that is getting done benefits the citizens of Bristol. Marvin Rees declared housing delivery a priority and points to cranes on the horizon as an indication of success. But his housing delivery targets have never been met and, while many struggle to find affordable housing, Bristol was recently named the UK's best city to be a buy-to-let landlord.

Local democracy

Following the vote in favour of a referendum, the mayor's Twitter account pronounced: "They are trying to take away your right to vote for who leads Bristol – and hit the voting rights of 340,000 Bristolians." This is an important issue, and voting rights are perhaps the crux of the debate. Whichever system is chosen, people in Bristol will retain their right to vote for 70 local councillors, but how is a 'leader' chosen and how is power distributed?

Under a committee system, the leader is chosen by the elected councillors who also contribute to decision-making through committees, balanced in terms of the political make-up of the council. Under an elected mayor, the mayor chooses up to nine councillors to form a cabinet but has the ultimate power over decision-making. Perhaps the most publicised example of this concentration of power was when Rees cancelled Bristol's city centre arena against the judgement of full council.

But those who observe council meetings have witnessed the marginalisation of backbench and opposition councillors, and the undermining of scrutiny, on a wide range of issues affecting the city and the people they are elected to represent. This has concerned members of all political parties so that even a Labour cabinet member stated (after his resignation) "we need to look at how those backbench councillors and opposition councillors can have more of a say". Given these concerns, I doubt if I am the only person who voted for the elected mayoral system ten years ago but welcomes another opportunity to reflect on what is best for Bristol.

March 2022: A vote for the Committee System would renew democracy in Bristol

At the 2012 referendum on Bristol's governance system, I voted in favour of an elected mayor. At the referendum in 2022, I will vote to replace the mayoral system with a committee system. Why?

It is worth remembering the purpose of local government: 'Local government is responsible for a range of vital services for people and businesses in defined areas. Among them are well known functions such as social care, schools, housing and planning and waste collection, but also lesser known ones such as licensing, business support, registrar services and pest control. Councillors work with local people and partners, such as local businesses and other organisations, to agree and deliver on local priorities' [9].

Those who argue in favour of an elected mayor tend not to focus on the delivery of vital services, or the ability of councillors to work with local people. Other 'strengths' are proposed: visible leadership, a vision for the city, and promoting Bristol nationally and internationally to attract investment. Before considering those strengths, two spurious arguments should be addressed: that Bristol would be 'leaderless' under a committee system, and that the four-year term of an elected mayor is responsible for greater stability in local government.

Under a committee system, full council would appoint a leader and deputy leader. The council would not be leaderless. As for stability, before the change to a mayoral system Bristol had been electing councillors by thirds for a four-year term: for three out of four years, a third of the council was up for election. This had the potential to change overall control more frequently. But Bristol now has whole-council elections for a four-year term, which will continue whether there is an elected mayor or a committee system. The four-year term of an elected mayor is no more stable than the four-year term of a council.

What about the other proposed strengths of the mayoral model? Our elected mayors have indeed been visible, providing a recognisable figure for press attention and those seeking to influence city issues. But this has been at the expense of 70 elected councillors whose role is to work with local people.

The diminishing power of councillors was eloquently expressed in 2021 by a Labour backbencher: 'There has been such a disparity between my hopes before I got elected and the reality of being a councillor under the mayoral system – it's been a demoralising experience... So much enthusiasm, talent and expertise has gone wasted... Our role is hollow, and our communities are let down' [8].

Similarly, an ex-cabinet member recently stated: 'The subversive element of the mayoral system is the lack of any effective democratic checks or balances... In the mayoral system almost every decision voted through in the council can be ignored' [10].

This constraint on local democracy is linked to the supposed benefit of having a mayoral vision. A leader who wishes to be visible is likely to prefer a grand vision. The daily grind of listening to and attempting to deliver for residents is not seen as visionary. When combined with a reluctance to engage backbench and opposition councillors, it is not surprising that research shows a decline in the number of citizens believing they can influence decision-making.

And what of the benefits of having a leader who attracts investment to our city by promoting Bristol on the national and international stage? One example is the 2017 *Bristol Development and Investment Hotspots* brochure which states: 'investors will benefit from rising Bristol rents and the value of their assets increasing over time as property prices continue to rise steadily' [11]. This is proving to be true. Meanwhile, promised targets for affordable housing have never been achieved, and research shows people in the less well-off parts of Bristol see mayoral governance more negatively than those in other parts of the city [12].

Crucial to a mayoral system are various scrutiny committees, intended to help 'the Council and partners make decisions that reflect the opinions, wishes and priorities of the people of Bristol'. But those who observe scrutiny committees have witnessed the difficulties councillors experience in accessing sufficient information to perform their role effectively.

Even proponents of the mayoral system suggest changes are needed to reduce the concentration of power in the mayoral office, strengthen the role of councillors and improve public trust. But the option of an elected mayor with more checks and balances will not be on the ballot paper in May. The choice is for Bristol City Council to be run 'by a mayor who is elected by voters' or 'by one or more committees made up of elected councillors'.

If the vote favours an elected mayor, there is no requirement (and arguably no incentive for the incumbent) to reduce the concentration of power. If a committee system is chosen, there will be two years to prepare for the new system during which Bristol City Council would adopt a new constitution detailing the functions of full council, the committee structure and terms of reference of the committees. This presents an opportunity for a city-wide debate to protect and improve local democracy.

2024: Postscript

In the run-up to the referendum, the electorate was sent a leaflet simply naming the two options and giving details of registration deadlines and polling day arrangements. In contrast to the 2012 referendum, no further information was included to explain the two different options for governing the city [13]. Some effort was made by other organisations in the city to provide information and encourage debate. *Bristol Ideas* commissioned and published a series of articles on the referendum [14]. Opposition parties campaigned for change, while Labour argued to retain the mayoral system. Meanwhile, *It's Our City Bristol* was established as an independent group to promote the arguments in favour of change to a committee system [15].

The 2022 referendum marked the demise of Bristol's mayoral system [16]. Despite limited information being provided by Bristol City Council, the turnout (29%) was higher than for the 2012 referendum that had introduced the mayoral system (24%), and the percentage of voters supporting the mayoral system (41%) dropped significantly when compared with 2012 (53%).

The 59% vote in favour of a new committee system was a clear indication of support for change. A cross-party Committee Model Working Group was established and met regularly to develop the new committee model, while the elected mayor continued in office until the May 2024 local elections. In May 2024, Bristol elected a new council of 70 councillors and the new committee system came into operation. ∎

ACKNOWLEDGEMENTS

I am grateful to the councillors and fellow citizens of Bristol who campaigned to improve scrutiny and for local democracy. Thanks are also due to Martin Booth, editor of *Bristol24/7*, and Andrew Kelly, former director of *Bristol Ideas*, for permission to reproduce the articles in this chapter.

REFERENCES

1. Statutory Guidance on Overview and Scrutiny in Local and Combined Authorities, May 2019. Ministry of Housing, Communities and Local Government. Available at: https://www.gov.uk/government/publications/overview-and-scrutiny-statutory-guidance-for-councils-combined-authorities-and-combined-county-authorities Updated 2023. (Accessed 5 June 2024)

2. Esme Ashcroft. Marvin Rees accused of 'disrespect' over council scrutiny process. *BristolLive*, 30 August 2018. Available at: https://www.bristolpost.co.uk/news/bristol-news/marvin-rees-accused-disrespect-over-1949544 (Accessed 5 June 2024)

3. Statement on behalf of the Overview and Scrutiny Management Board. Bristol City Council Cabinet meeting, 5 November 2019. Available at: https://democracy.bristol.gov.uk/documents/b18740/Supplement%20-%20Report%20from%20Scrutiny%20Commission%2005th-Nov-2019%2016.00%20Cabinet.pdf?T=9 (Accessed 5 June 2024)

4. Amanda Cameron. Marvin Rees calls councillors' plan to complain a 'fake debate'. *BristolLive*, 9 December 2019. Available at: https://www.bristolpost.co.uk/news/bristol-news/marvin-rees-calls-councillors-plan-3622276 (Accessed 5 June 2024)

5. Adam Postans. Row breaks out over future of Temple Island. *Bristol24/7*, 13 January 2020. Available at: https://www.bristol247.com/news-and-features/news/row-breaks-out-over-future-of-temple-island/ (Accessed 5 June 2024)

6. Local Government Association. Guidance for new councillors. Available at: https://www.local.gov.uk/sites/default/files/documents/11.101%20Councillors%27%20Guide%202018_v10_WEB.pdf (Accessed 5 June 2024)

7. Adam Postans. Bristol City Council cabinet member says mayoral system needs "more checks and balances".

BristolLive, 17 September 2020. Available at: https://www.bristolpost.co.uk/news/bristol-news/bristol-councillor-criticises-mayoral-system-4523855 (Accessed 5 June 2024)

8. Adam Postans. Motion to hold referendum on scrapping Bristol's mayoral system defeated. *Bristol24/7*. 17 March 2021. Available at: https://www.bristol247.com/news-and-features/news/motion-to-hold-referendum-to-scrap-bristols-mayoral-system-defeated/ (Accessed 5 June 2024)

9. Local Government Association. What is local government? Available at: https://www.local.gov.uk/about/what-local-government (Accessed 6 June 2024)

10. Paul Smith. Mayor vs Committee: Which System Delivers? *Bristol Ideas*. Referendum 2022, 17 January 2022. Available at: https://www.bristolideas.co.uk/read/referendum-paul-smith/ (Accessed 6 June 2024)

11. Esme Ashcroft. Concern as 'rising Bristol rents' portrayed as investment opportunity in Marvin Rees' China brochure. *BristolLive*, 28 September 2021. Available at: https://www.bristolpost.co.uk/news/bristol-news/concern-rising-bristol-rents-portrayed-911400 (Accessed 6 June 2024)

12. Robin Hambleton and David Sweeting. The Impacts of Mayoral Governance in Bristol. The Bristol Civic Leadership Project, September 2015. Available at: https://bristolcivicleadership.net/wp-content/uploads/2013/03/impacts-of-mayoral-governance-in-bristol-web-version.pdf (Accessed 6 June 2024)

13. Dawn Limbu. Lack of Bristol mayoral referendum information criticised. *BBC News*, 29 April 2022. Available at: https://www.bbc.co.uk/news/uk-england-bristol-61269802 (Accessed 6 June 2024)

14. Referendum 2022. *Bristol Ideas*. Available at: https://www.bristolideas.co.uk/projects/city-debates-referendum-2022/ (Accessed 6 June 2024)

15. It's Our City Bristol. Available at: https://www.itsourcitybristol.org (Accessed 6 June 2024)

16. Bristol mayor vote: City decides to abolish mayor post. *BBC News*, 6 May 2022. Available at: https://www.bbc.co.uk/news/uk-england-bristol-61336049 (Accessed 6 June 2024)

SOURCES

*   Suzanne Audrey. The New Year has not started well as far as scrutiny is concerned. *Bristol24/7*, 6 January 2020. Available at: https://www.bristol247.com/opinion/your-say/the-new-year-has-not-started-well-as-far-as-scrutiny-is-concerned/ (Accessed 6 June 2024)

*   Suzanne Audrey. Why is Bristol electing 70 councillors in May? *Bristol24/7*, 19 April 2021. Available at: https://www.bristol247.com/opinion/your-say/why-is-bristol-electing-70-councillors/ (Accessed 6 June 2024)

*   Suzanne Audrey. It is clear that Bristol's profile is not dependent on its electoral system. *Bristol 24/7*, 14 December 2021. Available at: https://www.bristol247.com/opinion/your-say/it-is-clear-that-bristols-profile-is-not-dependent-on-its-electoral-system/ (Accessed 6 June 2024)

*   Suzanne Audrey. A Vote for the Committee System Would Renew Democracy in Bristol. *Bristol Ideas*, 24 March 2022. Available at: https://www.bristolideas.co.uk/read/referendum-suzanne-audrey/ (Accessed 6 June 2024)

Epilogue

THE EVENTS DESCRIBED in this book relate to the kind of city we want to live in, and pass on to future generations. They tell of individuals, communities and organisations that have been willing to speak up, campaign, petition and protest. There are examples of solidarity, of learning from and supporting others. Even when the battle was 'lost', friendships have been formed and knowledge gained.

The campaigns and issues covered here benefitted from the support of allies who were willing to share information and experience, friends who made banners and turned up to protest, others who asked questions and made statements, 'strangers' who contributed to fundraisers and signed petitions, pro bono legal advice from experts who put people before profit, and good local journalism keeping important stories on the agenda. Such support has given people strength when the going got tough – and will continue to do so.

As this book goes to press, Bristol is adjusting to its committee system of governance, and the country has elected a new Labour government. The impact of these changes remains to be seen. Some of the challenges and campaigns described here will continue, some will be resolved, and new issues will arise as we go forward. There is a wealth of experience within these pages which we hope will inspire, inform and comfort future activists and citizens of our city. ■

Editor's acknowledgements

THANK YOU TO all the authors who contributed to this book, and the photographers and illustrators who gave permission to reproduce their work. I am grateful to *Bristol24/7, The Bristol Cable* and *Bristol Ideas* for permission to reproduce articles previously published by them. Thank you to all the activists and campaigners in our city, and those who support them. Thanks to the *WhatDoTheyKnow* website team for creating a wonderful resource for those wishing to submit or access Freedom of Information requests. Thank you to those councillors and officers at Bristol City Council who do their best to support the citizens of our city. Thanks also to the journalists who report on local activism, with special acknowledgement to the BBC local democracy reporters Adam Postans, Amanda Cameron and Alex Seabrook, *BristolLive* chief reporter Tristan Cork, *BBC* senior broadcast journalist Pete Simson, and editor of *Bristol24/7* Martin Booth. I would also like to thank Richard Jones and Joe Burt for advice on the publication. Finally, thank you to my partner Pete Corr for support as this book came to fruition. ∎